JAPAN, DISINCORPORATED

JAPAN, DISINCORPORATED

The Economic Liberalization Process

Leon Hollerman

HOOVER INSTITUTION PRESS

Stanford University ===== Stanford, California

Hoover Press Publication 363

Copyright 1988 by the Board of Trustees of the
  Leland Stanford Junior University

First printing, 1988

Manufactured in the United States of America

92 91 90 89 88   9 8 7 6 5 4 3 2

Library of Congress Cataloging-in-Publication Data
Hollerman, Leon.
  Japan, disincorporated: the economic liberalization process /
Leon Hollerman.
      p.   cm.—(Hoover Press publication ; 363)
  Includes index.
  ISBN 0-8179-8631-6:   ISBN 0-8179-8632-4 (pbk.) :
  1. Industry and state—Japan. 2. Japan—Commercial policy.
I. Title.
HD3616.J33H65 1988
338.952—dc19   87-25633
                CIP

To Peter F. Drucker

CONTENTS

INTRODUCTION AND OVERVIEW

Three phases of Japan's postwar transition form the framework of the present study. The first refers to Japan as a "small" nation following World War II, a phase in which it enjoyed the license of developing countries to practice protectionism without censure or retaliation from the world community. In this phase, the term "Japan, Incorporated," describes the alliance between government and business for the promotion of their mutual interests and the national interests of Japan.

In the second phase, consequent to its "economic miracle," Japan emerged as a major industrial nation. This was a phase in which economic liberalization was formally espoused. It included the episode of "Japan, Disincorporated," when the interests of business (especially big business) and the interests of government temporarily diverged. In addition to tension between government and the private sector, there was inter- and intraministerial conflict over the perceived threat of liberalization to bureaucratic vested interests. During that interval, the bureaucracy was besieged and distracted, its customary routines disrupted, the harmony of "Japan, Incorporated," dissolved.

The third phase, projected below in the final chapter as a scenario, is anticipated to ensue following the 1980s. In the scenario, government and business reach a new consensus, described here as "Japan, Reincorporated," in which the interests of the nation, of the bureaucracy, and of big business again coincide. The chief impact of this coincidence will be seen on the international plane, accompanying Japan's emergence as a "headquarters country." As projected in that role, Japan will control and manipulate an economic empire of foreign affiliates, subsidiaries, joint ventures, and cartel or quasi-cartel arrangements. Foreseeably, in an increasingly protectionist world, Japan's trade liberalization policies of the second postwar phase will have been reversed. The three phases overlap chronologically and are functionally entwined. It is the second of the two phases, namely that of "Japan, Disincorporated," with which the present study is primarily concerned.

Historically, within phase two, "Japan, Disincorporated," refers to an interval between 1980 and 1984 when Japan's liberalization process—especially financial liberalization—began to creep two steps forward and one step backward from theory to practice. At that time, there was a breakdown in the consensus and harmony that convention impels Japanese to contrive. The period 1980–1984 was an interregnum in which the bureaucracy inadvertently revealed to the world a great deal about its decisionmaking process and about the implications of financial liberalization from a Japanese government point of view. In particular, anticipated repercussions of economic liberalization had divergent implications for the vested interests of various bureaucrats.

In the interregnum, when markets were being forced open, the world saw a spectacle of interministerial rivalry, bureaucratic infighting, and conflict between government and business that normally would be papered over and concealed from public view. This suggests that the foreign image of Japan as a consensus society can be overdrawn. At home, Japanese are keenly aware of conflicts of interest and ideas in education, politics, and elsewhere. The phrase *sōron-sansei, kakuron-hantai* ("agree in principle, but disagree in particulars") refers to a Japanese practice that dissembles consensus. Moreover, consensus itself does not necessarily imply agreement. It may merely mean that "I accept your proposal now in return for your acceptance of my proposal on some future occasion." The artifact of agreement is presented publicly only after differences have been accommodated in private. During times of fundamental structural change, such as during the 1980s, forces promoting conflicts of interest multiply. Thus the liberalization process was not based strictly on economic logic: It was the result of a compromise among bureaucrats and businessmen in response to pressures on their respective interests and the national interests of Japan.

In sketching Japan's postwar phases, one can distinguish elements of continuity from elements of change. To recapitulate, the first phase, beginning with the occupation, was a period in which the economy was highly regulated, controlled, and planned. The system of control and planning was devised by the Supreme Command for the Allied Powers (SCAP) in accordance with its military mission. SCAP's primary objective was to demilitarize Japan, maintain order, and ensure that American aid (for relief and rehabilitation) was not wasted or stolen.

Next, to "take Japan off the back of the American taxpayer," it was the occupation's mission to help the crippled nation restore its capacity for self-support. The latter assignment was in the hands of expatriate New Dealers who formed the policymaking nucleus of General MacArthur's economic staff. Their program was based on the premise that "government is good, business is bad." Accordingly, besides dissolving the *zaibatsu*, or financial clique, they organized a system of direct government controls more comprehensive than anything the Japanese had seen during the war itself. These included price controls, wage controls, foreign exchange controls, interest rate and capital controls, allocation of scarce materials, allocation of credit and bank loans, licensing procedures, quotas, controls on inward and outward trade and investment, and restrictions on access by foreigners to the Japanese economy even in the form of visits by foreign salesmen or foreign buyers.[1]

In 1952, when the occupation ended, the control and planning apparatus was not dismantled but was handed over intact to Japan's civilian bureaucracy. The latter, having been the instrument by which SCAP controls had been exercised throughout the occupation, was ready, able, and eager to impose them in its own name. Meanwhile, as part of occupation reforms, the military bureaucracy, which for a decade before Japan's defeat had intimidated and overruled the civilian bureaucrats, had been abolished. (The institutional memory of that humiliation helps account for the present resistance of Japan's government to full-scale rearmament and the military bureaucracy that would be restored with it.) Thus in the bureaucracy, by courtesy of General MacArthur, the civilian bureaucrats "won the war" with the military brass.

Above all, the civilian bureaucrats were delighted that the legacy from SCAP included unconditional surrender of the Japanese economy to their rules, regulations, and interventionist authority. Their turf was vast; it was a domain of opportunities for status, power, and careers. Key members of the resurgent economic ministries, which had been barely touched by MacArthur's purge (the "Removal and Exclusion of Undesirable Personnel from Public Office") were former officials of the defunct empire, the Greater East Asia Coprosperity Sphere.[2] They had imposed Japan's rule as a headquarters country in the imperialist era when it mobilized the resources of the colonies. Hence they were proficient in techniques of planning and economic control. Moreover, in a nation whose politicians were relatively weak and of dubious reputation, the pre-eminence of the bureaucracy was institutionally well founded. Traditionally, in Japan's Tokugawa (feudal) period (1603–1868), the highest social prestige was attributed to bureaucrats. With the advent of the modern period under Emperor Meiji, their pre-eminent status was confirmed as they assumed a leading role in the modernization process.Thereafter, the bureaucracy constituted an elite of the best brains in Japan. Its chief career officials have been graduates of Japan's premier school, Tokyo University. In the planning process, moreover, during the first postwar stage that ran from the end of the occupation until the 1960s, the bureaucracy and big business enjoyed a symbiotic relationship in which they needed each other. Key industries were nurtured by the government, in return for which business submitted to the multitude of official rules and regulations that provided jobs for bureaucrats. In its oligopolistic characteristics, informally coordinated by the school tie, Japan's government ministries were complementary to the oligopolies of the private sector, which had their own Todai graduates. (This complementarity is restored in the scenario of Japan's re-emergence as a headquarters country described below in phase three of the postwar transition.)

Phase two of the transition began during the 1960s. Under a combination of internal and external pressures, the process known as economic liberalization (deregulation) had its beginnings in the period of Japan's economic "miracle" of 1955–1970. In the West, liberalization may be defined as a process in which government economic intervention is reduced and the principles of a free market system are employed. In Japan, where it is difficult to draw the line between direct and indirect controls, as well as between statutory and administrative controls, the process is more ambiguous. Nevertheless, in a desultory and roundabout way, and subject to Japanese objectives, liberalization has been pursued since the 1960s. Liberalization (jiyūka) and internationalization (kokusaika) go hand in hand. The latter refers to liberalization on the international plane.

As the economic miracle blossomed and corporate capital accumulated, the business community had less need of government subsidies and became less amenable to its intervention and administrative guidance. Among the public at large, a mood of impatience with the burden of government likewise mounted. In accord with the then popular American attitude, there was a growing conviction in Japan that government was bloated and inefficient. As publicly perceived, the private sector had adjusted well to new conditions created by the oil crisis of 1973 while the government had not. Taking these factors into account, in March 1981 the government of Prime Minister Zenko

Suzuki inaugurated the Provisional Commission for Administrative Reform (*Rinchō*). This successor to an unproductive series of previous postwar administrative reform efforts included proposals for reducing the size, scope, and expenditures of government, as well as for a transfer of domestic resources to the international sector. Partly, administrative reform was political theater. It was also adroitly consistent with the theory of economic liberalization and supportive of the strategy for Japan's emergence as a headquarters country. In practice, the *Rinchō* had little to its credit until the mid-1980s, and even then (as in the so-called privatization of national enterprises), there was less to its accomplishments than met the eye.

External, as a result of the economic miracle, Japan's economy was no longer regarded by Americans or Europeans as a tender plant needing shelter from world competition. Japan's trade partners began applying pressure for the removal of its barriers to entry of foreign goods and capital. (This was accompanied by pressure against Japan's "unfair" competition in its own external markets.) Japan's response to the impact of internal and external pressures was performed on a "step by step," "case by case" basis, with retrogression as well as progress, and with all deliberate speed. Indeed, economic liberalization is a classic case for study of the difference between appearance and reality in Japanese affairs. In general, foreign trade was liberalized earlier than international finance. Foreigners and foreign finance were the last to be relieved of government restrictions.

As a result of the Kennedy Round (completed in 1967), Japan reduced tariffs on 2,147 items; in 1972, there was an "across-the-board" reduction of 20 percent. In 1971, the Tariff Council recommended reductions in tariffs on manufactured consumer goods, simplification of customs procedures, and an increase in tariff exemptions. In the field of direct investment, following a tentative "yen-based" foreign investment program, the first rudimentary package of measures liberalizing direct foreign investment in Japan became effective in July 1967. The new policy was pursuant to the events of April 1964, when Japan acceded to International Monetary Fund (IMF) Article 8 and was admitted to full membership in the Organization for Economic Cooperation and Development (OECD), by which it became a member of the club of advanced industrial nations and subject to their codes of international behavior. Five further investment packages ensued, culminating by 1976 in permission (legally, if not administratively) for 100 percent foreign ownership in all but five industries. To a considerable extent, this was a "numbers game." As of 1987, it was clear that the Ministry of International Trade and Industry (MITI) still took a hostile view of direct foreign investment in Japan and employed measures to restrain it.[3] Meanwhile, the curtailment or repeal of statutory controls—although not "administrative guidance," which is non-statutory—was designed to give Japan the appearance of a Western-style, unplanned, free-market economy in the second, or deregulatory, stage of its postwar transition.

External financial liberalization (portfolio, or indirect investment) was the last and most imposing episode in the history of Japan's reluctant "market-opening" measures. Cumulatively, by the time this episode occurred, business had been unleashed to a considerable degree from government constraints in its everyday decisions. By the same token, shorn of much of its interventionist apparatus, the bureaucracy's prerogatives and turf were reduced in its relations with the private sector. The principal ministries, namely the Ministry of Finance and the Ministry of International Trade and Industry, were the main losers as a result of liberalization. In the contraction of their authority to ration credit, fix prices, assign quotas, license transactions, and the like, their stature within the government establishment was relatively diminished. Given the importance of hierarchy and status in Japanese government and society, this assault on the pecking order was indeed portentous.

In this study's review of the interregnum of the 1980s, the interaction between economics and bureaucratic politics in Japan is a principal theme. Another theme is the conflict between government and business in the liberalization process. Domestically, apart from instances in which business and banking were in effect subsidized by government controls, the demand for liberalization arose from the private sector. Externally, it was spurred chiefly by pressure from the United States.[4] In the form of adopted policy, however, liberalization may be at odds with the interests of officials charged with promoting it. While professing the proposition that free markets at home and abroad are in Japan's national interest, bureaucrats have their own stake in a mercantilist regime. In some cases, liberalization may be supported by those whose relative position in the pecking order would be improved by an absolute decline in the prerogatives of others. In the course of liberalization, there has been a merging of issues and breakdown of bureaucratic jurisdictions. Matters that formerly could be resolved at the discretion of a single Ministry of Finance official, for example, may now lie in a wider ministerial area or even in the realm of national politics.[5] The politicization of economic issues, an aspect of "Japan, Disincorporated," has been accelerated by the decline in the growth rate of gross national product (GNP).[6] Within the politicization syndrome itself, an additional aspect of "Japan, Disincorporated," arises from ambiguity concerning the role of the Liberal Democratic Party political leadership in the liberalization process.

On the international policy plane, Japan's chief preoccupation during the interregnum of the 1980s concerned the nature of its relations with the United States. In the latter 1980s, the question of whether Japan should behave as a "small" nation or as a "big" nation was no longer at issue. United States demands were sharply directed at Japan as a major industrial power. In the short run, Japan brooded about the optimal degree of acquiescence to U.S. demands. In the long run, especially in the framework of the scenario of Japan as a headquarters country, the problem concerned how it could best fulfill its objective of reducing the degree of its dependence on the United States as a market. (In 1985, Japan surpassed Canada to become the leading source of U.S. imports.) In the meanwhile, the pragmatic issue concerned how Japan could manipulate foreign pressures in such a way as to make them serve its own objectives and fulfill its own national interests. In this context, during the second postwar phase, the combination of Japan's formal endorsement of the liberalization program together with disingenuous backsliding in the implementation of it can be readily explained.

In its desultory approach toward liberalization, Japan's relations with the United States continued to be vexed by trade as well as financial issues. In the course of much U.S.-Japan recrimination, Japan's sincerity concerning trade liberalization was ostensibly demonstrated in its adoption of the July 1985 "Action Program" scheduled for results during the three years following. In 1985 as well, after a meeting between President Reagan and Prime Minister Nakasone, "market-oriented sector-selective" (MOSS) negotiations were inaugurated between the United States and Japan. The sectors subject to negotiation were those in which the United States was presumed to maintain a comparative advantage in international competition. They included telecommunications, electronics, forest products, medical equipment, pharmaceuticals, and transportation machinery. However, by 1987, in a review of the negotiations, the Office of the United States Trade Representative (USTR) was decidedly sour. "When we talk to the Japanese about semiconductors and superconductors, they say, 'Oh no, these are leading industries that will determine the fate of Japan. We can't make concessions.' When we talk to them about declining industries like shipbuilding and aluminum, we are told, 'We can't make concessions there because the costs of adjustment are too high.' And when we talk to them about agriculture—rice, beef, and citrus—

we're told, 'There would be political problems there; we can't make concessions.' "[7]

In April 1986, the Maekawa Commission, a private study group appointed by Prime Minister Nakasone, issued a report containing medium- and long-term proposals to "restructure" the Japanese economy. The report was ingenious in its apparent acceptance of U.S. demands while remaining compatible with strategy for Japan's emergence as a headquarters country. Noting that in 1985, Japan's current account surplus was unprecedentedly large, amounting to 3.6 percent of GNP, the report advocated a reduction in the export-orientation of the Japanese economy in favor of the expansion of domestic demand. The latter would include the improvement of domestic infrastructure and housing. "While paying due consideration to the impact on small and medium-size businesses," the report advocated the phasing out of declining industries and the promotion of large-scale projects, leading to economic concentration. Sunset industries to be phased out would include materials-intensive industries and low- and middle-technology industries that Japan as a headquarters country would assign to its agents in Third World nations or vouchsafe to mature countries such as the United States that protect and subsidize their declining sectors. While renouncing the mercantilist claim that Japan should maintain an established position in all export products across the board, the report argued in favor of concentration in the field of high technology products and international financial services. It further emphasized that Japan should promote international cooperation and make contributions to the world economy commensurate with its international status. From the headquarters country point of view, this would imply "promoting direct foreign investment," "conclusion of bilateral agreements," and contrivance of "a high level of policy coordination" among nations. In asserting its forward-looking view, the report argued for "liberalization of financial and capital markets and internationalization of the yen." By mid-1986, four of the world's five largest banks (in terms of assets) were Japanese; hence, in this field Japan had nothing to fear from liberalization. The Maekawa report said nothing about government procurement, the resistance of Japanese *keiretsu* (*zaibatsu* successor) groups to penetration by outsiders, or the difficulties of foreigners in becoming subcontractors in Japan. In general, the report was a masterly demonstration of the Japanese art of judo, in which the strength of the opponent is used *against* him. Foreign pressure (*gaiatsu*) for Japanese reform was utilized in the form of recommendations conducive to the fulfillment of Japan's indigenous goals and objectives.

By 1986, however, external pressure had advanced into a new

channel. While continuing to protest against restricted U.S. access to Japanese markets and excessive entry, dumping, and unfair competition by Japan in U.S. markets, the United States demanded that Japan should adopt expansionary monetary and fiscal policies; the latter would increase Japanese income, consumer spending, and imports, including imports from the United States. Thus at a delicate moment in the interval between phase two and phase three of its postwar transition, Japan was faced with a new challenge. Again the strategy problem concerned the optimal extent to which Japan should acquiesce to U.S. demands, or appear to do so, and how such acquiescence could be made to promote Japan's own national interests. Outright expansionary macroeconomic policies would jeopardize Japan's objective of achieving a balanced budget by 1990. It would jeopardize the objectives of the administrative reform program, which called for reduction of government spending. It would risk the outbreak of inflation. Moreover, the Japanese government felt that it had already made many concessions to the United States (for example, in the form of "voluntary export restrictions"), none of which had enabled the United States to overcome its trade deficit. On the other hand, by being uncompromising and intransigent, it would accelerate the passage of U.S. protectionist legislation directed primarily against Japan.

In either case, however—acquiescence or intransigence—there were possibilities for Japan to reap benefits. In the short run, acquiescence would retard the rise of protectionism in the United States and elsewhere. In the long run, intransigence, by provoking U.S. protectionism, would promote the expatriation of Japan's low and middle technology firms. By means of direct foreign investment, owners of such firms were already swarming to the newly industrializing countries as well as to the United States and Western Europe. It has been estimated that by the year 2000, if Japan can maintain the pace, as much as 30 percent of its productive capacity will be located abroad.

The ultimate disadvantages of protectionism to the United States, moreover, would conceivably redound to the benefit of Japan. For contrasting reasons, Japanese investment in the United States has occurred in high as well as in low and medium technology fields. In the high technology fields, its primary purposes have been to acquire technology, know-how, or distribution networks. In low technology, its primary purposes have been to liquidate Japan's own dual economy and to jump over existing or anticipated U.S. protectionist barriers. By attracting the expatriation of Japan's low and middle technology firms, the United States would be building and reinforcing its own dual economy while helping to liquidate the dual economy in Japan. (Indeed, by deliberate industrial policy, for more than two decades, Japan has already been liquidating its dual economy of coexisting backward and frontier firms.) Japan's resources would be allocated primarily to high technology while those of the United States would be dissipated in obsolete activities supported by the welfare state. Moreover, while Japan would welcome imports of low and middle technology manufactured products from the developing countries, the United States would increasingly resist doing so. This would create new areas of external friction for the United States to the indirect advantage of Japan. As the world's leading debtor nation, the United States would deepen its difficulties by closing its doors to developing nations that have their own debts to pay. Furthermore, U.S. protectionism would precipitate retaliation and the increase of protectionism in the world at large.

This conceivable course of events leads directly to the scenario of phase three, in which the United States is a beleaguered island in the world economy while Japan becomes a headquarters country. U.S. protectionism would antagonize the developing countries that now are building low and middle technology smokestack industries (in many cases with Japanese capital). Since Japan's markets would be open to their exports, they in turn would be a market for Japan's high technology products rather than those of the United States. In the financial field, the scenario takes account of the trend toward economic concentration by means of takeovers, leveraged buyouts, and megamergers that has "restructured" the industrial landscape of major industrial countries. In contrast with U.S. firms that merely seek promotional profits or short-term operating gains, Japanese firms are following their classic strategy of acquiring market share. In the shakeout of nonviable conglomerates that the future holds in store, major Japanese firms will survive (with the support of their *keiretsu* partners) and will consolidate their market positions. In terms of industrial structure, Japan will concentrate its resources in the fields of high technology and international financial services. It is in these areas that the ultimate showdown between the United States and Japan will occur.

Eventually, a protectionist world would give rise to bilateral relationships, countertrade, and cartels. In such a world, by virtue of its historical experience and centripetal propensities, Japan would fare much better than the United States. (Already, the 1987 semiconductor cartel arrangements between the United States and Japan turned out to be counterproductive for the United States.)

In the scenario sketched here, Japan as a rentier and high technology nation would flourish as England did in the nineteenth century, but in wider and deeper dimensions. The contemporary paradox of rising protectionism in the category of merchandise trade combined with progressive deregulation and liberalization in financial and capital markets gives Japan the best of both worlds. In phase three of its postwar transition, Japan would possess a world system of subsidiaries and affiliates, with headquarters in Tokyo. These would be controlled and coordinated by Japan's international financial institutions and its trading companies (sogo shosha). In operating its economic empire, Japan would have the advantage of being the world's foremost creditor nation, the advantage of exclusive relationships established by its trading companies, and the unrivaled information systems upon which the latter thrive. These networks would be utilized in behalf of the newly industrializing countries for the distribution of low and middle technology products such as those that generated Japan's economic "miracle." In particular, in a protectionist world, the capability of Japan's sogo shosha would be unexcelled in performing countertrade and switch transactions that overcome protectionist barriers and foreign exchange controls. Lacking comparable capability, the United States may itself become dependent upon these Japanese services. In implementing this scenario, Japan will adhere to its postwar precept of "friendship with all," namely with communist and noncommunist countries alike. Thus, Tokyo will preside over truly global channels for distribution of the products of its economic empire. In the present era, moreover, it is evident that control over distribution channels is often of more strategic importance than control over production facilities. These factors—together with structural trends in the world economy, such as bilateralism, economic concentration, and the dominance of financial over nonfinancial sectors—are the harbingers of the third phase of Japan's postwar transition.

In such circumstances, Japanese big business will again need the partnership of government in its transactions on the international plane. In a managed world economy, in which giant firms are engaged in life-and-death struggles, conflict is too deadly to be mediated at the private enterprise level; instead, it must be performed by means of government intervention. Traditionally, Japanese big business and the Japanese government have been closely associated, and their affinities contrast strongly with government-business antipathies in the United States. Internationally, the Japanese government will not only provide its good offices in resolving conflicts but also open doors at the political and diplomatic levels in search of special deals for the benefit of Japanese firms. The bureaucrat and the businessman once again will need each other in the era of "Japan, Reincorporated." Thus, bureaucrats will recover the turf they relinquished in the first phase of the postwar transition, the phase of "liberalization." Japan as a headquarters country will emerge in full flower.

In its approach to the ambiguities and conflicts of Japan's postwar transition, the present study concentrates on the liberalization or "Japan, Disincorporated" episode that precedes the headquarters country phase sketched above. It examines the relation between domestic and external liberalization and the institutional nature of policymaking in the Ministry of Finance. It also attempts to identify winners and losers in the power struggle. Domestically, that struggle is waged both between and within the public and private sectors. In the public sector, the players are politicians, ministries, and individual bureaucrats; there are conflicts both among and within ministries. Within the private sector, there are conflicts between rising and declining industries, between the banking industry and the securities industry, between manufacturing and agriculture, and between big business and small business.

The decline in Japan's growth rate following the first oil crisis imparted a dampening as well as a politicizing effect to the liberalization process. This can be attributed partly to the inverse cyclical relationship between two markets: first, the market for government services and, second, the market for commercial services and commodities. When the business cycle is at its peak, private sector demand for political and bureaucratic services is minimal; when the business cycle is at its trough, private sector demand for government support and assistance is at its peak. However, in responding to private sector demand, the government supplies intervention and controls as well as services and assistance. Consequently, after 1973, Japan's progress in economic liberalization was idiosyncratic and constrained. Formally, however, liberalization progressed while government bureaucrats clung to the residual controls they still possessed. Official landmarks of that progress included liberalization of the Foreign Exchange and Foreign Trade Control Law (effective December 1980), the new Banking Law (effective April 1982), and the administrative reform proposals (launched in March 1981). In various ways, these reforms were interrelated, especially in the realm of relations between the external and internal sectors of the economy. In the early 1980s, the chief issues of liberalization, issues with which this study is largely concerned, referred to money markets, capital markets, and capital movements.

The strategy of Japan's emergence as a headquarters country is implicit in the policies of the Ministry of Finance. Moreover, it is in the international financial sector, dominated by that ministry, that bureaucratic interests are most clearly at stake and in which the strategy and decisionmaking process of Japan's foreign economic policy may most clearly be observed. The decisionmaking process is described in the first chapter. Chapter Two, a study of the distinction between appearance and reality in Japanese economic affairs, shows how economic liberalization created a dilemma for the bureaucracy. The ambivalence of the bureaucracy with regard to liberalization is apparent in the inconsistent and devious measures that were adopted concerning financial liberalization. Chapter Three is a case study of the "Japan, Disincorporated," aspect of liberalization, in which the conflicting interests of the Ministry of Finance and the Bank of Japan are explained in the context of financial liberalization. Chapter Four concerns the role of administrative reform in Japan's emergence as a headquarters country. Although administrative reform was ostensibly launched for purposes of fiscal restraint, its ultimate economic implication is a switch in resources from the domestic to the external sector. Retrenchment in the domestic sector would facilitate that transfer. The Japanese government has made no secret of its wish to assume a higher posture in international affairs. Characteristically, however, as in the interregnum of liberalization, the approach to its objective is indirect.

In the present disorderly, protectionist, and increasingly risky international economy, it is clear that Japan's national interests require government and business to move in tandem. Thus, the goal of comprehensive economic security for the nation is a mandate for the emergence of "Japan, Reincorporated." In preparing an agenda for serving the nation, the bureaucracy is self-serving as well. Expansion of the government's role on the international plane would augment the functions, prerogatives, and staff of the economic and diplomatic establishment. The final chapter is a review and prognosis. With regard to the prognosis, Japan's emergence as a headquarters country is foreseen.

I am deeply grateful to those in the Japanese government, business firms, banks, and the universities who briefed me concerning the matters discussed here. For reasons that will be apparent, many of them cannot be named. By the same token, they are spared embarrassment for errors of understanding, interpretation, or perspective in my account. I am also grateful to the Hoover Institution for a grant in support of the research for this study.

═ 1 ═

THE DECISIONMAKING PROCEDURE

Although the terms *free enterprise, capitalism,* and *entrepreneurship* are used alike in both Japan and the United States, the phenomena to which they refer are not necessarily identical. At the government level, Japan's economic transition during the 1980s has been described as a process of liberalization, one where the government supposedly exercises less control over the economy. The meaning of the term is not self-evident. Accordingly, its results and their implications for U.S. policy are also not obvious. The rationale for liberalization in Japan begins with a decisionmaking procedure.

Pressures Impelling Liberalization

Following the occupation, the Japanese bureaucracy was reluctant to relinquish any sooner than necessary the bonanza of economic controls it had inherited from SCAP. By the 1960s, however, chiefly under pressure from the United States, many controls on international commodity flows had been removed, and progress was being made in the category of capital flows as well. At the same time, while controls were being removed in the external sector, Japan's domestic economy became increasingly centralized and subject to more, rather than less, official control.[1]

As the economy matured, the interests of the bureaucracy became increasingly differentiated. Some ministries, including the Ministry of International Trade and Industry (MITI), took an affirmative view of liberalization, while others, such as the Ministry of Finance, had mixed feelings. Although they were not prepared or presented as parts of a coherent liberalization program, it seems reasonable to classify three recent measures of the Japanese government as components of the liberalization process. These include the new Foreign Exchange and Foreign Trade Control Law, the Banking Law, and establishment of the Provisional Commission for Administrative Reform. Administrative reform implies reduction of the size and role of the government and the degree of its intervention, thus contributing to liberalization. Collectively, these measures embrace liberalization in both the domestic and international sectors.

In domestic affairs, demands for liberalization have been primarily indigenous, but foreign pressure on Japan's monetary and fiscal policy was heavy during debate on the "locomotive" thesis (1977–1979),[2] among other occasions. Although pressure from abroad has been directed mainly in behalf of liberalization of Japan's external sector, the interdependence of domestic and external policy has radiated that pressure into every crevice of the Japanese economy. As participants in international organizations and conferences, Japanese policymakers have been directly exposed to the demands of their foreign colleagues. Pressures have been applied in the councils of the Organization for Economic Cooperation and Development (OECD), the International Monetary Fund (IMF), and elsewhere.[3] Consequently, officials such as those in the Foreign Ministry and the International Finance Bureau (IFB) of the Ministry of Finance are among the most internationalist and liberal-minded members of the Japanese government.

Apart from uninvited pressures, sometimes external pressures are invited by interested parties in Japanese government or business. From time to time, "back-channel" information is leaked to the foreigner to be used as ammunition against the Japanese establishment.

The effectiveness of outside pressure on Japan may be decreasing because of resistance associated with rising Japanese nationalism. From a Japanese perspective, U.S. pressure is inappropriate because it has been (one) inconsistent or (two) unfair and (three) because U.S. credibility has been reduced by the failure of American domestic economic policies. In the "cheap yen" controversy of 1982, Japanese were indignant on all three points. On the one hand, they were urged by C. Fred Bergsten, then a Treasury Department undersecretary, to impose controls on capital outflows in order to reduce downward pressure on the yen.[4] Simultaneously, other American experts urged Japan to liberalize capital outflows in order to raise interest rates, which would strengthen the yen. It was argued in Japan that capital outflow would greatly weaken the yen before raising interest rates only slightly. Japanese believed that the undervalued yen was caused by excessively high U.S. interest rates and that it was unfair of foreigners to demand that Japan jeopardize the recovery of capital investment by raising its own interest rates. Moreover, Japanese felt victimized by the combination of various "voluntary export quotas" they had been forced to adopt together with the welfare loss implicit in their inferior terms of trade. Given the export quotas, there was no advantage to Japan in an undervalued yen, which moreover had inflationary potentialities because of its effect on the price of imports.

In summary, however, it seems fair to say that external pressures have led Japan to liberalize its international transactions before liberalizing its domestic economy. Private-sector pressure, rather than government initiative, has led to liberalization in the domestic economy. Thus, the bureaucracy followed rather than led in the liberalization process.

Patterns in the Wallpaper

The director of research and planning in the International Finance Bureau of the Ministry of Finance, Eisuke Sakakibara, was asked (one) who are the winners and losers because of liberalization and internationalization? (two) what changes have occurred in the decisionmaking process and in the procedures of the IFB because of liberalization and internationalization? and (three) what changes have occurred within the power structure of the Ministry of Finance and in its relation to the Bank of Japan because of liberalization and internationalization?

"Those questions are too broad," he replied, adding that these matters must be approached on a case-by-case basis.

Even the case-by-case approach cannot be too broadly conceived in the investigation process. Instead, when one is conducting economic interviews in Japan, it is necessary to ask very narrow and specific questions about the actual work of the organization. What happens in particular instances? How are these instances connected? What is the rationale of each instance? How has liberalization changed that rationale? When a mass of detailed facts has been collected and verified by several authoritative sources, the facts may be arranged in a mosaic that shows patterns of relationship. These are the "patterns in the wallpaper" from which the observer can draw his own conclusions about matters such as the nature and outcome of the power struggle. Various observers may see various patterns. The picture that emerges contains subjective as well as objective elements.

Within the Ministry of Finance, the subjective or interpretative element is substantial because the division of labor is not clearly defined even by the ministry itself. The responsibilities of the seven bureaus of the ministry are closely related. The IFB is a relatively young, newly emerging bureau. Its chief duties concern international financial problems and economic cooperation. Its power and scope are not conspicuously strong. Before it determines its policies, it confers with the Banking Bureau, the Securities Bureau, the Tax Bureau, or others as the case may be. In 1982, for example, in order to stem the outflow of capital (due to low Japanese interest rates) that was depreciating the yen, the director of the IFB recommended that interest rate restrictions authorized by the Interest Adjustment Law be abolished. To do so, however, would conflict with the artificially controlled terms of issue of national bonds and of some corporation bonds. The economic problem overlapped several bureaus.

Despite the adverse effect of interest rate restrictions on Japan's rapidly expanding international financial activities, the Financial Bureau and the Budget Bureau have resisted the suggestion that interest rates should be liberalized. This would reduce their turf and curtail their powers of control. Moreover, the Budget Bureau has resisted increasing the interest rate on national bonds because of the debt burden. The Financial Bureau opposed increasing interest rates because of its discouraging effect on domestic investment. Instead, these bureaus argued that the IFB should use its powers of administrative guidance (gyōsei shidō) to restrict international capital movements.[5] Thus, as one observer in the ministry remarked, "Even though realizing its defects, and aware that such restrictions should be imposed only in an emergency, as a result of decisions within the Ministry of Finance the IFB is forced to introduce foreign-exchange controls against its will." This reveals that in the decisionmaking process within the Ministry of Finance, domestic constraints may outweigh international considerations, despite Japan's dependence on the world economy. The Budget Bureau is pre-eminent in the decisionmaking process on the domestic side. Nonpecuniary income in the form of power and status constitutes an important part of the rewards the Budget Bureau enjoys.

The IFB is headed by the director general, followed by the deputy director general and the director of the Coordination Division, who is in charge of coordinating five principal IFB divisions. As described by an authoritative source, the most important of these is the Planning Division, which is in charge of matters such as the amendment of the Foreign Exchange and Foreign Trade Control Law. Second is the Research Division. Third is the International Organizations Division, which supervises Japan's relations with organizations such as the IMF, OECD, the International Bank for Reconstruction and Development (IBRD), the International Finance Corporation (IFC), the International

Development Association (IDA), and the Asian Development Bank (ADB). (The IMF executive director for Japan is a former Ministry of Finance official.) The International Organizations Division is also concerned with summit meetings insofar as they concern international financial affairs, and it prepares documents for international meetings. Fourth is the Foreign Exchange Division, which is in charge of foreign-exchange market intervention by the Bank of Japan. It also supervises the international business of Japanese banks. Fifth is the Capital Transactions Division, which controls the issuance by foreigners of yen-denominated bonds (Samurai bonds) in the Japanese market and issuance by Japanese of bonds in foreign markets. It controls portfolio investment in Japan by foreigners and portfolio investment abroad by Japanese. It also controls direct investment in Japan by foreigners and direct investment abroad by Japanese.

An example of how these divisions are coordinated is seen in the context of the recently increased international activities of Japanese banks. The Foreign Exchange Division is concerned with the country-risk and maturity-matching aspects of these transactions. It establishes rules, or "guidelines," about country limits, capital ratio, and liquidity ratio (the ratio of liquid assets to liquid liabilities). Before these banking guidelines are determined, however, the Research Division investigates the practices of other countries. The Coordination Division checks to see whether the collaboration between the Foreign Exchange Division and the Research Division is sufficient. It also consults with the Bank of Japan. After coordination has been completed, a policy draft is drawn up. At this stage, the director of the Coordination Bureau consults *informally* with the Banking Bureau. Next, an IFB meeting is held with its director general. After long discussion and further meetings, the consensus of the IFB is formed.

Another example of coordination among divisions concerns the prohibition in the summer of 1982 of purchases by Japanese residents of foreign zero-coupon bonds. The IFB was the bureau most concerned. The Tax Bureau was also concerned, but it lacked jurisdiction to restrict zero-coupon bond purchases. The IFB could have invoked its emergency powers, but it was reluctant to do so. Instead, it asked the Securities Bureau to restrict the purchases in accordance with its authority to regulate trading in securities. In receiving the cooperation of the Securities Bureau, which did comply with the request, the IFB incurred an obligation to return the favor on some future occasion.

In the summer of 1982, the IFB was also concerned about the outflow of capital resulting from the purchase of foreign bonds by life insurance companies. (Slack business conditions in Japan had reduced the domestic demand for their funds.) The insurance companies, however, are under the control of the Banking Bureau. The Banking Bureau acceded to the IFB's request to exercise guidance over the insurance companies to restrict purchases of foreign bonds. In so doing, the IFB again incurred an obligation to return the favor.

Within the IFB, each division has one director, three or four assistant directors, and five to ten section chiefs. In the formulation of policy, it is an assistant director who writes the draft. He consults with the director and with his colleagues before completing it. Thus, preparation of the draft is a collaborative process. In case of an emergency, this system is not efficient because it takes too long to form a consensus and arrive at a decision.

In the IFB, as elsewhere, the decisionmaking process depends on the type of personnel available; the career officials rotate rapidly, approximately once every two years.[6] Personnel are assigned to the bureaus of the Ministry of Finance by the Personnel Division in the Ministerial Secretariat. The Personnel Division makes its decision on the basis of personalities: it tries to balance innovative with passive types. It decides on where "strong," "complementary," or "conservative" types are necessary. Thus, the policymaking process in the IFB changes drastically, depending on personalities of the leadership assigned by the Personnel Division. The IFB can request the assignment of supervisory officials it prefers, but the decision rests with the Personnel Division.

Do noncareer personnel have any influence on policy? It depends on the case. Formally, noncareer personnel are specialists in the collection and processing of data, preparation of documents, and the like, and have no influence on policy. According to one interviewee, it is difficult to generalize about the decisionmaking process because there are no rigid rules. The process is ad hoc and depends largely on personalities and subjective judgments.

In the IFB, new policies are usually proposed at the level of the director of research and planning or at the level of the deputy director of the IFB. When they originate with the former, he generally consults with the director general or the deputy director general of the bureau to ascertain what they are thinking. Even when the research and planning people adopt an independent initiative, they generally know what opinion is held in the front office and know what that office approves of. This is consistent with consensus procedure. But the research and planning people say that they do not draft proposals under direct orders from the person at the top. The director general of the bureau has relatively independent power to make policy, although he is under the administrative vice minister (who mainly coordinates) and under the vice minister for international affairs. Usually, the director general takes the initiative himself. However, if the deputy director general wishes to take the initiative in introducing a new policy, he may do so, provided he has the consent of the director general. It is a flexible system, one in which there is no rigidly prescribed procedure. It depends basically on personalities. However, it is necessary to establish a mood, or create an atmosphere, before a new proposal can be accepted.

Understanding between the chiefs of divisions and chiefs of sections, and between section chiefs and division chiefs is very important. The most critical point in the decisionmaking process is the informal discussion. The formal disposition of a decision in an open meeting is preset and perfunctory. Real consideration of a decision rarely takes place at open meetings. The procedure is similar to that in the Japanese army, where in open meetings a general must accept the advice of his staff. If the general rejects that advice in an official meeting, relations with his staff will deteriorate, and morale will be poor.

Similarly, in the Japanese civil bureaucracy, if a section chief often rejects the decision of his subordinate division, human relations between the section chief and the division will deteriorate. These human relations are very important. Moreover, the way the section chief expresses disapproval is also important. If the section chief wishes to disapprove, he should inform the division indirectly or informally. A serious breach is caused if the decision of the division is rejected or "discussed severely." The decision of the division should never be rejected publicly in an open meeting. If good relations cannot be maintained, the section chief should ask to be reassigned to some other section.

The pecking order of the various bureaus within the Ministry of Finance has some bearing on how compromises are eventually negotiated. According to well-placed insiders, the bureaus rank as follows: (1) Budget Bureau; (2) Financial Bureau (which compiles the Fiscal Investment and Loan Program and which controls the Trust Fund); (3) Tax Bureau; (4) Banking Bureau (which supervises the Bank of Japan); (5) Securities Bureau (which supervises the stock market and securities firms); and (6) International Finance Bureau. In terms of status, there is a considerable gap between the Banking Bureau and the Securities Bureau; however, the latter is rising in relative prestige. During the past decade, the importance of the IFB has likewise increased. It will continue to do so inasmuch as the Banking Bureau and the Securities Bureau cannot do their work without IFB collaboration.

There are differences between the Ministry of Finance and MITI concerning the location of decisionmaking power. In MITI there is a preponderance of decisionmaking power in the lower levels of the bureaucracy. It so happens that this renders MITI more independent of the politicians than the Ministry of Finance, where decisionmaking is performed higher up in the bureaucracy. The reason for this is that political intervention normally occurs at the upper levels of the bureaucracy rather than at the lower levels. (In MITI, of course, the higher officials do possess decisionmaking powers comparable to those of officials in the Ministry of Finance, but they do not invoke them to the same degree.) Politicians are also more likely to intervene in domestic rather than in international affairs.

By the nature of its mission, the Ministry of Finance is more macro-oriented than micro-oriented, whereas in MITI it is the reverse. This does not imply, however, that the Ministry of Finance is more dedicated to the national interest than is MITI. In the course of bureaucratic politics, the Ministry of Finance is more likely to place its own interests ahead of the national interest in domestic rather than in international affairs.

In the Ministry of Finance, the process of negotiation among the bureaus involves technical, political, and economic factors. For example, were a politician to request the construction of a national railway spur in his home district, the first step would be to study whether such construction would be technically feasible. Second, economic factors, such as the phase of the business cycle, the level of unemployment, and other cost-benefit considerations, would be analyzed. Finally, the political influence of the Diet member would be weighed. When the Economic Planning Agency (EPA) sends a proposal to the Ministry of Finance, it may receive diametrically opposed responses from the various bureaus of the ministry. In matters involving statistical forecasts of national economic variables, the Coordination Bureau of the EPA enters the scene to work out differences of opinion. The EPA's Coordination Bureau also coordinates other economic matters among the various ministries.

When it comes to implementing policy, individual Diet members tend to identify themselves with whatever ministry has pork barrel potentialities with regard to the interests of their political constituents. The Diet member becomes a client of that ministry, as indeed the ministry in turn becomes a client of the Diet member. They support and mutually reinforce each other. Neither can disregard or arbitrarily oppose the other. In budget matters, for example, the percentage of increase in the appropriations distributed to the various ministries is no longer uniform, as it was formerly.[7] Thus, if a Diet member wants to get approval for a new hospital in his district, and if the Ministry of Finance is going to impose an absolute reduction in the budget of the Ministry of Health and Welfare, the Diet member cannot wait until the latter's budget has been submitted to the Ministry of Finance to argue his case. He must intervene with the Ministry of Health and Welfare at the point where proposals for hospital expenditures are being formulated and secure a disproportionately large share so that part of his project will survive even after the budget is cut.

The collaboration between bureaucrats and politicians is induced by the fact that, as individuals, bureaucrats are very weak and expendable. There are many bureaucrats contending for a limited number of opportunities for promotion. If a bureaucrat in the ranks conscientiously opposes the demands of twenty Diet members, he will never become a bureau chief, will never be promoted to vice minister or any other eminent appointment, and will not obtain a good position in the business world after he retires from the ministry. He will also never be permitted to become an LDP politician. It is more pragmatic to accede to the pressure groups than to be impartial. Thus, the equity of the decisionmaking process ultimately depends on the personal principles and integrity of only a few key people at the top of various strategic government pyramids, people who are in a position to resist political pressure.

The pyramids, moreover, are not well coordinated. Japanese government ministries operate as though they were firms in oligopolistic competition. On many issues, there is no single ministerial authority. Theoretically, the EPA is a coordinating agency in economic decisionmaking matters, but in practice it has little bureaucratic power. The Ministry of Finance is the coordinating ministry for budgetary affairs. In recent years, however, the Liberal Democratic Party's Policy Affairs Research Council (Seimu Chōsa Kai) has gained significant influence in the budgetary process.

Lack of coordination is also pronounced among the many advisory councils (shingikai) that give specialist advice to the various ministries. In 1982, there were approximately 212 such councils, officially established by laws, covering all important policy areas. In addition, there were numerous unofficial councils or advisory committees. There are various views of these councils and committees, which are not coordinated or organized in a hierarchy. One view is that the councils are appointed simply to define what the public or professional consensus actually is. This enables the government to determine whether its policies do or do not conform with that consensus. Within the government itself, economic planning is designed to form a consensus among the various ministries and to present that consensus to the public.

A second view of the advisory councils is that they lay out the array of options for the bureaucrats: they provide information about the range of opinion on those options. A third view is that the councils merely validate policies already determined by the government. For this reason, the council system is often called a cloak for the bureaucracy. This view assumes plausibility because materials for discussion and even drafts of reports are prepared by the bureaucracy before council meetings. The councils are said to contribute little of analytical substance. The bureaucrats often possess more specialist knowledge of the matters under discussion than the council members; moreover, the bureaucrats control the data provided to the council members. For the most part, council members are busy with their own work and often come to the meetings unprepared for more than casual discussion. This version of the councils is certainly not universally valid. In the IFB, for example, during the summer of 1982, the Study Group on Basic International Financial Problems, headed by Ryutaro Komiya, a professor of economics at Tokyo University, was discussing implications of the possible establishment of an international banking facility in Japan. Komiya could certainly not be described as a casual or passive commentator.

Japan lacks a political figure like the president of the United States, who acts as a coordinator on the political plane. Politically, even though the Japanese executive branch is stronger than its American counterpart, the Japanese prime minister is weaker than the U.S. president. Japan's comparative lack of machinery or institutional arrangements for coordination at the prime ministerial level make it highly vulnerable in a crisis, for it takes a long time to achieve consensus from below by means of the step-by-step procedure.

Personnel

What kinds of personnel are now being recruited by the Ministry of Finance, and how do they differ from those recruited in the past? Recruitment has been affected by the change in the environment surrounding the ministry—the environment with which it has to deal. Although the written examination is still of principal importance, the personality of the candidate has assumed relatively greater importance than in the past, and accordingly the interview has likewise assumed relatively greater importance.

The environment surrounding the ministry has become more pluralistic, more fragmented, more liberalized. In these circumstances, the ministry can no longer give peremptory orders either to its clients or to other ministries to the same extent as formerly. It must persuade, compromise, conciliate. The type of person being recruited must thus be capable of conciliation and persuasion. It remains true, however, that younger career officials are recruited from a dedicated, self-selected group that from an early age has aspired to enter the ministry. The candidates from this group are dedicated to the traditions of the ministry and to its established point of view. They look to their seniors for cues to correct behavior and thinking, and try to please them.

Are young Ministry of Finance officials more prone to liberalization and internationalization than their seniors? Perhaps half of the juniors are internationalist minded, while half are nationalistic. Among the seniors, perhaps less than half are internationalist minded. It does not follow that those members of the ministry who have gone abroad are necessarily more susceptible to internationalism. On the contrary, they may revert to nationalism *in reaction to* their experience abroad. Although young officials outwardly adopt the policy view of their seniors, inwardly they may feel differently in some respects. In particular, they may be less favorably disposed to the United States. They see Japan as strong, the United States as weak. Moreover, they see Japan as having practiced government intervention, and they associate controls and subsidies with Japan's success. (MITI, for example, believes that Japan's success is the result of its industrial policy.) On the other hand, while some young officials see nothing wrong with intervention, the free-market economists are likewise found primarily within the younger group. The latter have less confidence in the efficacy of controls and government spending. To this extent, they are in favor of liberalization and administrative reform. As a whole, the ministries are not advocates of administrative reform, because it threatens the survival of government jobs.

In the Ministry of Finance, the traditional policies are inculcated by means of an intensive six-month lecture and study course given to young officials after their second or third year of employment. The subjects include economic theory and economic policy; the lecturers include famous professors and specialists from other ministries.

As the top career personnel rotate from one assignment to another, do they carry their loyalties with them? What happens to institutional memory? In general, officials are loyal to the bureau to which they are currently attached. They regard it as a professional challenge to defend the turf for which they are presently responsible. In doing so, more-

over, they attempt—although not invariably—to fulfill their predecessor's commitments, such as trade-offs that have been agreed to in the
reconciliation or coordination process. The transfer of loyalties as well
as personnel from bureau to bureau may help explain the Japanese
dictum that "bureaus exist, but not ministries." The regular rotation
of career officials at two- or three-year intervals contributes to the
consensusmaking process because it helps them to understand each
other's problems. Thus, "We are friendly with each other," as one of
them explained.

What effect do noncareer personnel have on policy? In terms of
numbers, the percentage of noncareer personnel varies among agencies. In the EPA, it is between 30 and 40 percent. In the Japanese
National Railways and the Postal Service, it is about 90 percent. In
general, noncareer personnel are well disciplined and obedient to
policy, once the order has been given. With regard to liberalization,
however, the technician, the man-on-the-spot, often continues to operate by preliberalization rules. Technicians may feel threatened by
liberalization because it can destroy the basis for their interventionist
expertise. It may render their special knowledge obsolete or irrelevant.
It also prevents them from exercising their customary prerogatives. In
customs clearance, for example, the man-on-the-spot looks for a rule
that enables him to operate in the way he has always operated. Thus,
although liberalization is on the books, in fact it is not implemented.
The Ministry of Agriculture, Forestry, and Fisheries provides further
examples of resistance by noncareer officials to import liberalization.
Its officials are not economists; they are technical specialists in agriculture, forestry, or fisheries. As technicians, they exercise special
powers. The practice of these technical specialties may be jeopardized
by liberalization, which thus tends to be circumvented.

The noncareer official is normally rigid, conservative, and traditional. He is unsophisticated. He has not had a foreign education and
has not been exposed to international conferences. He is honest and
works hard. Moreover, it is the noncareer official who makes many of
the decisions that are issued by the government. The noncareer official
has had long experience in his particular duties. He knows what he
thinks about any possible contingency. The high career official is
rational, flexible, and may be friendly to liberalization, but he often
knows less about the actual details of his job than his subordinates.
Thus, he may avoid becoming involved in technical matters. Attempts
by outsiders to bypass noncareer officials may prove to be risky.
Salomon Brothers, for example, attempted to deal only with top
officials in pressing its application for a license to operate in Japan. In

doing so, the firm annoyed the lower officials, with the result that its application was held up for more than a year. It should be added that not all noncareer officials are opposed to liberalization on their own account. An increasing number of such officials are university graduates who have been educated to respect the market system. Those with a liberal attitude, however, are not free to express their opinions when these are at variance with the policy consensus.

Among the noncareer officials, the role of unions, although controversial, is of little decisionmaking concern. Legally, the chief assistant director of a division (which is below the bureau) is prohibited from being a union member. Everyone below him may join a union. The government unions are primarily concerned with pay and promotion. Therefore, although government unions may be left wing, they characteristically have no effect on public policy.

Policies

Japan's academic modern economists agree that the economic "miracle" was accomplished during the period of intensive government controls of the first two postwar decades. They maintain, however, that this does not imply cause and effect. Without government controls or guidance, Japan's performance would have been pretty much the same. In the future, they argue, continued maintenance of controls would place a constraint on the dynamism of the Japanese economy. Within the government itself, contradictory positions concerning controls and liberalization are held by officials of equivalent rank in various organizations. Their opinions reflect the jobs they perform and the vantage point afforded by the organizations in which they work. There may be a wide discrepancy, moreover, between the way the Japanese government describes its policy approach to outsiders and the way in which that approach is conceived by the government itself. In the international sector, the Japanese government contends that its policies are largely determined by the policies of the United States and that the scope of its independent policy options is small. In terms of its objectives, however, the government's goal is clear, namely, to become less visible and less susceptible to foreign protectionism in world markets. This may be accomplished first by shifting its industrial center of gravity from consumer goods to less conspicuous producer goods and from low-technology goods to high-technology goods.[8] Second, having grown to be a giant in physical production, Japan aims to become a giant in international finance and other services as well. This is the "external option." In effect, it would increase the dependence of other nations on Japan, thus relatively reducing its own dependence on the world economy. Moreover, the flow of finance is less visible in the marketplace (as well as being "invisible" in the balance of payments) than the flow of goods; this may make it more difficult for other nations to discriminate against Japan and may mitigate adversary relationships.

Priorities of the nation as a whole may or may not be apparent in those of the various ministries or those of the private sector. In the early 1980s, the principal objective of the Bank of Japan was to vanquish inflation.[9] It was less concerned about avoidance of financial loss. Ordinarily, the Ministry of Finance is keenly concerned about avoidance of inflation, but its chief aim is to balance the budget. In exceptional circumstances, these priorities may be reversed. For MITI, the principal objective is to achieve a good industrial structure and to establish strong firms. These policies are coordinated by the EPA, whose mission is policy adjustment. The EPA's objective is to make the priorities of the ministries compatible; it does not have strong priorities of its own. Contrary to what is often assumed, and despite Japan's enormous dependence on the world economy, priorities of the bureaucrats have hitherto been located primarily on the domestic rather than on the international plane. Bureaucratically, international problems receive chief priority only in critical cases.

In the private sector, there are several versions of the preferences of big business concerning the policy priorities of government. One story is that the *zaikai* are more unhappy about taxes than about regulations: they can be reconciled to the latter, but taxes eat up profits. The opposite version is that the zaikai know how to avoid taxes but find regulations onerous and expensive; thus, their principal aim is to shrink the size of the government and its power to impose regulations. Depending on circumstances, perhaps either may be valid. It is agreed that the zaikai would especially like the government to liberalize agricultural imports. This would make their own life easier in international circles.

Does the Ministry of Finance have an economic "Vision" of Japan corresponding to that of MITI? (Documents known as "Visions" are regularly published by MITI.) Perhaps there is a confidential blueprint within the ministry, but there would be reluctance to publish it because any government plan for the future implies the expenditure of money, and on this point the ministry is very careful.

The banks are ambivalent about economic liberalization. They may be in favor of it in one dimension but opposed to it in another. Even with regard to their reasons for opposition, they may not necessarily be losers in the long run. These reasons refer largely to the anticipated transformation of the banking business. In the future, city banks will become money changers rather than financiers. They will generate a host of off-balance-sheet activities. They will become consultants to financial managers of major companies. As suppliers of funds, they will principally serve small- and medium-size business. But as the city banks take away that small- and medium-size business, the regional banks will have to develop new products in consumer credit, housing loans, and the like. Before passage of the Foreign Exchange and Foreign Trade Control Law, the major banks were concerned that liberalization would allow securities houses, trading firms, and others to enter further into the foreign exchange business, which at that time was a monopoly of the foreign exchange banks and foreign exchange brokers.

In 1982, even the OECD was not in favor of Japanese economic liberalization if it implied that the Bank of Japan would abandon all controls over the exchange rate.The OECD wanted the Bank of Japan to intervene to reduce the violent fluctuations that were then occurring in the exchange value of the yen. In any event, recent financial innovations in Japan make the control process more complex; they also make it more difficult to evaluate the results of policy. During 1982, the OECD was also critical of Japan's policy mix—namely, tight fiscal policy combined with fairly easy monetary policy. The OECD preferred the reverse.

Although MITI's interventionist propensities are well known, the most highly regulated industry in Japan is banking, which the Ministry of Finance oversees. In 1963, when MITI sponsored a bill for "strengthening the international competitive power of Japanese industries," otherwise known as the "Specific Industries Promotion Bill," the banks were its most vociferous opponents. The zaikai at large were also opposed and at this relatively early date were strong enough to have it defeated in the Diet.

In terms of opportunities for intervention, MITI's fortunes rise as those of the economy fall. In 1982, MITI was engaged in preparing another bill with the ostensibly altruistic purpose of supporting Japanese industry but which would also expand its own powers of intervention. This was a bill to replace the Law on Extraordinary Measures for Specific Depressed Industries, otherwise known as the Structural Recession Law, due to expire on 30 June 1983. Following the oil crisis of 1973–1974, the law had been enacted for a five-year period beginning May 1978 to help industries in structural difficulties.

In the business community, there is an apparent division of opinion on this matter. Weak companies, especially in the basic materials industries, may favor renewal of the law. Strong companies, especially in the processing and assembling industries, are opposed. First, strong firms do not want to be controlled by MITI. Second, since under the Structural Recession Law antirecession cartels are established to protect the market shares of companies within a designated industry, strong firms feel that the law merely protects the weak. Although they too may fall into difficulties, strong firms do not usually need protection; on the contrary, during a recession they would like to push their competitors to the wall and swallow up the entire market.

Liberalization Versus Controls

An important official at the Bank of Japan was asked what plans the International Finance Bureau of the Ministry of Finance has for the coming five years. "It does not plan," he replied. When asked about the IFB's Planning Division, he said, "The Planning Division only plans for consensus."

It is no secret that the Bank of Japan and the Ministry of Finance are cordially contemptuous of one another.[10] In the context of liberalization and internationalization, their rivalry has undoubtedly increased. In terms of the division of labor, by law the Ministry of Finance is in charge of policy; it intervenes in daily operating affairs to the extent that it chooses to do so. The Bank of Japan is primarily in charge of operational matters; to the extent that it makes policy, it may be overruled by the ministry. As a loose generalization, minor matters are decided by the Bank of Japan, major matters are decided by the Ministry of Finance. In the course of liberalization, presumably there will be fewer major matters to be decided, implying a rise in the Bank of Japan's relative power. Legally, liberalization has diminished the power of the ministry; in practice, by means of administrative guidance, it exercises as much authority as before.

If we assume the *legal* progress of liberalization to be irreversible, what will be the effect on relations between the Ministry of Finance and the Bank of Japan? For many years, monetary policy, as formulated by the Banking Bureau of the Ministry of Finance, was Japan's paramount macroeconomic instrument. With the rising importance of fiscal policy, the Banking Bureau may find itself somewhat in eclipse. The International Finance Bureau will gain in the sense that its domain will widen and deepen. The Banking Bureau and the Securities Bureau will have to consult it more often than before. As the role of the international sector—especially with regard to capital movements—rises in importance, the Bank of Japan will have closer relations with the IFB; this will reduce the degree of its subordination to the Banking Bureau.

On the other hand, liberalization of foreign-exchange and foreign-trade transactions implies increasing difficulties for the Bank of Japan in the implementation of monetary and exchange rate policy. In 1982, for example, the effect of high U.S. interest rates was to depreciate the yen excessively. Not only currency speculators but also export and import industries increasingly feel the impact of international interest rate variations. Floating exchange rates compound the effect of liberalization on both commodity and capital flows. Private firms, because they have acquired substantial capital resources of their own, are increasingly independent of the banks and also have increasing access to funds from abroad.This in turn weakens the pressure that the Bank of Japan can put on the private sector through the banking system.

Whether the net impact of this evolution will redound to the benefit of the Bank of Japan rather than to the Ministry of Finance is problematical. The ministry as a whole is on the defensive with regard to liberalization, while the Bank of Japan is perhaps more receptive; this suggests that the latter may see itself as the potential winner.

From a national point of view, the case in favor of liberalization on the international plane argues that Japan's dependence on the world economy requires it to strengthen the multilateral free-market system. The opposing case simply argues the contrary: in contrast to the United States, which is relatively independent of other countries, Japan's dependence requires it to hold some discretionary controls in reserve. Furthermore, the Japanese economy is inherently subject to outbreaks of instability. Liberalization, including internationalization of the yen, implies problems in managing the exchange rate and domestic monetary policy. Even in the era of controls, Japan's domestic and international statistics reveal high volatility in the balance of payments as well as in output and prices. It is argued that the rapid pace of world events accelerates the degree of potential instability and makes it dangerous to relinquish controls too quickly. Within the Japanese government, these contrary arguments are being advanced for bureaucratic reasons by potential winners and losers in the power struggle.

Because it would be good for its big business clients, MITI is more favorably disposed toward liberalization on the international plane than is the Ministry of Finance.[11] Japanese firms that have established branches or subsidiaries abroad (as in Taiwan, Korea, and elsewhere) for export of light industrial products to Japan are among those that have an interest in Japanese import liberalization.[12] Although it is chiefly bureaucratic alumni of the Ministry of Finance rather than those of MITI that enter politics, it is MITI's constituency within the business community that finances those politicians. Thus, the primary loyalties of politicians with regard to the two ministries are not unambiguous.[13] It is clear, however, that politicians have gained power in relation to the bureaucrats as a result of Japan's economic transition. Liberalization and internationalization create a power vacuum into which they have been able to enter. Moreover, in the process of the transition, politicians have been able to play upon the rivalries among bureaucrats. They have been able to preside at the top level over negotiations to accommodate the differences among parties affected by the transition and to assume the role of reconcilers in the struggle for turf.

Policy Conflicts

In Japan's economic transition, various types of policy conflicts may arise. One type concerns the interests of Japan as opposed to the interests of other nations. Second is the conflict between Japan's internal and external policies. Third is the conflict among Japan's external policies; fourth, the conflict among its internal policies. Fifth is the conflict among ministries; sixth, the conflict within ministries. In addition, there are conflicts between government and business, and conflicts between big business and small- and medium-size business. In economic theory, division of labor contributes to efficiency in production. In terms of the bureaucratic facts of life, division of labor causes jealousy, rivalry, and struggles for status and turf. Interaction between the economic and political struggles affects the course of Japan's transition. A few of these struggles are as follows.

From 1945 to 1972 there were conflicts between Japan's domestic and international monetary affairs every three or four years. These were simple cases, however, because both domestic and external monetary affairs were controlled by the Japanese government. The difficult cases arose when external policy began to be liberalized while the domestic economy remained under control. Thus, when internal conditions were inflationary while the balance of payments was in surplus, internal conditions called for contractionary domestic policies while the balance of payments surplus called for expansionary domestic policies. Correspondingly, if internal conditions were in recession while the balance of payments was in deficit, internal conditions called for expansionary domestic policies while the balance of payments called for contractionary domestic policies. The regime of fixed exchange rates prevailing before 1973 made it difficult to resolve these dilemmas without recourse to policy-induced recessions.

In 1982, there was a conflict between domestic monetary and fiscal policy. On the one hand there was the need to finance the government's debts and stimulate private investment, which implied maintaining a low interest rate policy; at the same time, though, the government wanted to resist inflation and reduce capital outflow, which implied keeping interest rates high. Japan was not alone in this dilemma.

Interministerial conflict may arise where MITI and the Ministry of Finance attempt to impose inconsistent policies in a common jurisdiction. In the first instance, the conflict may be handled at the section chief level; if not resolved there, it may move up to the division chief level. Next it may move to the bureau chief level. The more important the case, the higher it is likely to go. If very important, it may require a conference between the MITI minister and the Minister of Finance. At the same time, as the case moves up the ladder, politicians enter the scene. The politicians can have a decided impact on the decisions of the bureaucrats. Moreover, money will flow to the politicians as a result of their efforts to intervene in behalf of important constituents.

MITI is careful not to violate the antitrust law. What it fears is not Japan's Fair Trade Commission (FTC) but the possibility that in the event of a fight between MITI and the FTC, journalists will get hold of the story and present it to the public as a scandal. Although after the first oil crisis the Antitrust Law was amended to give the FTC more power, it is not a strong agency. It is especially weak in its powers of enforcement on the international plane. The personality of the FTC chairman may make some difference, but this is not a major factor.

MITI criticizes the Ministry of Finance as being too conservative and too slow to liberalize, and it cites services as an example. Foreign securities companies and insurance companies are subject to onerous official barriers to entry into Japan. The Ministry of Finance is also criticized for maintaining the "convoy" system, under which the speed of the fleet is determined by the slowest ship. This is seen, for example, in the banking sector, where Ministry of Finance protection of small, inefficient banks redounds to the disadvantage of large, efficient and innovating banks. MITI further criticizes the Ministry of Finance for authorizing nonbank enterprises to enter the banking field. Department stores have inaugurated Sunday banking and credit cards, moves that place the stores in direct competition with conventional banks.

Primarily, however, MITI's criticism of the Ministry of Finance concerns its guidance rather than its protectionism. MITI itself practices protectionism with regard to the interests of small- and medium-size manufacturers.

The resistance of the banks to the government's insistence that they subscribe to national bonds yielding subequilibrium interest rates has caused a deterioration in relations between the banks and the Ministry of Finance. By 1982, the banks had financed more than two-thirds of the government deficit. (Of course, this contribution by the banks was more apparent than real. The true cost was borne by the banks' depositors, who received artificially low interest rates on their savings.) Until 1982, about 90 percent of the bonds issued by the national government had ten-year maturities. When these mature from 1985 on, they will have to be refinanced. At that time, the previous subscription system between the government and the banks is bound to break down.

In this controversy between the banks and the Ministry of Finance, the principal bureau adversely affected is the Banking Bureau. This bureau is also losing clout within the ministry itself because of the rise of the Securities Bureau (which once was merely a part of the Banking Bureau). Thus, the Banking Bureau is doubly a loser. The shifting balance of power between the Banking Bureau and the Securities Bureau reflects the shift in the balance of power of their respective clients. The increasing number of arguments between the Banking Bureau and the Securities Bureau is not primarily due to liberalization but rather to changes in the behavior of the banks and the securities companies. The minister's secretariat of the Ministry of Finance attempts to perform "coordination and adjustment" among the bureaus, but it is not very strong. The coordination divisions of the various bureaus are confined to similar duties within their respective bureaus. "Fights are traditional within the Ministry of Finance," said one interviewee.

Being responsible for a wide assortment of activities—including money and banking, public finance, securities, and insurance—the Ministry of Finance is not necessarily a loser when one of its clients gains at the expense of another. In discharging its own responsibilities—as distinguished from those of its clients—in the field of fiscal policy, the ministry is clearly a loser. The ministry has also been directly in charge of the controversial Japan Tobacco and Salt Public Corporation.[14] Among the clients of MITI, on the other hand, there are likewise winners (such as the processing and assembling industries) as well as losers (such as the basic materials industries). However, by means of increased opportunities for legal intervention in behalf of distressed industries, MITI is more likely to be a gainer bureaucratically because of difficulties among its clients.

MITI has definitely less to lose from liberalization and internationalization than does the Ministry of Finance. In former days, during the infancy of its key industries, there was a split in MITI over the merits of liberalization, and a great deal of consequent factionalism arose within the ministry. At present, when its major clients are mature and internationally competitive, MITI is of one mind on the matter. There is now less factionalism in MITI than in the Ministry of Finance, whose Budget, Tax, International Finance, and Financial Bureaus are prone to have inconsistent views. Indeed, apart from the interests of its clients, MITI may be in favor of liberalization and internationalization because they may diminish the bureaucratic power of the Ministry of Finance.

In cases affecting clients, trade-offs may be arranged among the various bureaus of the ministry. For example, the law prohibiting banks from selling securities was stretched in a compromise that allowed the banks to sell newly issued national bonds to the public in return for the banks' acquiescence in continuing to accept quotas for the purchase of government bonds. In the struggle between the securities companies and the banking industry over this matter, there was an open confrontation between the city banks and the Ministry of Finance. Such an open breach was unusual and a violation of Japanese mores. The ministry was embarrassed at its failure to keep the matter private until a resolution had been achieved.

Concerning decisionmaking in intraministerial affairs, attempts are made to resolve conflicts first at the policydrafting level, next at the level of bureau deputy director general or director general, and then at the vice ministerial level. In the summer of 1982, there was considerable difference of opinion within the Ministry of Finance concerning the use of fiscal, budgetary, and monetary policy to correct the unduly low exchange value of the yen. The Banking Bureau and the Securities Bureau opposed raising the discount rate or the prime rate. In a case of this sort, there is much *nemawashi*—conversation and informal consultation among the bureaus in anticipation of a formal meeting with the vice minister or minister. If no consensus emerges, then one or the other of these officials makes the decision at the formal meeting. However, this is a rare event. Usually there is a consensus before the meeting.

The Postal Savings system (under the Ministry of Posts and Telecommunications) purchases about half of the national bonds issued by the government, and these in turn help finance the expenditures of the Fiscal Investment and Loan Program (FILP), which is controlled by the Financial Bureau of the Ministry of Finance. Consequently, the Financial Bureau supports the expansion of the Postal Savings system. The Banking Bureau, however, opposes the Postal Savings system, which is a rival to the private banks, and the Banking Bureau wishes the Postal Savings system were curtailed. The Securities Bureau also opposes the Postal Savings system, but its reasons are further in the background. The Ministry of Agriculture, Forestry, and Fisheries likewise opposes the Postal Savings system because the system, as a lender, is a rival to the agricultural cooperatives, whose funding sources are the savings deposits of farmers.

The private banking system in Japan argues that it is a victim of double discrimination. First, the Postal Savings system, which is authorized to pay a higher interest rate on savings than the banks, takes away its depositors. Second, although the deposits in the Postal Savings system are used to buy government bonds, the banks themselves are nevertheless required to buy government bonds as well. (The fiscal aspect of this is a further anomaly. The deposits in the Postal Savings system are an obligation of the government. But the bonds that are bought with these deposits are also a debt of the government. Thus, in a sense the government has a double obligation based on public deposits.)

The Postal Savings system has flourished because it provides favorable terms, special tax treatment (as well as opportunities for tax evasion), and convenience to depositors. The principal advantage of the Postal Savings system, however, is not its popularity but rather the votes of politicians in the Diet to whom it contributes support. Its network of about 22,000 branches compares with about 17,500 branches of the private banking system throughout Japan. The Postal Savings system's deposits are about five times greater than those of Japan's largest private bank, the Dai-Ichi Kangyo. In 1984, the Postal Savings system held approximately 30 percent of all personal savings deposits, and it has the competitive advantage of bearing no tax burden. The relative independence and oligopoly power of the Postal Savings system also reduce the control of the Ministry of Finance over monetary policy. Without the cooperation of the Postal Savings system, the rate of interest on deposits cannot be liberalized.

The lender is usually in a stronger position than the borrower. Because the Postal Savings system lends to the government, its strength is augmented by its political support from the public. City banks, on the other hand, have no mass voter support. For national influence, they rely on their large financial contributions to the politicians. The various local bank associations (*Shinyū Kumiai*), however, have strong local political power.

The conflicts and antagonism that lie behind the scenes in the Ministry of Finance are usually concealed by the cosmetically united position that the ministry presents to outsiders. In the Ministry of Finance, the Bank of Japan, and elsewhere, the official story of the organization is conveyed to outsiders by designated spokesmen. They are especially concerned that they present a single face to the foreigners. There may be a consensus behind the united front they present. However, consensus does not necessarily imply agreement; it may merely mean that trade-offs have been arranged. In Japanese decisionmaking, compromise plays an important role. In ministerial conflicts, bureaucratic politics is being exacerbated by the growth of economic liberalization. As a result, personal prejudice and personality may become more important than official or substantive matters.

The Bank of Japan, for example, possesses an "institutional memory" of its relations with other Japanese government organizations. Before its abolition in 1968, a Council on Fund Allocation of Financial Institutions existed under the control of the Ministry of Finance, the Bank of Japan, and a few representatives of major financial institutions. Its job was to perform the supply-side function of carrying out the fund allocation decisions of the Committee on Industrial Funds. On the demand side, MITI was dominant in the Committee of Industrial Funds of the Industrial Rationalization Council, which guided investment and financing schedules. On both the demand and the supply sides of the financial system, the Bank of Japan played a passive role. Thus, the bank particularly relished its adoption of monetarism (which it professes not to practice) in the mid-1970s, which enhanced its economic role.

Institutional memory likewise enters into relations between the private and the public sectors. While bureaucrats seek to retain their prerogatives of control, big business was the boss of government in previous eras. *Keidanren*[15] wants to be free of government regulations. ("If the truth were told, it wants to get rid of environmental controls as well," said one official of Keidanren.) It wants economic liberalization because it would be profitable. In particular, contrary to the agricultural lobby, it wants import liberalization to safeguard its own exports from abroad to Japan and to protect its foreign investments.

Among ministries, common jurisdictions are a source of policy conflict. Overlapping occurs at the international level, for example, where MITI's role is primarily on the trade side, while the Ministry of

Finance is primarily on the financial side. Especially in large projects, trade and finance are required to accommodate one another, as in the ill-fated Mitsui Bandar Khomeini petrochemical project in Iran. Another example of overlapping jurisdiction involves Nippon Telegraph and Telephone Public Corporation bonds issued overseas. NTT is under the jurisdiction of the Ministry of Posts and Telecommunications; the bonds, however, are guaranteed by the Japanese government, which involves the Ministry of Finance. Again, if MITI wants to extend a subsidy, it may do so in the form of a tax cut or provision for accelerated depreciation. To extend the subsidy, however, MITI has to argue for it with the relevant bureau of the Ministry of Finance.

Among ministries, lack of consensus may be expressed publicly as well as privately. There have been many discrepancies in the public statements of government leaders as well as conflicting statements of the LDP and the bureaucrats on the trade friction problem. There have been open conflicts between MITI and the Ministry of Foreign Affairs; between the Finance Ministry and the Foreign Ministry; and between MITI and the Ministry of Agriculture, Forestry, and Fisheries. Some of these conflicts and discrepancies can be accounted for by efforts on the part of the various spokesmen to manipulate foreign rather than domestic opinion. When the ministries are dealing with the United States, for example, there may be an attempt to please the Americans in one respect as an alternative to pleasing them in another. This may give rise to conflicting ministerial statements.

=== 2 ===

APPEARANCE VERSUS REALITY: THE FOREIGN EXCHANGE AND FOREIGN TRADE CONTROL LAW

Administrative Criteria

The Foreign Exchange and Foreign Trade Control Law (1949) was amended by Law No. 65 (dated 18 December 1979); the latter came into effect on 1 December 1980. The amended law, known as the "new law" (hereinafter "Foreign Exchange Law"), has been represented as a reversal of the old law by 180 degrees. Whereas the old law stated that external transactions were to be "prohibited in principle, with freedom of transactions as an exception," the new law was to provide "freedom in principle, with prohibition of transactions as an exception."[1] In its published version, however, the new Foreign Exchange Law refers to "freedom of exchange, foreign trade, and other external transactions, with necessary but minimum control"; it does not contain the phrase "freedom in principle."[2]

The Foreign Exchange Law, moreover, contains many articles authorizing the government to screen, delay, or license (that is, prohibit) transactions that, in its judgment, "might" lead to certain undesired results. For example, Article 21 provides for licensing of any capital transaction that "might" lead to the following: "(1) It might make the maintenance of the equilibrium of our country's balance of international payments difficult; (2) it might result in a drastic fluctuation of our currency's foreign exchange rates; or (3) it might result in transfers of funds between Japan and foreign countries in a large volume, and thereby adversely affect our money or capital market." In discussions concerning the Foreign Exchange Law, the above provisions are usually described as "emergency" provisions.[3] The term "emergency," however, does not appear anywhere in the law itself.

When an executive director of the Bank of Japan was asked to name the criteria for invoking the so-called emergency provisions of the Foreign Exchange Law, he replied, "There are no defined criteria." Then, when asked who identifies an emergency, he answered, "We all do."[4]

From the government's point of view, officials offer various reasons for declining to define emergency criteria. Liberalization is a new game, one in which the government is making up the rules as it goes along. It would be premature to specify criteria for an emergency before the government itself understands the new game and how to defend its interests in that game. In particular, the government is reluctant to inform speculators concerning its intervention points, as well as who pulls the strings, when, and under what circumstances. The emergency criteria should be like a *denka no hōtō*, an heirloom sword that lies in the *tokonoma*—the alcove in which family treasures are displayed; the sword is not on active duty, and you would like never to use it, but everyone knows it is there. The IFB maintains that no emergency criteria for the Foreign Exchange Law have been formulated even intramurally for its own information. It explains that liberalization progressively creates new loopholes for the businessman; these are not easily anticipated by the IFB. Thus, it would be useless to prematurely define emergency criteria for the restriction of transactions. Even with full knowledge of the loopholes, the IFB would be reluctant to declare an emergency because of the difficulty of closing them completely. Furthermore, "now that we have opened up long-term capital outflows, we cannot officially disrupt them," as one interviewee put it.

The fact that the government has no hard and fast rules, no specific triggers, means that it can act pragmatically and respond flexibly to various situations. Concerning "equilibrium" in the balance of payments, for example, the Ministry of Finance could declare an emergency on the basis of the overall balance, the trade balance, the current account balance, or the capital account balance. Ultimately, of course, the emergency provisions are spurious inasmuch as the Ministry of Finance can *create* an emergency or refuse to acknowledge an emergency should one arise. In any event, partly because it gives bureaucrats a feeling of importance to possess discretionary powers and partly for more professional reasons, the ministry does not want to be bound by indicators or rules that automatically trigger its response. In this sense, the new Foreign Exchange Law is a glorified legal authorization for more administrative guidance. Controls may be imposed for the same reasons they were imposed before liberalization: external pressure, personal judgment on the part of the "competent authorities," and personality factors. As a practical matter, in cases where there is no clear criterion, the bureaucracy usually enforces the standard of "behavior as in the past." This is one reason why precedent is so important in the government's decisionmaking process.

Even when criteria for official action have been determined and openly revealed, the authorities retain a considerable amount of discretion in deciding how the criteria will be applied. This includes what may be described as "control by definition or redefinition." For example, although some particular activity may be permitted in principle, in practice only a specified type of bank or firm may be eligible to participate in it. Moreover, the definition of "eligibility" is subject to change at the discretion of the "competent authorities." To stem capital outflow, the Ministry of Finance in the summer of 1982 manipulated the criteria for eligibility on the part of foreign companies seeking to float Samurai bonds in Japan. The new criteria referred to size of shareholder equity, ratio of long-term debt to total capitalization, ratio of working capital to total assets, the interest coverage ratio, and the ratio of long-term debt to cash flow. It was estimated that only 70 companies in the United States and Europe would qualify under those criteria as defined. Even assuming that eligible companies applied, the number of permissible Samurai offerings was restricted to one each calendar quarter. Furthermore, the total value of each offering was limited to ¥ 20 billion (about $83 million in 1982 dollars).

To lean on the foreign-exchange rate, the authorities may use definition or redefinition to cut off or open up channels for capital flows. In May 1979, the bond repurchase (gensaki) market was opened to nonresidents by redefinition of eligible participants. This induced capital inflows to support the exchange rate. To discourage capital outflows, the authorities in March 1982 redefined the provision for the exemption of capital gains from income tax so as to exclude appreciation on deep-discount (zero-coupon) bonds.

Another example concerns the barrier between the banking business and the securities business. According to Article 65 of Japan's Securities and Exchange Law (patterned after the United States' Glass-Steagall Act), banks are prohibited from acting as underwriters. In defining the law's area of coverage, however, the Ministry of Finance has ruled that the law does not apply overseas. This concession to the banking community was in return for its continued willingness to accept subscription quotas of national bonds that yield artificially low returns. Rarely does the maintenance of one control lead to the abandonment of another, as occurred in this case. In the upshot, the banking industry and the securities industry are increasingly entering into each other's territory.

Still another case of control by the manipulation of definitions shows how the ministry can liberalize with one hand while it deliberalizes with the other. Under the new Foreign Exchange Law, Japanese residents were given permission to hold savings deposits in foreign currency without limit. Before the new Foreign Exchange Law, deposits of foreign currency by Japanese residents were restricted to the equivalent of ¥ 3 million. Such deposits were clearly attractive because the interest rate on savings was controlled only in yen accounts. Since dollar interest rates were much higher than yen interest rates, and since interest earned on the first ¥ 3 million of savings deposits was exempt from withholding tax on interest earned, the Ministry of Finance feared that dollar savings accounts would become too popular. Accordingly, they were defined as ineligible for the exemption from withholding tax. Japanese banks (but not foreign banks) abetted the ministry in this tactic by charging depositors a "lifting fee" for the "new service" of providing facilities for foreign-currency savings deposits.[5] Thus, unless the foreign-exchange value of the dollar were to appreciate, the advantage of holding such deposits was eliminated.

Theory Versus Practice

How has "freedom of transactions" in principle been observed in practice? Officially, what remains unliberalized? Why does the Ministry of Finance periodically announce further measures of liberalization about matters that already were presumably covered by "freedom in principle"? Which types of transactions that were officially liberalized have been deliberalized by administrative guidance? How can the extent of liberalization be quantitatively evaluated?

Among the elements or dimensions of liberalization in external financial transactions are the following: permitted size and frequency of transactions, reporting requirements, reserve requirements, maturity limits, licensing requirements, quota allocations, requirements for collateral in financial transactions, definition of eligible participants in specified markets, designation of lines of specialization among financial institutions, definition of eligible financial instruments in specified markets (as in definition of types of bonds eligible for use in the bond repurchase market), designation of ceiling or floor limits (as in administration of interest rates), treatment of residents as contrasted with that of nonresidents, the degree of market intervention by the Bank of Japan, and the degree of administrative guidance that replaces overt legal controls.

Incomplete liberalization. What remains unliberalized? "It depends on your definition," responded a Ministry of Finance official. In some cases, it is difficult to draw the line between prudential regulations and outright restrictionism. Some examples of remaining controls are as follows.

In many cases, documents must be filed with the Ministry of Finance before a transaction. There are three types of filing: (1) ministerial permission required, (2) reporting plus waiting period, and (3) reporting ex post. Legally, a Japanese nonfinancial company can raise capital overseas without government permission. In practice, however, it cannot do so. The company must notify the Ministry of Finance that it plans to raise capital abroad. The notification must then be *accepted* by the ministry; this acceptance constitutes *approval*. Thus, in reality there has been no change from the previous version of the Foreign Exchange Law, which specifically required "approval." Foreign-currency swaps (simultaneous spot purchase and forward sale of yen against dollars) by commercial banks are subject to swap limits. (The criteria for assignment of swap quota limits by the Ministry of Finance to individual banks are not public information.) Issuance of yen securities by nonresidents in the Japanese market (Samurai bonds) is largely restricted to international financial institutions and foreign governments. Before July 1982, permission for overseas yen lending was limited to "top-ranking" financial institutions, namely, long-term credit banks, city banks, trust banks, the six principal life insurance firms, and the two principal regional banks. Thereafter, the list of eligible institutions was extended to include two dozen banks and insurance companies of lesser rank.

Syndicated foreign lending by the banks, moreover, is subject to restrictions by administrative guidance. The framework of control includes restrictions on aggregate permissible lending of the banking system as a whole, restrictions on the eligibility of individual banks to participate in syndicate lending, restrictions on the amount of permissible lending by an individual bank,[6] and restrictions on the amount of lending to individual countries.[7] In the case of portfolio investment, if the transaction is performed through one of four specified major securities houses, no documents need to be filed with the government; however, if any other securities house is involved, documents must be filed. For direct investment abroad by Japanese or for direct investment in Japan by foreigners, documents must be filed in advance. Specified Japanese companies are subject to a maximum foreign ownership percentage of 25 percent.

In practice, the degree of liberalization is either increased or decreased from time to time by administrative guidance. Increasingly, policy shifts as expressed by guidance are a response to shifts in the balance of forces in the private sector rather than being autonomously determined by the government in accordance with a preconceived plan. Administrative guidance is also constrained by the government's appraisal of how far it can go without incurring foreign criticism.

"Continuing liberalization." Although "freedom in principle" was theoretically granted to all external transactions by the new Foreign Exchange Law, in practice the Ministry of Finance periodically announces further measures of liberalization. In June 1981, the Ministry of Finance granted the overseas subsidiaries of city banks the privilege of issuing bonds abroad and allowed them to be guaranteed by the parent bank in Japan. The city banks needed the long-term funds provided by the bonds in order to finance their increasing long-term international business. This outcome was a defeat for the long-term credit banks (Industrial Bank of Japan, Long-Term Credit Bank of Japan, Japan Credit Bank, and the Bank of Tokyo), which enjoyed a monopoly in issuing such bonds domestically and which did not wish to see that monopoly diluted by competition from the city banks. As a compromise, the ministry simultaneously denied the city banks the privilege of bringing the proceeds of the bond issues of their foreign subsidiaries into Japan. The privilege of establishing Japanese bank subsidiaries abroad remained subject to permission by the Ministry of Finance.

In October 1981, the ministry for the first time allowed the formation of a financial product similar to the U.S. money-market fund. It took the form of a "Foreign Securities Fund," a type of investment trust, established by the Nomura Securities Company. In December 1981, the Ministry of Finance raised the ceiling on the monthly volume of yen-based bonds issued by foreigners through public offering or private placement in the Japanese market. This was undertaken partly in response to foreign pressure for more access to the Japanese capital market and partly to reduce the "embarrassing" balance of payments surplus on current account.

Offshore yen lending by Japanese commercial banks is divided into two categories. The first includes loans to international agencies to which the Japanese government provides capital contributions or credit facilities for political purposes (such as to the People's Republic of China). These loans are made available at the initiative and under the guidance of the government. The second category includes loans extended at the discretion of the banks themselves. Before 15 May

1982, these loans were restricted to the financing of resource-development projects that would produce exports to Japan, to financing trade in which Japanese firms were involved, or to loans to international agencies to which the Japanese government made no capital contribution. On that date, restrictions on the purpose of commercial bank loans abroad were abolished. Banks were also given permission to make yen loans to foreign private enterprises. However, these loans were subject to the restriction that they must be guaranteed by a foreign government export-import bank or foreign trade bank. On the other hand, the Ministry of Finance simultaneously refused to increase significantly the city banks' individual six-month quota for total overseas lending (which it prefers to call "loan programs"). The queue of potential foreign borrowers was very long during this period. The ministry also announced a relaxation (though not abolition) of guidelines on the timing of Samurai bond issues. Before January 1982, a maximum of one Samurai issue per month, not to exceed ¥ 10 billion, was authorized. Thereafter, the limit was raised to three issues per month, but each issue was limited to ¥ 10 billion. Ceilings on foreign currency swaps by foreign banks were said to have been raised, but foreign banks still received secret individual quota assignments for the amount of dollars they could convert.

In the six-month period ending March 1982, the aggregate quota for yen lending by Japanese banks to foreign borrowers was limited to ¥ 350 billion. However, in January 1982, the Ministry of Finance permitted the export credit agencies of foreign governments to be included among eligible borrowers of yen funds from Japanese banks.The number of yen bond issues in Japan by all foreign borrowers was limited to one or two a month. In fiscal year 1981, 50 such bond issues were permitted.

"Deliberalization." The above were examples of increasing liberalization in practice. On the opposite side, some external transactions have been liberalized in theory but deliberalized in practice. This may be accomplished by administrative manipulation of criteria and definitions of criteria, as mentioned earlier.

The official reasons for deliberalization may differ from the real reasons. Internationalization of the yen, for example, produces an unwelcome complication in the management of domestic monetary policy. In the summer of 1982, restrictions on capital outflow were represented by the authorities as beneficent measures to support the yen. However, those restrictions also suited the strategy of the Ministry of Finance in slowing the rate of accumulation of yen by foreign financial institutions. This slowing helps insulate Japan's domestic monetary policy from outside disturbance. Not officially mentioned, moreover, is the fact that restrictions on capital outflow also bottle up the surplus of domestic financial resources that have accumulated since the first oil crisis of 1973, making those funds available for the purchase of national bonds.

There is, of course, an official rationale for administrative guidance. In the early postwar decades, that rationale was based on the assumed superior wisdom of the bureaucrats. At present, it is based on their supposed superior information. The prime minister's office, for example, receives privileged communications from the government of the United States. It passes these on to the Ministry of Finance, which is thus in a position to provide its clients with special policy advice. (This procedure also helps to explain why "there are no secrets in Japan.") The following example shows the link between ministerial information and administrative guidance. When an eminent Ministry of Finance official was asked the extent to which the IFB engages in direct operational control of individual banks or firms, he replied: "Before revision of the old Foreign Exchange Law in 1980, all foreign transactions were subject to Ministry of Finance license. At present, the prior notice system replaces the license system. Primarily, this is for statistical purposes. However, we can use this information to apply our influence to individual cases. For example, if a Japanese bank would like to extend a loan to a less developed country (LDC), we may be aware that it has already borrowed heavily from other banks. Or for other reasons known to the Japanese government but not to the bank, there may be a great deal of country risk attached to the proposed loan. In this situation we may say, 'This transaction would be against the national interest.' By means of administrative guidance we can achieve consensus with banks and corporations. Thus, we can use our information to apply influence to individual cases."[8]

Among its various interventions at the micro level, the IFB controls the international lending of individual banks. In the case of securities companies, it controls issuance of bonds abroad and issuance of bonds by nonresidents in the Japanese capital market. It advises manufacturing companies that plan large projects abroad requiring financial assistance from the government or the city banks. In the case of trading companies, it gives advice on lending rates and on interest rates associated with export credit. If a trading company considers making a heavy investment in a developing country with which it is not familiar, or if that investment is partly financed by the Export-Import Bank or the Overseas Economic Cooperation Fund (OECF), that company must stay in close touch with the IFB. In general, individual firms and banks receive more guidance from the Ministry of Finance in their international transactions than in their domestic transactions. In the present stage of Japan's transition (but not necessarily in the future), the ministry is resigned to further liberalization and internationalization as all but inevitable. "But we wouldn't do anything to accelerate the trend," commented an official of the IFB.

One of the ways in which liberalization is reversed is through "self-restraint" in the business community. This self-restraint is induced by invisible means in the administrative guidance process. (The same process may have served as a model for the anomaly in U.S.-Japan relations by which Japan adopts "self-imposed" restrictions on various of its exports to the United States.) In April 1982, five major Japanese life insurance companies were requested by the Ministry of Finance to impose self-restraint on their purchases of foreign-currency-denominated bonds.[9] In the same month, the aggregate issues of Eurobonds by Japanese corporations were restricted to a maximum of $1.5 billion during each quarter; the number of issues was limited to one each week. After negotiations between representatives of the securities industry (which arranged the bond issues) and the Ministry of Finance, these restrictions were likewise described as "self-imposed." As a third event in April 1982, each individual offshore yen loan and each individual Samurai bond issue became subject to approval by the Ministry of Finance.[10] (Samurai bond issues and offshore yen loans had previously been subject to aggregate limits, but not to individual approval.) All of these measures were imposed without the declaration of an "emergency."

In March 1982, the Securities Bureau of the Ministry of Finance summoned 26 securities companies to a meeting at which it announced that they would terminate sales of foreign-currency-denominated zero-coupon bonds. These discounted bonds had aroused great enthusiasm in Japan following the announcement that a so-called Green Card system (subsequently shelved) was being prepared for adoption in 1984. This proposed system was a device to reduce tax evasion occurring when an individual held multiple Postal Savings accounts but registered them under spurious names. If each account contained less than ¥ 3 million, it was exempt from income tax. Since the return on zero-coupon bonds (if redeemed before maturity) constitutes a capital gain—which is likewise exempt from tax—liberalization had provided a convenient alternative loophole.

Within the Ministry of Finance itself, there were various motives for the injunction against zero-coupon bonds. The Securities Bureau was not worried about tax evasion; it was concerned about the flight abroad of savings that otherwise might have been used to purchase national bonds. The Budget Bureau was not concerned about capital flight; it was opposed to tax evasion. From the point of view of the IFB, capital outflow had the effect of depreciating the yen, which was already undervalued; this would further reduce Japan's already inferior terms of trade, causing real losses to the economy. In its public explanation, however, the ministry alleged that the reason for stopping the purchase of foreign zero-coupon bonds was that the firms that issued them could go bankrupt and that the Japanese purchasers could be fleeced. Thus, the ministry was acting in the interests of the innocent purchaser.

When a Ministry of Finance official was asked whether the ministry's suspension of foreign zero-coupon bonds was inconsistent with the liberalized Foreign Exchange and Foreign Trade Control Law, he replied that the securities companies had "voluntarily" stopped selling them. On 1 February 1983, the Ministry of Finance withdrew in part its restriction on the domestic sale of foreign zero-coupon bonds.

Evaluation of liberalization. During the early 1980s, the period of "Japan, Disincorporated," the bureaucracy resisted financial liberalization for reasons described above in the Introduction. As a net outcome, how may the degree of liberalization during that period be evaluated? The observed magnitude of transactions in supposedly liberalized categories does not tell the whole story. Administrative "guidelines," which in any event were unquantifiable, shifted frequently with regard to coverage and degree of permissiveness. In its differing impact by size of firm, liberalization presented a further complication. As an exception to the rule, ironically, it was sometimes more difficult for large firms than for small firms to "pass the gate" of Ministry of Finance scrutiny. Before presuming to avail itself of ostensible new privileges, a large firm might wait until small- or medium-size firms had established precedents that it could use in arguing its case with the ministry. In explaining this, a Ministry of Finance official pointed out, however, that the large firm's application would not be rejected outright. "We haven't turned anyone down," he said, "and therefore we can't be accused of undermining liberalization."

One of the main results of the new Foreign Exchange Law was liberalization of impact-loan transactions. (Impact loans are loans in foreign currency that are converted into yen for use in Japan. Long-term impact loans must be used for capital investment, but short-term impact loans may be used for general operating purposes.) Residents can take out impact loans without restriction and without notifying the government. Banks that issue impact loans, however, must notify the Bank of Japan. Although foreign banks in Japan had been among the most vociferous in their demands for liberalization, an ironic effect of the new law was to deprive them of their monopoly on impact loans; before 1980 these loans had been their most lucrative source of profit. When impact loans were decontrolled in accordance with the new law, the volume of such loans outstanding nearly doubled from $10.7 billion at the end of 1980 to $20.3 billion at the end of 1981. At the end of 1982, the outstanding total was $27.4 billion. Most of the increase was accounted for by loans from Japanese banks rather than by foreign banks.[11]

Another major result of the new Foreign Exchange Law was the permission granted to Japanese residents to deposit foreign currency in Japanese banks. From 1980 to 1982, the interest rate on dollar deposits was uncontrolled and thus higher than that on deposits of yen. However, as mentioned above, Japanese banks receiving such deposits charged a "lifting" fee for the new service, which wiped out the differential. Thus, in 1981, the outstanding balance of foreign-currency deposits in Japanese banks began to decline since the yield on such deposits was about the same as that on yen deposits. Moreover, foreign-currency deposits are not eligible for the exemption from withholding taxes on interest equivalent to ¥ 3 million, as is the case with yen deposits.

The fact that Japanese domestic interest rates have been controlled at subequilibrium levels creates a built-in predicament for the task of external liberalization. Since market-determined interest rates have not been allowed to emerge, implicit arbitrage opportunities continue to exist in Japan to an extent that exceeds that in other major industrial countries. To maintain interest rates at the desired levels, the authorities must offset these arbitrage opportunities. The bureaucratically congenial method of doing so is to impose administrative (rather than legal) controls on capital movements. The government defends itself against accusations on this score by citing statistics of increased foreign-exchange market activity and increased capital flows since December 1980. The foreign-exchange statistics, however, are primarily non-trade-related and do not reflect an increase in commodity-import liberalization. The increased capital outflows are evidence chiefly of the government's need to balance its current account surplus with a capital account deficit, without which its foreign-exchange reserves would rise. A substantial rise in the foreign-exchange reserves would be an embarrassment to the government in its relations with debtors among its trade partners. Thus, the dimensions of Japan's international accounts—which may seem commensurate with those of other major economies, such as West Germany—may or may not be comparable.

Apart from comparability, there is the matter of inclusions in the long-term capital account. Those who defend the government's record point to the fact that in calendar year 1981, outflow amounted to $22.8 billion (compared with West Germany's $12.4 billion) and inflow of $16.4 billion (compared with West Germany's $16.8 billion). For purposes of balance of payments statistics, however, external transactions in securities are classified as long-term capital movements even though they may be traded on a short-term basis. In calendar year 1981, long-term capital outflow attributable to purchases of foreign securities amounted to $8.8 billion; capital inflow for that purpose amounted to $15.1 billion.[12]

Apart from factors that interfere with external liberalization, such as the government's efforts to keep interest rates low in behalf of encouraging business investment and to reduce the burden of financing the national debt, in practice international liberalization is easier to achieve than domestic liberalization. The reason is that liberalization is a political as well as an economic matter. For example, in Gumma Prefecture, located in the Kanto region north of Tokyo, many farmers grow a potato used in making konnyaku (a traditional Japanese edible paste). This region is powerfully represented in the Diet by its politicians, who successfully defend the inclusion of konnyaku in the list of items subject to "residual import restrictions." However, there is no powerful representation in the Diet in favor of limiting capital flows. Thus, the Japanese government can more easily liberalize capital imports than agricultural imports.

Liberalization on the international plane is also facilitated by the change in priorities of the Bank of Japan since the days of "miraculous" economic growth. In the 1960s, the primary rationale for external controls was the preoccupation of the Bank of Japan with equilibrium in the balance of payments. At the end of the 1960s, the Bank of Japan shifted its priorities in favor of the suppression of inflation. Japanese authorities have made much of the implication that Japan's capital market is fully liberalized because some of the indicators of activity in that market show that it is "not closed."[13] As logic, this is incomplete. Moreover, although some statistics have improved since the advent of the new Foreign Exchange Law, they are not unambiguous indicators of progress in liberalization.

What is arguable is not whether liberalization has occurred, but how much and to what extent increases in volume should be attributed to economic growth as distinguished from economic liberalization. Some sample statistics follow. Foreign equities acquired by Japanese residents in calendar year 1982 (on a settlement basis) amounted to $1.13 billion, compared with $1.07 billion in 1980. Foreign bonds and beneficiary certificates acquired by Japanese residents in 1982 (on a settlement basis) amounted to almost $17 billion, compared with $9.40 billion in 1981. (Data for 1980 were not comparably compiled.) Through foreign currency bonds, Japanese industrial firms raised ¥ 1.23 trillion in fiscal year 1982, compared with ¥ 683 billion a year earlier. Issues of yen-denominated bonds by nonresidents amounted to ¥ 856 billion in calendar year 1982, compared with ¥ 261 billion in 1980. Acquisition by foreign investors of shares in Japanese companies amounted to ¥ 184.4 billion in calendar year 1982 (on a notification basis), compared with ¥ 76.5 billion a year earlier. The share of yen-denominated foreign bonds in relation to the total of new international bond issues amounted to 4.3 percent in calendar year 1982, compared with 2.6 percent in 1980. International lending by banks located in Japan (loans to nonresidents plus foreign-currency-denominated loans to residents) amounted to 7.5 percent of international lending in the world at large at the end of September 1982, compared with 6.2 percent at the end of December 1980. In December 1982, only 12 foreign corporations were listed on the Tokyo Stock Exchange. The share of foreign investors in total sales of public and corporate bonds amounted to 5.8 percent in calendar year 1982, compared with 4.2 percent in 1980. The average share of nonresidents in total bond repurchase market operations during 1982 amounted to 14.0 percent, compared with 4.0 percent during 1980. The year-end share of foreign banks in total call and bill market operations amounted to 6.4 percent in 1982, compared with 4.3 percent during 1980. As a settlement currency in Japanese foreign trade, the yen was used for 38.2 percent of exports in 1982, compared with 28.9 percent in 1980. Settlement in yen for imports was approximately 2.4 percent in both years. At the end of 1982, the share of the yen in total identified official holdings of foreign exchange of all countries amounted to 3.9 percent, compared with 3.5 percent at the end of 1980.[14]

Speculation. One of the statistics often cited as a measure of liberalization is the level of transactions in the Tokyo foreign exchange market. In 1981, total transactions there amounted to $3.3 trillion, an increase of about eight times compared with the 1976 total. However, a large proportion of the foreign-exchange transactions in 1981 and

1982 were a reflection not of liberalization in the constructive sense but rather of overt or covert speculative activity in the financial sector. Because of the 1982 recession, many business firms and banks were doing poorly in the activities in which they were formally engaged. As an alternative, they were prone to seek profits through speculation. This propensity was fueled by the volatility of the yen during that period. And with the advent of electronic banking came increased access to facilities for speculation. Treasurers of multinational corporations have the information and the means within their own offices of instantaneously arranging transactions with their subsidiaries and affiliates abroad. Indeed, the cost of installing these computer and telex systems, and the cost of the personnel hired to operate them, gives a strong inducement to private firms to justify the expense. This leads them to "play banker" and thus to speculate. It could be said that international electronic banking and its maintenance cost give the business community a vested interest in the continuance of speculation. Likewise, some have a vested interest in the floating exchange rate system, which increases the range of potential speculative activity.

Foreign-exchange activity resulting from speculation is not something the authorities intended or of which they are proud. Indeed, statistically there is no way for the Ministry of Finance or the Bank of Japan to even distinguish between speculative and nonspeculative foreign-exchange transactions. What they do know is that in 1981 only 40 percent of the foreign-exchange transactions of Japanese banks with domestic customers were trade related. (Banks aver that it is their customers, not they, who are doing the speculating.)

The most informed source of opinion regarding the amount of foreign exchange speculation in Japan comes from the *tanshi* firms, the short-term money brokers who execute the bulk of foreign-exchange transactions. According to the president of one of the six tanshi in Tokyo, 70 percent of all Japanese foreign exchange transactions in 1982 were speculative. There are many ways in which speculation can be performed. For example, a Japanese bank may use the telex to arrange fund purchases and sales between its subsidiaries or branches in two different foreign countries. Because no record of these transactions is received by the Japanese government, they cannot be controlled. Unhedged commodity contracts, such as uncovered commitments to pay for future deliveries of petroleum in dollars, likewise constitute currency speculation.[15] Japanese oil refiners lost $930 million in fiscal year 1981 because they bet that the yen would appreciate; instead, it declined.[16] Other examples of losses due to exchange speculation have also come to light.[17] These are probably only the tip of the iceberg. There has been a tremendous increase in the amount of currency speculation through mismatched maturities in the obligations of Japanese financial institutions. There is speculation through leads and lags in payments for commodity transactions. There is speculation through investment in foreign-currency-denominated securities and deposits. Much speculation is invisible to the authorities because banks in Japan can pass their speculative holdings to their overseas branches and affiliates to avoid actual or potential restrictions at home.[18] Apart from their Eurodollar transactions, which are well matched, speculation also occurs when the banks lend long and borrow short, especially through syndicated loans denominated in dollars.

Speculation by foreigners in Japan's capital markets contributed substantially to the statistics cited as evidence of the "openness" of those markets. In 1981, net bond repurchase agreements by foreigners reached a record high of $3.22 billion, reflecting their attempts to gain foreign-exchange profits.[19] (In 1982, the total was one-third less.) Largely for the same reason, purchases of Japanese securities by foreigners in 1981 amounted to $12.52 billion, a record level.

Japan's foreign-exchange brokers are perhaps the chief beneficiaries of the volatility of the yen and the currency speculation it has engendered. The volume of their business has increased tremendously, and their commissions have not declined much.

International Banking Facility

Japan has arrived at a node on the path from economic control to liberalization. It must choose whether or not to follow the example of other financial centers that have inaugurated facilities for "offshore" international banking, otherwise known as international banking facilities (IBFs).[20] The decision has both economic and bureaucratic implications.

The IBF promotes a specific aspect of liberalization, namely, internationalization of the yen. Clients of the IBF are exclusively nonresidents, including foreign subsidiaries of domestic corporations, from which the IBF accepts deposits and makes loans in terms of authorized currencies. The IBF's transactions are restricted exclusively to those between nonresidents and other nonresidents: thus, they are described as "out-out" transactions. These transactions are exempt from various domestic restrictions. The New York IBF, for example, enjoys freedom from U.S. taxation,[21] freedom from maintaining reserves,[22] freedom from regulation of the interest rate on loans, and freedom from exchange control.

In 1982, the economic implications of a Japanese IBF were not yet fully understood. They would vary in accordance with the specific rules it would observe. What effect would establishment of an IBF have on the ability of the Ministry of Finance to control monetary policy? For example, a resident corporation might evade government regulations by converting domestic funds into offshore money through overseas intermediaries. Would there be "spillover" from the external market into the domestic market? Theoretically, spillover would be minimized by the requirement that every IBF transaction must be channeled through an authorized foreign exchange bank, which would determine the eligibility of each transaction.

When first established, a Japanese IBF would presumably exclude transactions in yen,[23] but yen transactions might gradually become permissible. If so, Euroyen transactions all over the world might shift to Japan. The expanded volume of transactions between the Euroyen and other currencies could induce a high degree of volatility in the value of the yen, causing repercussions on Japan's domestic economy. Further effects would result from the impact of a Japanese IBF on the IBFs of other countries. Singapore and Hong Kong, for example, would be greatly concerned about the loss of business to Japan. Asian feelings already run high about Japanese "economic imperialism." In the opinion of an official at the Bank of Japan, the London Euroyen market would probably not be much affected.

Other aspects of the organization of an IBF would have political and bureaucratic implications at home. Would its functions be confined to commercial banking, or would they include merchant banking as well? The latter implies the issuance of debentures, which would be strongly favored by the securities companies.[24] Even alternative housekeeping arrangements for the IBF are of consequence. Would IBF banking and domestic banking be housed in a single structure? If so, domestic customers would see that the withholding tax on interest income is rescinded for the offshore accounts, and they would cry "unfair." On the other hand, if the offshore market accounts were to be maintained in an entirely separate banking institution, that new bank would be under the jurisdiction of the International Finance Bureau rather than under the Banking Bureau. The former would be the winner, the latter would be the loser. Thus, there is strong resistance from the Banking Bureau to this type of innovation. There is also opposition from the Tax Bureau, which would receive no revenue from the international banking facility.

Despite the lack of unanimous opinion within the Ministry of Finance, on the whole the ministry was more favorably disposed to the establishment of an IBF than the Bank of Japan. Some ministry officials believed that with an IBF the domestic yen could be more effectively controlled than before. An official in the International Finance Bureau said, "The reason is that we could watch the Euroyen transactions more closely." Asked whether administrative guidance would be imposed on the IBF, the same Ministry of Finance official said, "Some officials of the Ministry of Finance think so." However, excessive restrictions on the IBF would be of no avail, if not actually counterproductive.

In the summer of 1982, insiders and outsiders held remarkably different opinions about the potential bureaucratic effects of an IBF. According to one well-placed observer in the foreign banking community in Tokyo, establishment of an international banking facility would diminish the authority of the International Finance Bureau. "At present, the IFB checks and controls the quality of the international lender and borrower; it determines *when* the parties can come to market and *who* is eligible to do so." If it lost its checking and approval functions, what would the IFB do? "I can't think of anything," said the outside observer. An official of the IFB, on the other hand, had a different opinion. "Officials of the Japanese government are very flexible," he said. "I am not worried about working myself out of a job as a result of economic liberalization or the establishment of an offshore market."

Among insiders, chief proponents of the IBF included Takashi Hosomi, a former vice minister of the Ministry of Finance who later was head of the OECF. Another was Tsuneo Fujita, director of the Coordination Department of the OECF, formerly an official of the IFB. These men argued that if due to protectionism Japan could not earn sufficient export income from commodities, it would have to turn to services. Within the IFB itself, an official enumerated the following functions of the bureau that would remain after establishment of an IBF: It would collect statistics, make policy concerning intervention in the foreign-exchange market, help determine Japan's official economic cooperation policy, and give guidance to individual firms about their plans for financing large overseas projects. The Ministry of Finance, moreover, like MITI, might thrive on what is seen as misfortune in the private sector. Liberalization will presumably be accompanied by more uncertainty and instability in the economy at large, which will give the ministry a larger stabilization role to play and more opportunity to impose administrative guidance on the private sector. In the banking community, Japanese banks were passive and apprehensive about the IBF. It was the foreign banks that were clamoring for its establishment because they believed that their greater experience in international markets would give them an advantage over Japanese banks.

The Bank of Japan was not enthusiastic about establishment of an international banking facility. This was delicately expressed by a senior official of the bank, who said, "Our basic principle is to *not* promote the yen artificially or deliberately as an international currency." On the contrary, the bank maintained that it had a great deal to do in first liberalizing the domestic market. It argued that it would be inappropriate to artifically superimpose a new fully liberalized external market on the existing semi-liberalized domestic market. "Let's catch up with domestic liberalization, and then we can create the IBF as a natural next step," is how the Bank of Japan official put it. In a fully liberalized domestic money and banking system, the Bank of Japan's operating functions as manager of the system would assume relatively greater importance in relation to the diminished policy functions of the Ministry of Finance.

In the International Finance Bureau there was approval of the IBF proposal as well as opposition for bureaucratic reasons. As opposed to the research people, who were in favor of it, the operations people were opposed because they would have to listen to complaints, such as those of the small regional banks that would not be able to compete effectively in the proposed institution. The operations officials, however, hold their jobs for only two years or so, during which time they adopt the adversary attitude.When transferred elsewhere, they might change their opinion.

When asked what effect establishing an IBF would have on the ability of the Ministry of Finance to enforce emergency controls, an International Finance Bureau official said that although theoretically the IBF would be subject to the Foreign Exchange and Foreign Trade Control Law, in practice the law would be difficult to apply. With regard to official thinking, the same official remarked that "when we discuss the IBF, we limit it to banking. The Nomura Securities Company would like securities companies to be eligible to participate." (As established in December 1986, one of the restrictions imposed on the IBF was the prohibition of securities transactions.)

It was unclear to the Ministry of Finance, moreover, what effect an IBF would have on Euroyen transactions. Some officials expected that Euroyen transactions all over the world would shift to Japan. Others believed that if the IBF were heavily regulated, it would not attract as high a volume of Euroyen activity. According to the same International Finance Bureau official, the London Euroyen market would probably not be much affected. However, Singapore and Hong Kong would be considerably affected, and therefore in his opinion they were apprehensive about the establishment of an IBF in Japan.

Trade Liberalization

In their respective views of trade friction (*bōeki masatsu*), the contrast in the U.S. and Japanese positions is stark. From the Japanese point of view, in raising barriers against Japanese merchandise it is chiefly the West that is illiberal. This matter was discussed with a retired professor of economics, who said: "Japan regards itself as the victim in the struggle between the White Demon and the Red Demon. 'How can we harmonize their struggle?' the Japanese ask. Japanese intellectuals are divided between the two. The Western world does not accept our superior productivity; therefore, we must achieve rapprochement with Russia and China.They will accept our productive power . . . this is what Russia and China are saying to Japanese politicians. Indeed, a Diet member recently said this very thing in the Diet. Publicly, he was criticized. But this was not his opinion alone; privately, it is shared by others. . . . Moreover, Japanese sense that Germany is doing the same thing. They ask, 'Why don't we?' "

It is interesting to examine the course of trade liberalization as formulated in cabinet orders implementing the Foreign Exchange Law. These mainly confer new liberties on Japanese in their trade transactions with foreigners rather than on foreigners in their trade transactions with Japanese.[25] Chiefly, new departures under the Foreign Exchange Law are as follows: (1) Exports no longer require certification by a foreign-exchange bank; (2) the "standard method of settlement" for exports is (with some exceptions) no longer required; and (3) in general, it is no longer necessary to declare imports to a foreign exchange bank.

Nevertheless, until 1 June 1985, when a yen-denominated bankers' acceptance market was inaugurated, domestic encumbrances to trade remained. The financing of Japan's imports was at a disadvantage because of the Bank of Japan's reluctance to allow the establishment of a bankers' acceptance market. The bank feared that the activities of such a market would be incompatible with its control of credit conditions, especially if it wished to impose a tight money policy.[26] A constraint on imports also remained in the form of a potential limit on commodity import financing. Trade financing was defined (again, control by definition) as falling within the category of "general domestic loans," which were subject to Bank of Japan ceilings, including limitations on loans to any individual borrower. Even in instances where foreign suppliers requested payment in yen, Japanese importers were unable to receive accommodation at the banks.[27] Thus, only 2 percent of Japan's imports were financed in yen, compared with approximately 40 percent of exports.

As of January 1982, Japan maintained residual import restrictions on 27 commodities, of which 22 were agricultural. In terms of the U.S. balance of payments, their existence may be symbolic rather than substantive. It has been estimated, for example, that complete removal of Japan's agricultural import quotas would after five years result in an increase of U.S. agricultural exports to Japan of only $500 million.[28] In defending these residual restrictions, the Japanese do not allude to "freedom of transactions in principle." Instead, they invoke the argument that the restrictions make little difference. For example, "if Japan were to remove all restrictions on imports of beef, Australia would benefit more than the United States. Or if Japan were to import more beef from the United States, it would import less grain. If it were to abandon all import restrictions on oranges, Brazil would benefit more than California." Concerning the U.S.–Japan trade imbalance, the Japanese point out further that for a Japanese, it is more difficult to expand market share at home than abroad, whereas in the U.S. market, the opposite holds. These mutually reinforcing factors help increase the U.S.–Japan imbalance.[29]

Why, even for a Japanese, is it so difficult to expand sales at home? Two opposite reasons are often given. The first is that due to the free-market system, competition is more ferocious in Japan than elsewhere. The second, on the contrary, is that market share is frozen by means of artificial and arbitrary restrictions. For example, in some sections of Japan the trading companies have attempted to enter into the production of eggs in order to reduce their cost and selling price. But this would cause too much competition for established rural egg producers. Because of political intervention, it has therefore not been permitted.

Japan's remaining import restrictions are explained at least as much by political as by economic considerations. Although consumer groups 30 years ago favored import liberalization, they now officially oppose import liberalization. This comes despite the fact that Japanese families spend approximately 32 percent of their disposable income on food (compared with 20 percent for Europeans and 17 percent for Americans). Consumer groups talk about maintaining Japan's food producing capacity in order to reduce dependence on the outside world. They remember President Nixon's soybean embargo of 1973; some also remember the privations of World War II. On the other hand, the bureaucrats of the consumer movements do not necessarily represent all consumers.

Among other pressure groups, big business, as represented by Keidanren, is urging removal of all 27 residual import restrictions.[30] In the nonagricultural category, the items include only coal and several types of leather goods, which are of little concern to Keidanren. What it mostly fears is that in retaliation for Japanese residual agricultural import barriers, Western trade partners will impose restrictions on their own imports of manufactured goods from Japan. In this respect, there is no consensus between Japanese agriculture and export-led industry.

As reflected in bureaucratic politics, lack of consensus is readily apparent. In the controversy over specific items in the step-by-step approach to liberalization, each ministry calls for liberalization of products under the jurisdiction of some other ministry. Thus, in the interest of its own clients, MITI calls for liberalization of agricultural imports. It also calls for liberalization of data communications services, which are under the jurisdiction of the Ministry of Posts and Telecommunications. With regard to other services under the jurisdiction of the Ministry of Finance, liberalization has been slower than it has with commodities. Thus, MITI criticizes the Ministry of Finance for being "conservative." Unlike MITI, other ministries have few clients whose interests are subject to foreign retaliation. The nontariff barriers imposed by those ministries, however, provoke protectionist countermeasures abroad that are directed against clients of MITI.

How will the agricultural import question be solved? It will be solved by the demographic transition and the migration of young people from rural to urban areas. Most farmers today are elderly. After 1990, most of them will have retired. Their children will not be available to take over the farms. At that time, many will sell or rent their land to others who will consolidate the plots and undertake extensive cultivation, as distinguished from the traditional intensive mode of Japanese agriculture. If Japanese agriculture can become more mechanized and efficient, it will not need protection. The moral of the story is that the United States must be patient for another decade.

The demographic transition and its implications for agriculture have corresponding implications for the Liberal Democratic Party (LDP). The decline in the size of the rural community reduces the importance of that group's vote. LDP dependence on the farm vote has already declined from about 50 percent in 1955, when the party was formed, to about 20 percent in 1983. In the future, the LDP will attempt to recruit urban rather then rural supporters. (Thus, at present it is cultivating constituencies among small- and medium-size businesses, small banks, and even labor unions. To some extent, it is doing so by providing protection against the adverse effects of premature liberalization.) The paradox is that by dedicating itself to reform (fiscal, administrative, etc.), the LDP will become a progressive party while the communist and socialist parties, which defend the status quo (such as subsidies for agriculture) become reactionary.[31] At present, resistance to progress in liberalization is waning, but the central location of that resistance is in the Diet. Theoretically, and at the top of the hierarchy, politicians are in favor of liberalization. But for the insecure rank and file in the Diet, it is necessary to seek votes. This means that they must appeal to their constituents in terms of resisting liberalization.

In surveying this scene, an old friend, a professor, observed, "Struggle and opposition are everywhere in Japan. But consensus and 'groupism' are also everywhere. Thus, it is difficult to determine what Japan is. Even though 'number one,' Japan is a divided nation." In this nonhomogeneous Japan, it is difficult to discern not only what Japan's intentions might be but even where its leadership lies. What does this imply for U.S. strategy in coming to an accommodation with Japan? Where Japanese are of two minds on a particular issue, it would appear that opposition between the United States and Japan might be reduced: Trade-offs might be more readily arranged. Absence of unanimity on the part of the Japanese toward U.S.–Japan issues, moreover, increases the possibility that in the universe of issues, an individual Japanese may entertain a mixture of pro–U.S. and anti–U.S. attitudes. In the Diet, for example, some of the leading defenders of agricultural protectionism are simultaneously hawkish in matters of military defense. This would apparently enhance the possibilities for linkage agreements,[32] to which the Japanese are in general highly opposed. The reason is that linkage opens fathomless possibilities for further demands on Japan by countries other than the United States. In the step-by-step dialectic, each concession to the United States creates a precedent that other countries might attempt to invoke.

Alternative approaches by the United States in the attempt to overcome trade friction with Japan include the "package" approach, the "specific issue" approach, the "summit" approach, formal protests to General Agreement on Tariffs and Trade (GATT), "trial by media," "talking rather than listening," "scapegoating," legal harassment by private corporations, congressional pressure, labor union pressure, and delivery of threats and ultimatums by administration officials. In response, the Japanese have used the "numbers game," mobilization of

Japanese pressure groups, passive resistance, and leaks of inside information to the press. They have also acquiesced in "orderly marketing agreements," "voluntary export restraints," "adjustment of standards," and establishment of an Ombudsman Office. They have also established production facilities in the United States as well as export platforms in third countries. In addition, they have used an ingenious device, the "iridescent solution" (*tamamushi iro no kaiketsu*), which is an agreement in which each party can see what he is looking for.

The General Trading Company

The distinction between appearance and reality is of special interest in connection with one of Japan's greatest institutional innovations, the general trading company (*sōgō shōsha*). In the early postwar period, Japan's foreign exchange and foreign trade controls contributed to the prosperity of its major trading companies. Later, on the contrary, they prospered through liberalization. In the period of direct controls, the power of the nine major trading companies was based on their privileged access to scarce credit, to allocations of scarce commodities, and to valuable import quota assignments. These advantages were the foundation for their dominant positions in both the domestic and foreign sectors of the economy. When credit became more accessible and quotas began to be phased out by liberalization, the pre-eminence of the major trading companies came to depend primarily on their information networks and the exercise of sheer business power. In the early 1980s, they favored comprehensive liberalization, which would provide an environment in which that power could be exercised without restraint. In the case of the trading companies, as elsewhere in the Japanese economy, liberalization was in the interest of big business, while weaker and less efficient firms sought shelter in government protection and restraint of competition.

In the course of Japan's postwar transition, a coincidence of micro and macro interests is very clear in the case of the trading companies. In the period of the economy's enhanced growth, trading companies centered their efforts in the materials industries, such as petrochemicals, iron, and steel. As these materials industries reached their ceiling, the center of gravity of Japan's industrial structure shifted to new star performers in the processing and assembling industries. The general trading companies shifted as well. They established positions in high technology, backed venture firms, and became investors and project coordinators as well as traders.[33] This familiar story emphasizes the fact that although Japan's national interests remain fairly fixed, its innovative strategies for fulfilling those interests have undergone rapid evolution.[34] At present, both in terms of fundamental economic planning and administrative reform, Japan's national priority lies in transforming itself from an industrial and commercial giant into a financial and high technology giant in world markets. Here again, there is a coincidence of national and private interests, for with the decline in the domestic growth rate the trading companies' role in international finance and international investment has become more important than ever to those firms.[35] The general trading companies are increasingly involved with money itself, including international money, as a "product." For the general trading companies, as for the nation at large, liberalization in the form of internationalization takes a high place on the agenda.

As a result of the Foreign Exchange Law, financial arrangements have become more flexible. For example, because there is no longer a "standard method of settlement," payments can be made by the installment method. Formerly, to circumvent payment restrictions, trading companies frequently resorted to switch transactions. There is less need for that now. The permissible limit for in-house "marrying" of foreign currency obligations and export receipts (kōgō keisan kanjō) has been raised so that trading companies have less need to pay for the foreign exchange services of the banks.[36]

Although negative controls on trading company operations have legally been largely abolished, those operations remain susceptible to official controls in the form of administrative guidance. Trading companies are not legally compelled to comply with the guidance, but they do so because it is dictated by "traditional mentality" and is customary. Likewise, the mentality of the bureaucrats remains predisposed to imposing guidance. In particular, as an offset to the contraction of their legal powers of indiscriminate intervention, and in the name of the national interest, government officials attempt to recover the scope of their authority by extending "protection" to weaker enterprises. This is a major obstruction to the further advance of liberalization. In accordance with the increasingly financial nature of trading company operations, the Financial Bureau of the Ministry of Finance is the source of most of the direct guidance they receive. On overseas investment, they may also receive guidance from the Bank of Japan. Indirectly, guidance is imposed by means of the External Trade Association, whose membership includes the major trading companies and major manufacturers. The association receives instructions from the government that it passes on to its members. The process is accentuated by the fact that the secretariat of the External Trade Association includes many former government bureaucrats.

At the commodity level, many nontariff barriers remain. One of these is administrative guidance imposed by MITI. Concerning the import of "sensitive" items, the trading companies receive messages relayed through manufacturers or through phone calls directly from MITI. The messages are often ambiguous: "You should know that we are concerned . . ." What are they concerned about? This may not be clear, but the trading companies surmise that matters such as the general condition of Japanese industry, the problems of a particular industrial sector, priorities within MITI itself, or diplomatic negotiations may be involved. MITI also supervises trade credit, and most trade credit is extended by the trading companies. Some of the most effective nontariff barriers are unintentional, such as those arising from classification criteria embodied in old laws that were framed with no reference to international trade whatsoever. In the case of sake, for example, the law provides classification criteria only for sake that has been produced in Japan; those criteria cannot be applied to sake produced in California. The Pharmaceutical Control Act presents similar barriers to foreign entry into the Japanese domestic market, although in this case the difficulty is intentionally compounded by the way the law is administered.

Among the key elements of the Japanese genius for institutional innovation are its resourcefulness and flexibility. There is, however, a fundamental difference between businessmen and bureaucrats in the nature of these aptitudes and the objects to which they are applied. In the government, resourcefulness arises from improvisation, extemporaneous decisionmaking, absence of criteria, and the case-by-case approach. In the private sector it arises from the creative response of entrepreneurs to new situations through the production of new products and new techniques. Government officials may feel a complacent sense of personal security. They are satisfied with the status quo and, they are not required to show profits. Their improvisations often take the form of interference with the actual details of private business transactions. Since the demise of the economic miracle, the days of the bureaucrat as hero were in eclipse during the 1980s.

=== 3 ===

BANKS—
FACING INWARD AND OUTWARD

Banks mediate between the internal and external sectors of the economy. Thus, they occupy a strategic position in the liberalization process. By the same token, they will be assigned an instrumental role in fulfilling the international proposals of the administrative reform program. The latter (of which more in the following chapter) contemplates a shift of resources from the domestic to the international sector of the Japanese economy and an expansion in Japan's activities in investment, finance, and information on the international plane. In this respect, the following account may be regarded as an introduction to what Chapter 4 refers to as Japan's "external option."

The Bank Law

Due to external pressures during the postwar period, international liberalization preceded domestic liberalization in Japan. Domestically, the most formidable remaining body of controls lies in the monetary and banking sector under the jurisdiction of the Ministry of Finance. The banking system, however, faces both inward and outward. Thus, even the degree of external liberalization has remained ambiguous.

The new Bank Law (not to be confused with the Bank of Japan Law[1]) came into effect in April 1982, superseding the former Bank Law of 1927. It is liberalizing in appearance but not in reality. Legally, the range of permissible action on the part of the banks has been widened, but administrative guidance by the Ministry of Finance will determine the actual outcome much as before. The ministry, for example, may impose regulations on the banks either in accordance with the Bank Law or with the Foreign Exchange and Foreign Trade Control Law.

Thus, the ministry possesses strong powers of retaliation in case a bank fails to comply with the ministry's guidance in either domestic or international matters.

In accordance with the trend of recent legislation, the new Bank Law is more specific than the old. Formerly, laws were written in a vague and comprehensive manner. (In style, all laws nowadays are written in *kanji* and *hiragana*, whereas formerly they were written in kanji and *katakana*.). Under the former law, the boundary between the banking business and the securities business was not clear. City banks argued that because securities transactions by banks were not forbidden, those transactions were therefore permissible. Securities companies argued the opposite: Permission was not specifically given to the banks to engage in securities transactions; therefore, they were forbidden to do so. (Incidentally, this is the opposite way securities firms interpret the law as it concerns their own activities.) The new law specifically allows banks to engage in securities transactions, limiting this to the sale of government bonds. Initially, the banks were restricted to selling new issues of long-term government bonds; selling medium-term government bonds and dealing in previously issued bonds were to be authorized later. By giving banks explicit permission to engage in government securities transactions, the new Bank Law implicitly prohibits them from dealing in all other types of securities. This in effect nullifies the implication that could be drawn from the previous Bank Law; namely, that by not mentioning the matter, it authorized the banks to engage in any kind of securities transactions. In effect, the explicitness of the new Bank Law constituted a defeat for the banking industry in its rivalry with the securities industry.[2]

Among its other ostensible dispensations to the banks—dispensations that formerly would have been conferred by administrative guidance—the new Bank Law authorized the sale in Japan of commercial paper (CP) and certificates of deposit (CDs) issued abroad or denominated in currencies other than the yen. (The inaugural date for such permission, however, was postponed until April 1983.) In April 1982, banks and securities houses were authorized to sell gold, in bar or coin form, over the counter. The law provides for adoption of a five-day banking week and for settlement of bank accounts once a year instead of semi-annually. The new law also specifically mentions foreign banks in Japan, which were not referred to in the former law.

On the other hand, in contrast to the old law (which did not mention the matter), the new law restricts the size of loans a bank may extend to any single borrower to a proportion of the bank's equity capital that will be specified by the government. This gives legal sanction to a method of control that formerly had been enforced only by administrative guidance. Article 13 of the Bank Law reads as follows: "A bank shall not extend credit to anyone or any organization exceeding an amount that is to be calculated by multiplying the value of capital and reserves of that bank by a fixed figure. The definition of credit, reserves, and the fixed figure will be determined by further regulation." This article constitutes a countermeasure to the increasing independence of private banks from the central bank that occurred during the 1970s because of an increase in the private banks' nonborrowed reserves.

The new Bank Law also imposes a heavier burden of disclosure and auditing requirements than its predecessor. It requires the banks to provide more information about their business transactions, balance sheets, income statements, and personnel than formerly. This additional information, of course, is grist for the mill of administrative guidance.

The Bank of Japan Versus the Ministry of Finance

Although liberalization is in the national interest, the bureaucracy seeks to maintain its control over the banking system much as before. How the Bank of Japan pursues the national interest is highly conditioned by how it pursues its own interests, especially in relation to those of the Ministry of Finance.

As mentioned above, MITI and the Ministry of Finance dominated the policy framework for the allocation of funds following World War II. This was done through councils established at the initiative of those authorities. During the first half of the 1960s, for example, the Council on Fund Allocation by Financial Institutions (*Kinyū-kikan Shikin Shingikai*) of the Ministry of Finance and the subcommittee on Industrial Finance of the Council on Industrial Rationalization (*Sangyō-Gōrika Shingikai Sangyō Shikin Bukai*) of MITI coordinated the funding and fund allocation of the private banks. In the capital markets, the Council for Coordination of Stock Issues (*Zōshi tō Chōsei Kondankai*) and the Council on Bond Issues (*Kisai Kai*), composed of representatives of the leading financial institutions, intervened in the allocation of capital funds. The last two councils were likewise dominated by the ministries. The Bank of Japan played a subordinate role to MITI and the Ministry of Finance in these arrangements. It was obliged to control money and credit through window guidance imposed on the private banks in accordance with the wishes of the Ministry of Finance. In the future, due to financial innovation and to internationalization of the money market, window guidance is likely to be less effective. Accordingly, this will shrink one of the channels by which the ministry can impose its will on the Bank of Japan.

Since the mid-1970s, among other attempts by the Bank of Japan to achieve autonomy, it has increasingly invoked the doctrine of monetarism. Hitherto, the money supply has been controlled primarily through the quarterly quota on lending limits that the Bank of Japan imposes on the city banks. (No lending limits are imposed on foreign banks, but these banks account for only about 3 percent of the banking business.)[3] However, the same factors that are diminishing the effectiveness of window guidance will diminish the Bank of Japan's ability to control the money supply. In the past, Japan's money and banking system was highly controllable due to the dependence of firms on bank loans, to functional segmentation of the banking system, to the simple structure of the money market, and to Japan's insulation from international financial disturbance.[4] Each of these factors will be less effective in the future. In a sense, the weakening of the Bank of Japan's own powers of intervention in the market is the price of the bank's emancipation from control by the Ministry of Finance. Being willing to settle for this result may be one of the reasons the bank favors deregulation of the domestic market. In practice, the Bank of Japan enjoys a good deal of discretion in the implementation of policy, if not in the formation of policy itself. As seen from outside, however, it is not always clear to what extent its actions reflect independent judgment rather than dictation by the ministry. Monitoring and intervention by the Ministry of Finance vary drastically from time to time in accordance with the ministry's policy shifts.

Banking and Administrative Guidance

Publicly, the city banks profess to want more independence from the government. They say they want liberalization of interest rates and banking controls. Privately, they are not so sure. While interest rates on national bonds remain under control, the city banks are coerced into subsidizing the government by buying its bonds at a loss.[5] On the other hand, if interest rates are liberated and rise, the value of the city banks' entire portfolio of outstanding loans declines. The cost of new funding would also rise. By depriving the banks of guaranteed market shares, liberalization would tend to force them to shift their traditional emphasis from long- term to short-term banking objectives. Hitherto, even the rank order of the size of banks has been controlled by the Ministry of Finance. When that order is disturbed, the ministry takes forceful steps to restore the customary lineup. In a free market, as well as in a country that is "overbanked," banks fear that "more competition every day—chiseling on each other's margin—is not a comfortable way to live," as one Sanwa Bank official put it. The ministry uses this ambivalence (especially on the part of weak regional banks) for its own purposes in slowing down the rate of liberalization. It asserts that in order to achieve a "soft landing," it must proceed at deliberate speed.

Deterioration in some of the basic conditions that confront the banks has increased their apprehension. In recent years, profits have declined because business firms are less dependent on bank loans than formerly. The owned capital resources of firms have increased, and their sources of funds, both domestically and abroad, have been diversified. The wild fluctuation of foreign-exchange markets has been a burden. Because of the decline in income increases, depositors have become more yield sensitive and are shopping around more than ever for higher returns on their savings. (In favor of liberalization, the banks feel they have to be free to offer securities as well as savings accounts.) In the international sector, the banks are even more insecure than domestically. They especially fear potential competition from the securities companies, which are more venturesome than the banks.

As suggested above, the new Bank Law is new mostly in form rather than in substance. It publishes procedures that had already been approved through administrative guidance. However the law itself is subject to interpretation by further administrative guidance. Whether or not the law proves to be liberalizing will depend on how the authorities choose to interpret it. Because the government is itself ambivalent about liberalization, administrative guidance is likely to become more vexed than ever before.

From the government's point of view, there is no consistent rationale for the liberalization of banking. Fighting among the bureaus of the Ministry of Finance is traditional, but recently consensus has been even more difficult to achieve because of the liberalization process. Some bureaus, such as the Tax Bureau, are reluctant in principle. Because of the antagonistic interests of their respective clients, the Banking Bureau and the Securities Bureau have been increasingly at odds. The Overall Coordination Division of the Minister's Secretariat is supposed to perform coordination among the various bureaus, but it lacks the strength to do so effectively.

The economic rationale for the government's maintenance of its controls contains several elements. The administered low interest rate policy, combined with the system of allocating quotas of its bonds to the city banks (but not to the regional or foreign banks), has benefited the government as a means of reducing the cost of servicing the national debt.[6] The increasing size of government bond issues, however, is undermining this control. In the early 1970s, when the size of issues was modest, the secondary market for national bonds was likewise small. In those circumstances, the terms established in the issuing market were predominant. The entire issued amount of government bonds was purchased by the city banks and ultimately absorbed by the Bank of Japan, leaving little scope for a secondary market. But as the size of issues grew, the secondary market also grew because it was impossible for the Bank of Japan to absorb all the bonds from the city banks, which were unable to hold them for ten years to maturity. (The banks were required to hold the bonds for a year before selling them.) The Ministry of Finance could maintain its control over the issuing market, but 1975 was the turning point at which the issuing authority could no longer disregard the secondary market.

Another element of the economic rationale for administered interest rates is the government's attempt to encourage private investment. This is fundamental to Japanese supply-side economics. A third element (political as well as economic) is the government's professed aim of forestalling the bankruptcy of inefficient minor regional banks that survive mainly because of the artificially low interest rate on deposit accounts. City banks will regret the loss of this cheap source of funding as well. As mentioned above, it is in the government's economic interest to prevent the unrestricted outflow of savings abroad in order to dam up a pool of private financial resources that can be diverted into purchasing the national debt. A complementary reason for restricting capital outflow is the government's desire to prevent foreign financial institutions from acquiring substantial supplies of yen, which would promote internationalization of the yen and subject domestic economic policy to further external constraints. In this respect, among others, the Ministry of Finance has an incentive to implement the new Bank Law restrictively in coordination with restrictive implementation of the Foreign Exchange and Foreign Trade Control Law.

Besides imposing additional constraints on domestic policy, internationalization of the yen tends to undermine the domestic controls of the Ministry of Finance. Already, however, liberalization in the external sector has preceded and exceeded liberalization at home. Overseas, for example, segmentation of Japanese financial and investment activities has broken down to a considerable extent, which threatens the domestic barriers against universal banking. As a countermeasure, the Ministry of Finance has used administrative guidance to project its domestic controls onto international terrain. The Japanese government has no legal authority to inquire into activities of foreign corporations, even those that are subsidiaries of Japanese parent companies. However, when the banks have their regular "hearings" at the Ministry of Finance, they may be asked about their "total position," which is a way of asking about the operations of their branches and subsidiaries abroad.[7] The government contends that such inquiries are purely for statistical reporting purposes. In fact, however, the Ministry of Finance has even restricted the amount of borrowing from local markets abroad by foreign branches of Japanese banks. The overlap between the economic rationale and the bureaucratic rationale for maintenance of controls is ambiguous in these cases. In any event, it is clear that the government is just as ambivalent about liberalization as are the banks.[8]

An Interview on Intervention (July 1982)

The government's ambivalence toward liberalization may be illustrated in the following interview with a senior official of the Bank of Japan.

Q: *As seen from the Bank of Japan, what are the major trends in liberalization and internationalization?*
A: So far as the Bank of Japan is concerned, the liberalization is taking place primarily in the domestic money market, not so much in the international market. We want more liberalization of the interest rate, but not a radical change. We want steady, gradual change.

Q: *To what extent does the Bank of Japan intervene in short-term money markets?*
A: We intervene in order to keep the short-term interest rate a little higher than expected in order to reduce the differential between the U.S. and Japanese interest rates. But this sort of intervention is universal. We intervene by change of attitude towards the market: we supply less than it wants. There is no way to directly intervene in the gensaki market. But if we sell a large amount of TBs, the money-market rate will increase. Thus, the Bank of Japan can intervene *indirectly* in the gensaki market.

Q: *In what way is the Ministry of Finance too strong?*
A: In some sense. . . . this is too difficult to answer at once.We respect the market mechanism. So the tendency of liberalization is a

benefit to us. The IFB likes liberalization: they are exposed to foreign pressure; they are concerned about what foreigners think. The Banking Bureau does not feel foreign pressure.

Most operating matters are handled by the Bank of Japan. These are subject to review by the Ministry of Finance. The ministry determines policy and monitors to see that its policy is being observed. The banks still accept guidance from the Ministry of Finance, just as they did in the days when they were wholly dependent on Bank of Japan discount facilities for their money supply. But they also protest now, as seen in their resistance to underwriting of low interest rate government bonds.

Q: *Because of liberalization, what changes have taken place in the administrative procedures of the IFB?*

A: There is now more discussion among the Ministry of Finance bureaus than before. For example, when the Ministry of Finance advised against the purchase of zero-coupon bonds, all the bureaus had to discuss it. The decision was done by guidance rather than by law. Guidance requires more consultation than before the liberalization, and there is more guidance now than formerly. This is difficult to explain to foreigners. I do not like too much guidance. When a bureau can exercise its functions under law, there is no need for consultation among bureaus. But when it has no law to back it up, it must get a consensus among other bureaus that possibly may be affected, so liberalization of the law gives rise both to more guidance and to more consultations among the bureaus concerning guidance.

Q: *Because of liberalization, what changes have taken place in the relations among the bureaus (especially Banking, International Finance, and Securities) of the Ministry of Finance? What changes have occurred in the power structure of the ministry?*

A: In the long term, IFB power will increase, but not as a result of liberalization. The reason is that at present most Japanese companies are in the international field, so IFB has an increasing number of clients. The scope and importance of their clientele are increasing.

Q: *Legally, the Ministry of Finance has lost some of its authority to intervene. Does the ministry actually have less power than before?*

A: Yes and no. We have a long history and tradition of government guidance in Japan. In this sense, the liberalization of the Foreign Exchange Law did not change the situation much. But some changes have occurred. It depends on the situation. In particular, the government is much concerned about criticism from abroad.

Q: *To what extent does the IFB engage in direct operational control over individual banks or firms?*

A: It is difficult to say. This is a very sensitive matter. It relates to trade friction between Japan and the United States in goods and services. In the matter of syndicated loans in foreign currency or in yen, the Ministry of Finance performs close consultation with Japanese banks, but not with foreign banks. The Ministry of Finance realizes that foreigners are critical of its administrative guidance, so they don't like to use the term and don't like to talk about it. However, when Japanese want to lend money abroad or subscribe for Samurai bonds, the Ministry of Finance does exercise control. Indeed, all over the world, there is fine-tuning of the capital market by the authorities. In the case of Samurai bonds, the volume to be issued is more important to the ministry than the degree of eligibility of the borrower. The Ministry of Finance likes to form a queue of borrowers.

Q: *To what extent has the political role of the Diet members changed because of liberalization?*

A: Very interesting question. Very private. The increasing role of the Diet is *not* a result of liberalization, but rather it is due to increasing controversy regarding trade friction. The Diet is much concerned about the low value of the yen. It is more concerned about foreign criticism than ever before. Thus, the Esaki mission went to Europe and the United States to explain about Japan. [Masumi Esaki, chairman of LDP Special Committee for International Economic Measures, went abroad in July 1982.]

Q: *What is the division of labor between the Ministry of Finance and the Bank of Japan in the guidance of foreign lending by Japan?*

A: Here, guidance is by the ministry rather than by the bank. Every six months, a rigid ceiling is placed on the total banking system and on each bank individually concerning the amount of yen loans that may be made to abroad. The Ministry of Finance gives guidance to each bank on the terms of the lending rate, on the maturity of the loans, on the syndication of loans, on the front-end fee (the management fee for lenders). In fact, the Ministry of Finance controls every aspect of lending of yen to abroad. On the other hand, every three months the Bank of Japan determines the total amount of yen lending, both at home and abroad, that may be done by each bank. The Bank of Japan is also in charge of implementation. For an outflow of less than ¥ 3 million, it gives automatic approval. For an outflow of ¥ 3 million or more, you have to file a prior notification, and this notification has to be approved by the Bank of Japan. There is no clear criterion regarding the way of determining the ceiling on yen loans to abroad by individual banks. [In the issuance of CDs, there is a clear criterion: it is determined as a ratio to the bank's capital.] In cases where there is no clear criterion, we usually adopt the criterion of "behavior as in the past." We attempt to maintain consistency with whatever that behavior happened to be.

Q: *Do individual firms receive more administrative guidance in their international transactions than in their domestic transactions?*
A: Ah! It is very difficult to answer correctly. In my personal opinion, they receive much guidance as to prudentiality. That is, they are encouraged to have "good ratios." In domestic transactions they get lots of administrative guidance from MITI and the Ministry of Finance. We still have lots of regulation of interest rates: there is a ceiling on deposit rates, and there is a close relation between the official discount rate and the prime rate. Although banks in theory can independently determine their own prime rate, they do not do so. In fact, there is only one short-term prime rate in Japan, one-half or one-quarter percent over the official discount rate. The long-term prime rate is market determined; however, it is related to the interest rate on government bonds. The TB (treasury bill) rate is not liberalized, even today. The interest rate system is very narrow.

Q: *Is it correct to say that the International Finance Bureau has gained wider jurisdiction because of internationalization but has lost operational authority?*
A: Yes, as a total answer it has more jurisdictional scope, but it has lost operational control.

Q: *What has happened to the ability of the Bank of Japan to impose a tight money policy?*
A: Since liberalization, we have more difficulty imposing a tight money policy. If we did impose a tight money policy, we would have trouble with impact loans and other types of avoidance. According to our younger staff, we could still control the situation by means of the interest rate, that is, by controlling some particular rate and inducing arbitrage in the short-term money markets around that controlled rate.

Q: *How would you forecast the relative degree of liberalization in the domestic as compared with the external sector?*
A: Although international liberalization comes first, in ten years

probably the domestic side will be more liberalized than the international side. Domestically, we have an important problem in liberalization of the deposit rate of interest because of the Postal Savings system.

Q: *How does liberalization affect the stability or instability of the Japanese economy?*
A: Liberalization helps stabilize the money market. But if liberalization takes place during a time of inflation, it creates instability in the market. We fight inflation as a precondition for further liberalization. If we liberalize during inflation, this increases expectation of further inflation.

Q: *Are there any legal barriers against long-term lending by the city banks?*
A: There is no legal prohibition against it. However, they would have to lend at the long-term interest rate. If they were to lend long on the basis of the short-term rate, the Long-Term Credit Bank, the Industrial Bank of Japan (IBJ), and the other long-term credit institutions would strongly object, because short-term rates are lower than long-term rates, and the city banks would be taking customers away from the long-term credit banks. Inside Japan, the city banks have no instrument [such as the debentures issued by the long-term credit banks] by which to fund long-term loans. The long-term interest rate is not officially determined; it is regulated merely by custom among the debenture-issuing banks themselves. The custom is that the rate on debentures issued by long-term credit banks plus 0.9 percent is the amount of the long-term interest rate on loans.

Q: *Do Japanese syndicated loans require the borrower to provide collateral?*
A: Syndicated loans are exclusively loans to abroad. They never require collateral, but these loans are confined to sovereign borrowers or government agencies. Inside Japan, loans always require collateral.[9]

Q: *What is the division of labor between the Ministry of Finance and the Bank of Japan with regard to main types of transactions?*
A: Since liberalization, the Bank of Japan monitors every foreign-exchange transaction and foreign-currency deposit. Many people come to the Bank of Japan to consult about how to invest in foreign currency or foreign securities. So we have lots of work to do in advisory functions. Some sections of our bank are busier than [they were] before the liberalization—for example, in collecting reports from the author-

ized foreign-exchange banks. Nevertheless, the number of people in the [bank's] Foreign Department has decreased 20 percent. In practice, but not in law, the Ministry of Finance concentrates largely on Japan's international transactions, such as syndicated loans, and the Bank of Japan concentrates on domestic transactions. By means of quarterly "window guidance," the Bank of Japan assigns the total lending level of each bank. The Bank of Japan also has to be consulted each time a very large loan is extended to an individual customer.

Q: *Because of liberalization and internationalization, has the main incentive of Japanese banks shifted from emphasis on service to emphasis on profit?*
A: Yes, very true. The ratio of the banks' international transactions is rising. Accordingly, the role of the "intimate relation" with domestic clients has been reduced. Moreover, international transactions are the most profitable of the transactions of Japanese banks.

Q: *Who will be the winners and losers because of liberalization?*
A: On the whole, it is too early to answer. However, the Bank of Japan will gain. We respect the market. Liberalization of the market will contribute to the well-being of the Bank of Japan. With regard to foreign-exchange control, there has been no clear change in the power of government officials as yet.

Foreign Banks in Japan

Foreign banks play a marginal role in the Japanese economy. Their share of total loans and discounts has never been much more than 3 percent.[10] Although Japanese banks used to rely on foreign banks as a source of dollars, the Eurodollar market is now the Japanese banks' main source of dollars.[11] Foreign banks are no longer needed by Japanese banks for any major purpose.[12] Among their difficulties, the foreign banks lack substantial yen deposits as a funding base, and they have meager contacts with major Japanese firms as customers for loans. They lack deep roots within the economy and the bureaucracy due to the shortage of Todai graduates among their personnel. Thus, they lack access to the pipeline of information from *Kasumigaseki* that is available to insiders who have known Ministry of Finance officials since their schooldays.

As a marginal factor in the Japanese banking community, the foreign banks serve an ironically interesting function: They are the last to feel the benefit of improvement in the business climate and the first to feel an adverse development. Thus, their performance is a leading indicator of business decline.

The foreign banks are perhaps even more ambivalent about liberalization of banking than the Japanese banks. According to an American banker, "We make more money in the regulated market than in an unregulated market because smart operators profit as a result of the inefficiency of others in that market. Weak banks are *protected* by the regulatory franchise; they can stay alive even though inefficient. We benefit as well because we can get around the restrictions faster than anyone else." In the new era of deregulation, it will not be possible to make profits by finding loopholes. Thus, foreign as well as Japanese banks are going to have to rely on pure efficiency and competitive power. Liberalization will make all participants in the market more efficient, just as the textbook says. Already, both customers and competitors are more sophisticated than before.

Profits, however, have been whittled down to the bone, and probably they will be reduced further.[13] In the game of seeking low-profit business, U.S. banks are at a disadvantage in competition with Japanese banks. The latter often perform transactions with no profit for the sake of expanding their market share.[14] U.S. banks, however, cannot do so because this would reflect adversely on their home offices and would disappoint their shareholders. (The shareholders of major Japanese banks are primarily institutions with which they do business.) U.S. banks are subject to the evaluation of foreign rating agencies; Japanese banks are not. Moreover, U.S. banks are constrained by the rules of the U.S. Federal Reserve Board as well as by the rules of the Japanese government.

Although foreign banks complain about Japanese government regulations, some find them more onerous than others. Indeed, it is the structural environment rather than the regulatory system itself that often causes their difficulties.[15] For various reasons, the structure of the environment is not neutral in its impact on foreign as contrasted with Japanese banks. In the matter of funding, for example, U.S. banks lack the branches and the deposit base of Japanese banks.[16] They also lack connections with the industrial groups that yield deposits from major firms and insurance companies.[17] The limitation on access to yen funds through branches was compounded in 1982 by the limited permissible amount of dollars that could be brought into Japan for conversion into yen, the so-called swap operation.[18] (There is no limit on the amount of dollars that can be brought into Japan to be held as dollars.) This restriction had no legal sanction; it was enforced purely by means of administrative guidance. Furthermore, the government imposed limits on the extent to which banks had recourse to the short-term money markets for yen funds. Even assuming nondiscriminatory restrictions on all banks with regard to money-market funding, such restrictions had a relatively adverse impact on foreign banks because their source of yen in the primary form of household deposits was itself relatively meager.[19]

Another example of how identical regulations applied to all banks may have a relatively adverse impact on foreign banks can be seen in the case of certificates of deposit. The CD market in Japan was inaugurated in May 1979. Its characteristics, however, differ from those of the American CD market. In particular, the minimum permissible transaction size was ¥ 500 million, or about $2.5 million. A CD of this size was just about right for Japanese city banks, but for foreign banks, as well as for Japanese regional banks, it was much too large. (Thus, the supposedly "more liberal framework" of approval for issuance of CDs by foreign banks as contrasted with that for Japanese banks was merely a hypothetical advantage.) A smaller minimum amount would be appropriate to the typical customer of foreign and regional banks. The rules may have been designed to keep regional banks out of the CD market, but they had the same effect on foreign banks. Whereas the CD business of domestic banks was limited to 50 percent of their net worth, the CD business of foreign banks was limited to 20 percent of their outstanding yen loan balance, which was supposed to give foreign banks an advantage. In terms of maturity requirements, the Japanese CD was limited to a period longer than three months but less than nine months. Foreign banks would have liked the maturity period to be more flexible.

Concerning the permissible size of CDs there was a related, behind-the-scenes matter. Foreign banks would have preferred a minimum of about ¥ 10 million. If that limit were adopted, many Japanese would withdraw their savings deposits and buy CDs in order to obtain higher interest returns. The shift of time deposits to the CD market, however, would tend to raise the cost of funds to the banks. Banks, in turn, would raise their lending rates, which would be reflected in further pressure for an increase in the interest rate on national bonds. But an increase in the cost of servicing the national debt would not appeal to the Ministry of Finance.

Outright discrimination against foreign banks can be seen in the participation in lending syndicates sponsored by the Japan Development Bank or the Japan Export-Import Bank. The Ministry of Finance issues blanket licenses to domestic banks for participation in such syndicates. Foreign banks, however, must apply for a separate license for participation in each syndicated loan. The situation has improved somewhat from how it was in the late 1970s, when foreign banks were completely excluded from participation.[20] Part of the appeal of participation in these syndicates is the implicit subsidy to private banks provided by the Japanese government. Government bank money is contributed to the syndicate at a low interest rate, allowing the private bank lenders to charge a higher interest rate while still maintaining a competitive aggregate lending rate on the syndicated loan as a whole. The Japanese may be reluctant to share this subsidy with foreign banks.

Another aspect of outright discrimination concerns the relatively greater access accorded domestic banks to the discounting facilities of the Bank of Japan. The discrimination occurs in practice, not in law. The funding problems of the foreign banks involve not only the availability of yen but also interest rates and maturities. In each of these matters, restrictions by the Ministry of Finance or the Bank of Japan apply in one way or another.[21]

To a considerable extent, the yen deposits of foreign banks arise in the form of compensating balances. (This is partly because the foreign banks' clients are among the weaker and smaller companies upon whom such conditions may be imposed.) The extent of such balances depends on the terms of loans negotiated between the banks and their clients. If a bank agrees to lend at a low interest rate, it insists on a higher compensating balance. This arrangement may suit the purposes of firms attempting to improve their credentials for loans from Japanese banks. A firm that must pay a high interest rate on loans (as revealed in its accounting statement) is not regarded as a first-class firm. But if it can show that it has obtained loans at a low rate of interest from a premier foreign bank, its bargaining position with Japanese banks may be enhanced.

Some Japanese officials maintain that foreign banks in Japan have received the benefit rather than the brunt of discrimination. In the opening of new branches, for example, Masumi Esaki, former minister of International Trade and Industry, said that where "there is no problem regarding the reciprocity principle . . . applications have been accepted" from foreign banks that meet "the minimum soundness requirement." Moreover, "Approval of the opening of branches offices of foreign banks is given every year, whereas that of Japanese banks is given once every two years."[22] In view of the permission that has been given to foreign banks to establish branches without limit, the fact that few such branches have been opened prompts Japanese bankers to observe that former complaints of foreign banks about the withholding of such permission were spurious.[23] An American bank official expresses it differently. "Liberalization means that you are let into the Japanese economy after all the opportunities there have dried up. When there is nothing left to be gained by entry, you are allowed to enter." In the present instance, opening of many new branches by foreign banks would not be profitable. As lenders, foreign banks are marginal, especially in a highly liquid economy. When Japanese firms pay off their loans, they retire their (more expensive) loans with foreign banks first. Moreover, more than three-quarters of the business of the principal American banks lies in the Tokyo area; most of the remainder lies in the Kansai area (Osaka and its environs). "There is nothing for U.S. banks to develop in Hokkaido or other outlying areas," said one observer.

On the deposit side, U.S. banks are at a disadvantage in relation to Japanese banks for various reasons that inhibit the opening of new branches. Japanese nationals have a natural preference for doing business with Japanese banks, especially in regional areas where attitudes are more traditional. Perhaps the decisive handicap, however, is the impersonal nature of foreign banking. As seen by a Japanese economics professor at Hitosubashi University, "In Japan, the basic problem of the foreign banks is their rationalism. Foreign banks are not accustomed to giving free service, as Japanese banks do. For the purpose of collecting deposits, Japanese banks send excellent young men to the offices of Japanese companies—sometimes monthly, weekly, or even daily. Thus, the firm and its employees are saved the trouble of visiting the bank. The excellent young man is friendly; he becomes acquainted with the personnel of the company. He not only collects deposits, he also collects information. He learns that the company is planning to build a new plant. He learns that the company is planning to transfer some of its business from Bank A to Bank B. He scouts out the territory. In this sort of practice, there is no barrier to foreigners. However, even if the chief of a foreign bank knows that he must conform to Japanese business practices, he must persuade his home office. But the home office officials can't understand giving free service. They are rational. These are matters that liberalization cannot overcome. Given such difficulties, foreign banks can be losers in the Japanese market despite liberalization. On the other hand, if the foreign bank does not want to do domestic business, but merely wishes to be the second, third, or fourth bank of a Japanese company, doing international business exclusively, then the foreign bank can be successful in the Tokyo market." Indeed, even if American managers fully perceive the imperatives of banking Japanese style, many cannot afford to take a long-term view of profits because their post assignments may be as brief as two or three years. Thus, they insist on profit from each individual transaction.

The philosophy of American banking is thus not conducive to business development in Japan by opening regional branches. Be that as it may, the Japanese government, as seen by the American banking community, was cynical in its liberalization in 1982 of the rules for branch banking and for takeovers of Japanese banks.[24] The senior vice president of an American bank in Tokyo said, "If an American bank wanted to open ten new branches next year, the Ministry of Finance would find reasons to explain why this would not be desirable. Concerning takeovers, there are no healthy Japanese banks for sale. They don't want to be taken over. And we wouldn't want to take over weak Japanese banks that are failing and acquire their shaky loans, such as those in Latin America."[25] If an American bank took over a regional bank, the American bank would become a competitor of other regional banks and would thereby lose those regional banks' correspondent business. (Some regional banks prefer to entrust their foreign business to foreign banks since they fear that if they entrusted it to a Japanese city bank, the latter might muscle in and take away some of their domestic clients as well. Foreign banks lack the connections with which to do this.)

One of the chief complaints of foreign banks about funding is that they are not allowed to issue debentures. The government insists that there is no discrimination here because "ordinary" Japanese banks are likewise forbidden to issue debentures. Apart from a few government banks such as the Shoko Chukin Bank, only three long-term credit banks and one specialist foreign-exchange bank (the Bank of Tokyo) are allowed to issue debentures. Being deprived of debentures as a funding source, foreign banks have practically no means of extending long-term yen loans (except by rollovers of short-term loans). The longest term deposit that a city bank can accept is for three years. (In their foreign branch operations, Japanese banks lend long on the basis of short-term funding in the Eurodollar market.) From the government's point of view, however, separation of long-term from short-term banking is an important part of its scheme for segmentation of the banking system as a means of facilitating economic control. American banks observe that this domestic strategy conflicts with the principle of international reciprocity. In the United States, branches of Japanese city banks, as well as of long-term credit banks, are permitted to issue debentures and have already done so. In the summer of 1982, the topic of debenture issuance by branches of foreign banks was being discussed by the Banking Bureau, the Securities Bureau, and the IFB of the Ministry of Finance.[26]

Some American bankers report no great change in administrative guidance (gyōsei shidō) since December 1980. The government asserts that foreign banks receive less administrative guidance than Japanese banks. As mentioned above, however, in the case of yen lending by banks from Japan to abroad, major Japanese banks receive a six-month quota. Minor banks and foreign banks must apply for government authorization in each individual case. In applying for permission, American banks prefer dealing with the Bank of Japan rather than the Ministry of Finance, because the former is said to be friendlier.[27] Sometimes the Ministry of Finance gives its guidance in clear language. Its officials may say, "We do not approve." Sometimes they are Delphian, saying, "This matter does not interest us." Translated, this could mean "not approved." Equally, however, it could mean nothing at all. The use of ambiguous language by the Ministry of Finance, as well as by MITI, may be a deliberate strategy to induce their clients to be consistently cautious. It also shifts the responsibility for restrictive action to the client by inducing "self-restraint" or the adoption of "self-imposed guidelines." The result may be a lesser degree of liberalization than would be achieved if the full burden of saying no were to be placed clearly on the government. Domestic as well as foreign banks have problems interpreting what the Ministry of Finance means. Japanese banks, however, have better pipelines into the ministry for the clarification of instructions. One way is through the banks' *amakudari* personnel—former officials of the Ministry of Finance who take positions with Japanese banks after retirement from the ministry. According to the senior vice president of an American bank in Tokyo, "Japanese banks are always out there probing to ascertain what the attitude of the government really is, and what are its limits of tolerance." Administrative guidance, incidentally, may arrive not only from the Ministry of Finance or the Bank of Japan but also by way of communications from the Bankers' Association.

Even with the benefit of impartial intentions on the part of the government, the impact of administrative guidance is relatively adverse on foreign banks by virtue of their position and role within the Japanese banking structure. Lacking "pipeline" assets, American banks complain that guidance is inefficient and that it increases uncertainty. "You never know what the result will be. Guidance is erratic and vague." The most serious objection of American banks, however, is that the emphasis and deleterious effect of guidance seem to fall primarily on the new and the untried. For it is precisely through innovation and creative techniques that American banks attempt to overcome their handicaps in the Japanese milieu.[28] The government is not impressed. It takes the position that the primary purpose of regulation is to ensure a *sound* banking system, not to promote innovative, creative, or aggressive banking, or searches for loopholes. The high velocity of turnover of career bureaucrats reinforces this official attitude. Newly installed supervisors tend to be cautious, to resist new or unique forms of financing. Thus, they are slow in responding to requests by impatient American bankers in need of speedy decisions. In so doing, they simultaneously protect themselves from undue divagations by Japanese banks that closely follow the financial innovations of foreign banks and that quickly adopt any new idea the foreign banks introduce.

On the other hand, if officials are too repressive, the foreign banks call in the press and complain about the inferior treatment they have received. Such interviews are embarrassing to the government. Foreign banks also pursue the opposite tactic of providing expensive entertainment to government officials in the attempt to establish connections and to ingratiate themselves. This procedure may be useless because government decisionmakers are often anonymous. Indeed, crucial decisions are often made by junior personnel who are not among those invited to dinner.

On balance, one American banker contends that the net effect of liberalization on foreign bankers is zero, that in some ways the situation has improved while in others it has worsened. Partly, for example, the demand for "equal treatment" with Japanese banks has boomeranged. As mentioned above, under the new Bank Law, foreign banks must now comply with the same disclosure requirements as Japanese banks. They must also set aside a proportion of their profits as reserves for losses. Foreign banks complain that their overnight uncovered position limit is too restrictive. After a grace period of five years, the new Bank Law requires them to restrict their loans to any single customer to a maximum of 20 percent of the bank's net worth. For branches, this ratio is calculated on the basis of the sum of the equity and reserves of the branch and its head office abroad. This formula in effect makes the restriction for branches of major banks purely nominal. At the same time, it neatly cancels the value of the new equality that permits foreign banks to establish domestically incorporated Japanese subsidiaries. Such a subsidiary would have to raise substantial capital to make substantial individual loans. Moreover, if foreign banks were to become truly equal with domestic banks, they would be obliged to purchase their share of Japanese government national bonds.

"Equal treatment" has also terminated the monopoly that foreign banks formerly enjoyed in the issuance of impact loans, which before the new Bank Law constituted the bulk of their business and which was very profitable. The impact loan is defined as a foreign-currency loan extended to a Japanese nonfinancial corporation. When Japan was a capital importer, and especially during periods of tight money enforced because of balance of payments deficits, the impact-loan monopoly of the foreign banks provided a safety valve for firms that could not obtain loans from Japanese banks. American banks would lend dollars (at a substantial spread), which would then be converted to yen (at a further profit to the American bank). In other instances, Japanese firms would borrow dollars and hold them as a hedge against dollar receivables. (Under the new Bank Law, other hedging devices became available, thus reducing the importance of the impact loan.)

As a financing device, the impact loan was of course in conflict with government tight money policy. But when a tight-money policy was imposed to reverse a balance of payments deficit, the positive contribution of the capital inflow outweighed the offense in the form of expansion of domestic credit. During the period of tight money policy following the second oil crisis (1979), impact loans had precisely this desirable effect. It was then that the government decided to allow Japanese banks to share with foreign banks the privilege of issuing impact loans. With the inauguration of the new Foreign Exchange Law in December 1980, Japanese banks entered actively into the impact-loan business. Their avidity in doing so was stimulated by the fact that impact loans are not subject to restrictions on total lending volume through Bank of Japan window guidance. The effect on foreign banks was fairly devastating. Calling on their entrenched connections with major companies, Japanese banks were in a much stronger position than foreign banks to find customers for impact loans. Offering characteristically more attractive terms, the Japanese banks also took away customers already secured by the foreign banks. This predatory behavior was further impelled by the fact that liberalization was enabling Japanese companies to reduce their dependence on indirect finance by means of bank loans in favor of direct financing by means of bonds and shares floated both at home and abroad. In 1981, more impact loans were issued by domestic banks than by foreign banks in Japan.[29]

In a free market, which is what the foreign banks profess to desire, foreign banks are singularly ill-equipped to compete for impact loans, as suggested above. Ironically, at the same time that Japanese firms have become less dependent on the banking system, impact loans have become an increasingly large component of the banking business. In

1981, the sum of foreign bank lending to all Japanese firms amounted to ¥ 5 trillion. Impact loans accounted for ¥ 3 trillion of this amount.[30] Since the impact loan is a more competitive, less traditional, and cheaper form of financing, this situation is not good even for Japanese banks. Firms that borrow through impact loans are very cost conscious. They have less concern—especially during periods of easy money, when the borrower has the upper hand—about the "close personal relationship" that is typically nurtured between Japanese firms and their main bank. Moreover, even if the price of the impact loan were the same at both a foreign bank and a Japanese bank, a prospective Japanese borrower would typically choose to do business with the Japanese bank.

Since Japan's emergence as a capital exporter rather than a capital importer, the anomaly of the foreign banks being primarily dependent on impact loans—that is to say, capital imports—has become increasingly inappropriate. In a larger sense, the problem of American banks in Japan is the problem of banking in general as an intermediary function. Intermediation is a dying business in a world where firms in the physical operations sector have the same information as the intermediaries. Electronic facilities instantly provide the banks' customers with all the national and international information to which the banks themselves have access. At a moment's notice, the banks' customers can ascertain where their money is, what it is earning, where else it could be placed, and what conditions prevail in any part of the world. Banks thus become mere order takers, executing the decisions at which operating firms have independently arrived. The same is true of other intermediaries, including trading companies of the traditional type. In what direction, then, can foreign banks turn?

As the yen becomes a more fully international currency and as Japan's financial markets become more liberalized, small firms in the hinterland and small regional banks that hitherto have had only domestic experience are increasingly entering the international arena. Major foreign banks, through their networks and contacts abroad, are finding a role for intermediation in behalf of small- and medium-size firms and banks outside of Tokyo and the Kansai area. (Even with help, minor Japanese banks have a dim future.) Major foreign banks are also innovating new services and products, including "off balance sheet" types, such as factoring and leasing.[31] Thus, they are helping small firms develop business abroad. By putting a foot in the door with these innovations, foreign banks hope to establish relationships with Japanese firms and to develop spin-off business of other types. Spin-off is exactly the strategy used by Japanese banks, except that they started with "free" services, and started first.

Not all foreign banks perceive their difficulties in Japan in the same way. French banks, being accustomed to a high degree of arbitrary government intervention at home, see nothing unusual in the Japanese environment. German banks feel that the Japanese government is too restrictive. U.S. banks are the most dissatisfied of all foreign banks in Japan.

Money-Market Innovations

Before World War II, Japan's only short-term money market was the yen call market, established in 1902. Its chief function was to control the balance of fund demand and supply between minor and regional banks that were in chronic surplus and city banks that were in chronic deficit. Because of the financial practices and regulations prevailing in Japan at that time, no further money-market arrangements were needed for the implementation of monetary policy. Among those arrangements was the monopoly assigned to the Yokohama Specie Bank for the handling of all foreign-exchange transactions. Thus, the domestic economy could be effectively quarantined from external monetary effects to the extent necessary. Following the war, the Foreign Exchange and Foreign Trade Control Law (1949) and the Foreign Investment Law (1950) restricted access by business to funding from abroad. Lacking adequate capital supplies of their own, businesses relied on indirect financing through the banking system. At the government level, balanced or overbalanced budgets prior to fiscal year 1965 precluded the Ministry of Finance from deficit financing that could have been monetized. Thus, the Bank of Japan was able to control both the money supply and the interest rate by means of credit rationing to the banks and by controls over bank lending to firms (madoguchi shidō or window guidance). The system constituted a quasi-monetarist regime.

During the expansion of the 1960s, however, the authorities were impelled to increase the economy's competitive power by increasing its international exposure. (Response to pressures from the United States was merely the public or "official" explanation of liberalization.[32]) In the meantime, because of a growing stock of owned capital accumulated from the profits of the 1960s, major firms were becoming less dependent on the banks; and the banks, with increasing access to funding from abroad, were becoming less dependent on the Bank of Japan. With the inauguration of floating exchange rates in 1973, accelerating activity occurred in the capital account of the balance of payments. In part, this activity reflected increased volatility of interest rates and exchange rates in the world economy, volatility associated with deficit financing by the governments of major industrial nations. Because of capital movements that occurred for purposes of interest rate arbitrage, it became increasingly difficult for the Bank of Japan to enforce the low interest rate policy that had been maintained for the benefit of private business investment. This was awkward because the Japanese government itself had become the principal beneficiary of that policy after abandonment of the balanced budget principle in fiscal year 1965.

Even during the 1960s, lack of sufficient money-market instruments had inconvenienced the Bank of Japan in its attempts to control seasonal fluctuations of the money supply. The inconvenience became a calamity during the dollar crisis of the early 1970s, when Japan's trade surplus produced a huge inflow of inflationary foreign funds. Moreover, in the recession following the oil crisis of 1973, the government's reflationary efforts produced enormous budgetary deficits. These compounded the problem of interest rate management by the Bank of Japan. With the liberalization of its instruments of direct control, the Bank of Japan was increasingly obliged to rely on indirect controls. On the latter score, however, it lacked adequate instruments for intervention through open-market operations. Coincidentally, the private sector was demanding permission to employ new financial products. Thus, in the 1970s, while ostensibly yielding to those demands, the Ministry of Finance authorized the establishment of new money markets in which the role of financial innovation, and its effects on interest rates, could be managed by the Bank of Japan.

In permitting the establishment of additional short-term money markets and expansion in the scope of Bank of Japan open-market operations by means of those markets, the Ministry of Finance inadvertently created space for new maneuvers in the power struggle between itself and the Bank of Japan. Under the regime of direct controls (lending quotas, window guidance, interest rate controls), the Bank of Japan largely followed orders as an agent of the ministry, acting as a channel for the ministry's administrative guidance. In that system, the ministry could anonymously, particularistically, and extemporaneously intervene at will in any of the bank's activities. In a liberalized world of indirect controls, there would be less operational scope for such intervention. Instead, pursuit of financial stability and equilibrium would depend primarily on technical matters, about which the Bank of Japan would be the pre-eminent authority. For example, the bank would be the arbiter of open-market operations in the new money markets. Moreover, if interest rates were determined in the market, the bank would be relieved of pressure from the ministry to support the price of government bonds. Hence, the Bank of Japan took the position that interest rates should be liberalized.[33] Because of the increased independence this would confer on the bank, liberalization would promote a shift in bureaucratic power from the ministry to the bank. Furthermore, by manipulation of eligibility rules and by guidance and supervision of the brokers (tanshi) through whom money market transactions were performed, the Bank of Japan would be able to augment its own administrative guidance while that of the ministry was being shrunk. Incidentally, this is an example of how new methods of control may be devised and implemented in terms of the liberalization process itself.

The new short-term money markets include the bills discount market (inaugurated in May 1971), the dollar call money market (inaugurated in April 1972), and the negotiable yen CD market (inaugurated in May 1979). The bond repurchase (gensaki) market was inaugurated in 1949; the treasury bill market was inaugurated in May 1981. Bank of Japan money market operations are conducted by means of six brokerage firms (tanshi), which are intermediaries between the bank and the private sector. (The six tanshi plus four other firms act as foreign exchange brokers as well.) The tanshi perform transactions in the several money markets simultaneously; thus, they constitute an instrument by which the Bank of Japan can coordinate monetary policy. In the short-term money markets, control is also maintained by segmentation of the market in terms of definitions of eligible participants. This segmentation is not imposed by legal restrictions but merely by restrictions in practice, or "by custom." Banks, securities companies, insurance companies, finance corporations, residents, and nonresidents are subject to various degrees of eligibility for participation in the several markets. Nonfinancial corporations are eligible to participate only in the gensaki and CD markets. The Bank of Japan discourages money market activity that does not pass through the hands of brokers, because it can control the activities of brokers and thus invisibly control the money markets. For this reason, the Bank of Japan discourages interbank deposits and interbank lending, where the role of the brokers is superseded. Disintermediation occurs in the gensaki market and in the CD market, in which transactions may occur directly between the parties, including nonfinancial corporations, without the intermediation of brokers. Thus, these markets threaten the Bank of Japan's control.

In terms of the degree of intervention by the Bank of Japan, the bills discount market is the market most highly regulated. Next is the yen call market. Although the Bank of Japan may deny it, the bank also controls rates in the CD market. The dollar call market, being linked to the Eurodollar and Asiandollar markets, is more free. Moreover, the Bank of Japan is less concerned about transactions denominated in foreign currency than those denominated in yen. The gensaki market, which is the only market in which all parties may participate, is the most free; however, it may also be controlled as a residual by arbitrage. Moreover, the Bank of Japan may intervene in the gensaki market through Japanese treasury bills.[34] Nonresidents may enter the gensaki market through the securities companies.

The Bank of Japan tries to achieve countervailing power in relation to the Ministry of Finance by means of its daily operating functions. Markets that are nominally "free" are in fact manipulated by the Bank of Japan. In the CD market, for example, the Bank of Japan may whisper to money market brokers that it is not happy to see the interest rate on CDs higher than a certain level. The brokers oblige and reduce the interest rate; but then they cannot find customers for the CDs, so the banks stop issuing them. "Nothing is written down about the Bank of Japan's control over the CD market, but the bank controls it even though the law says that the market is free," an important Bank of Tokyo official said.

The six tanshi companies perform a vital role in the institutional arrangements by which the money markets are controlled. The Bank of Japan is in daily contact with the tanshi companies, to which it imparts meticulously detailed instructions on how they are to perform their duties. Moreover, the Bank of Japan's control is facilitated because the same tanshi companies operate in all money markets as well as in the foreign-exchange market. Thus, they can coordinate policies in all markets simultaneously. Besides their brokerage function, the tanshi take positions in the call market and in the CD market. Although rates may be quoted in the bills discount and CD markets, the president of a tanshi company said "there may be no business at the quoted rates. If you try to borrow excessively [beyond your implicit 'quota'], you may find that there is an availability problem."

For intervention in the foreign-exchange market, the Bank of Japan uses domestic and foreign banks as surrogates. For example, it may tell the Mitsui Bank to enter the market to buy dollars. Later, the Bank of Japan will buy the dollars from Mitsui at the same price Mitsui paid for them. The government is reluctant to internationalize the yen because foreign money markets are free and very volatile. If the yen were internationalized, there would be arbitrage between the domestic yen market and the Euromarkets; thus, the yen interest rate would likewise become free and volatile. Domestic control over the monetary system would become very difficult. Before establishment of the dollar call market, Japanese residents were prohibited from engaging with each other in foreign exchange transactions. Banks with excess dollars on hand had to sell them for yen in the local foreign-exchange market or lend them in New York or London. Similarly, banks requiring dollars had to buy them in the local foreign-exchange market or borrow from abroad. The Ministry of Finance authorized establishment of the dollar call market in order to reduce the necessity of borrowing from abroad. When the dollar call market was established, however, the authorities took stringent measures to insulate it from the yen call market.[35] By 1982, the dollar call market had expanded approximately to its limit, giving rise to demands by the commercial banks for inauguration of full-scale offshore banking facilities.

In appearance, the Bank of Japan's open-market operations progressively bear a resemblance to those of the United States. The Bank of Japan influences money-market interest rates by its adjustment of demand and supply of funds through purchases and sales of government bonds (two to four years, or ten years in maturity terms) and increasingly by use of treasury bills.[36] During the early 1980s, funds entering the market as a result of government public works expenditures reduced the need for funds supplied by the Bank of Japan; thus, the money-managing role of the bank was correspondingly diminished. As a money manager, the Bank of Japan possesses potential means for discrimination among financial institutions because of its purchases of government bonds from individual banks and insurance companies.

As participants in the money markets for purposes of yen funding, foreign banks are primarily concerned with matters concerning the rate of interest, the availability of funds, and the spectrum of maturities. Each of these is restricted by the Bank of Japan in one way or another. In the case of a particular leading American bank, availability is not a serious problem.[37] Its primary source of yen is the bills discount market, which provides up to 50 percent of its funding needs. Second is its swap limit, which in general provides one-quarter to one-third of the funding needs of foreign banks in Japan. Third is the call market, which can provide up to 25 percent of the bank's funding needs. Since 1979, CDs have provided between 15 and 20 percent of its funding, and to the extent the bank holds a portfolio of bonds, it can obtain approximately 10 to 15 percent of its funds in the gensaki market.[38]

In structural terms, Japan is overbanked. In some respects, this strengthens the hand of the Bank of Japan in maintaining control. In its guidance of the city banks, for example, the Bank of Japan asserts that its monetary policy is conditioned by the fact that it must protect the small- and medium-size regional banks. Well-placed observers, however, maintain that this is only an excuse the Bank of Japan uses to justify its prerogatives and to maintain the policy it would impose even if there were no regional banks. To some extent, the bloated banking structure itself facilitates the Bank of Japan's control. The intense competition among banks, for example, induces them to keep their prime rate very close to the Bank of Japan's discount rate. If one bank tries to increase its prime rate, it will be undercut by others. Thus, it is competition rather than guidance that maintains uniformity in the prime rate. Characteristically, the prime rate is one-half percentage point above the discount rate.[39] Consequently, the Bank of Japan can effectively control the prime rate without appearing to intervene.

Because banks cannot deal with one another directly for most purposes, the reality of the Bank of Japan's management of the money markets depends heavily on its control of the tanshi intermediaries, through which most money-market transactions are performed. The tanshi officials are mainly former Bank of Japan people who are strongly sympathetic to the bank's policies. In promoting an easy money policy, for example, the Bank of Japan may ask the tanshi to tell the banks to sell bills to the bills discount market. The banks will do so even though they may not need any more funds. They comply because they know the request really comes from the Bank of Japan. Alternatively, to enforce a tight money policy, the bill brokers may ask the banks to buy bills to tighten the money supply.[40] The same procedure occurs in the call market. Long-term money markets are more controlled than short-term markets; accordingly, the Bank of Japan is more concerned about developments in the latter.

The tanshi themselves take positions in the markets in which the Bank of Japan intervenes most, thus contributing to the effectiveness of the Bank of Japan's policy. In the call market, for example, the tanshi may take a position, or they may merely arrange a deal between a lender and a borrower. In the bills discount market, the tanshi may collect many small bills, aggregate them, and sell them to some major buyer. In the treasury bill market, although taking a position, the tanshi may have previously lined up a buyer and seller on both sides of a prospective transaction before doing so.

A Questionnaire on Banking and Foreign Exchange

The "monolithic" reputation of the Japanese government is belied by the fact that, as seen above, its various experts may express inconsistent or even diametrically opposite opinions about the liberalization process and its implications. Differences in analysis arise largely from different interests of the bureaucrats concerned. Although Japan's national interest is a meaningful concept, there is no such animal as "the" Japanese government in pursuit of that national interest. This is revealed in further detail by a collation of responses from officials of the Ministry of Finance, the Bank of Japan, the Economic Planning Agency, and the Bank of Tokyo to the author's questionnaire on banking and foreign exchange.[41] All respondents did not reply to all questions. Some interesting replies don't pertain to the questions asked.

Q: *Who are the winners and who are the losers as a result of the liberalization of the new Foreign Exchange Law and the new Bank Law?*

A: Your questionnaire is very interesting. These are the questions we ourselves would like to ask. If we knew the answers, we could write a big book.

A: The commercial banks were losers in relation to the securities companies. The foreign banks were losers to the domestic Japanese banks.

A: The foreign banks are losers in the sense that they did not gain, while the Japanese banks did gain. The liberalization did *not* make it easier for the foreign banks to raise yen funds in Japan. The foreign banks can get yen funds from the life insurance companies and from the trust banks, but the rates charged are not competitive.

Japanese banks, on the other hand, have gotten into the impact market. They are lending to both big business and small- and medium-size businesses. More than half of the loans of some city banks are now extended to small- and medium-size firms.

Concerning easing of controls, there is now more outflow of capital without forward cover. Both long-term and short-term outflow of yen are subject to government approval. Capital flows may be subject to approval without being subject to license. In effect, regardless of the formalities of "notification," anyone who wants to extend a yen loan overseas has to talk it over with the Ministry of Finance people beforehand and get their informal "understanding." *Then* you go through with the notification process.

A: It seems natural that liberalization would result in more interministerial conflict. MITI is positive as regards trade liberalization, while the Ministry of Agriculture, Forestry, and Fisheries adopts a defensive posture. Thus, it is left to the politicians to seek some compromise. Some politicians seek to promote the interest of the Postal Savings system, some promote bank deposits, and some the savings vehicles of securities firms. They will all have to work harder to achieve compromise.

In the securities industry, various kinds of controls and guidance still exist. These include control over the dividend rate of securities firms, the number of branch offices, and restriction of new issues in the over-the-counter market.

Banks will soon be allowed to sell new government bond issues, which until now has been exclusively the domain of securities firms. Banks further want to deal in existing government bonds for their clients. This should not be allowed. Since banks also make loans, they may combine loans and bonds into a single package, thereby giving their bonds the appearance of being more attractive (through manipulation of the loan conditions) than those offered by securities companies. The loan conditions included in such transactions would not be known to outsiders, and hence the fair pricing of bonds in the market would be precluded.

Operationally, it is difficult for the government to be consistent in introducing liberalization measures. The interest rate on CDs, for example, is free of control, so it is in contradiction with deposit rates and other controlled rates. It was feared that if CDs were introduced without any restrictions, a large amount of money would suddenly shift from deposit accounts to CDs, thereby unduly disturbing financial order. Therefore, restrictions were imposed so that each certificate would be ¥ 500 million or more, with maturity of three to six months, and the issue amount limited to 10 percent of equity capital. [As of April 1985, the minimum permissible size of CDs was reduced to ¥ 100 million. In April 1986, the maximum maturity was extended to one year. In September 1986, the permitted combined amount of issuance of CDs and money market certificates (short-term financial instruments similar to CDs but with floating market interest rates) was increased to 2.5 times the amount of bank shareholders' equity.]

Barriers between the banking industry and the securities industry have been lowered primarily as a result of the need to digest an increasing amount of government bonds. Moreover, it is the issuance of government bonds rather than liberalization or internationalization that has prompted an increase in economic concentration in Japan. For example, three medium-size securities firms, which were all affiliates of Nomura [Securities], were merged into one big firm. Several major banks strengthened their ties with their own affiliated securities firms.

A: There are only winners, no losers.

Q: *Within the Ministry of Finance and the Bank of Japan, what are the administrative rulings, regulations, and interpretations that explain what can and what cannot be done under the new Foreign Exchange and Foreign Trade Control Law?*

A: It depends on the item. If impact loans increase greatly in volume, the authorities may ask that borrowing be constrained. You can't find these regulations in published form. There are a great many "invisible handshakes" in Japan. Administrative guidance is one form of the invisible handshake.

The new law permits unrestrained lending and borrowing between parent companies and their subsidiaries abroad. This is new. No license and no notification to the government are necessary.

A: Prior licensing was formerly required of a Japanese company that wished to issue securities abroad. Since liberalization, only a prior report is filed. But in actuality, guidance by the government continues.

Q: *Which officials in the International Finance Bureau (IFB) of the Ministry of Finance give instructions to the Bank of Japan?*

A: On what occasions? In emergency conditions, it is the Minister of Finance himself that gives the instructions. Otherwise, we don't know who gives the instructions. With regard to swap quotas, the Short-Term Capital Department of the IFB makes a recommendation to the director general [*kyokuchō*] of the IFB. The swap quota for each individual bank is reviewed every two years. Impact loans are within the jurisdiction of the same department. But there are no longer any restrictions on impact loans.

Concerning intervention in the foreign exchange market, the Short-Term Capital Department handles this as well. It determines the amount of government intervention. The same department controls the foreign exchange reserves. If it decides that the government should intervene, it informs the Bank of Japan accordingly. Then the Bank of Japan uses the hot line to the Bank of Tokyo, telling us to make the actual trade in the market. The Bank of Japan also gets in touch with other banks and with foreign exchange brokers, telling them likewise to intervene in the market and to what extent.

Q: *What role does MITI play in the implementation of the new Foreign Exchange Law? What effect has the law had on MITI's power in relation to that of the Ministry of Finance?*

A: MITI plays only a small role in implementing the new Foreign Exchange Law.

A: Legally, the administration of the law is in the hands of the Ministry of Finance. But they consult MITI with regard to matters that concern it. Concerning interest rate policy, for example, MITI is primarily concerned with the cost of long-term trade finance; therefore, MITI is influential in the determination of long-term interest rates, in applying OECD guidelines on long-term export credits, in determining Export-Import Bank interest rates on export of capital equipment, and in setting the terms for supplier's credit. MITI operates the export insurance system, which further enhances its influence in long-term finance. MITI, as well as the Ministry of Finance, is influential in determining the policies of the Export-Import Bank.

Up to now, the banks have been more important than the securities companies in terms of their influence within the Ministry of Finance. Article 65 of the Securities Law corresponds to the U.S. Glass-Steagall Act, separating banking from securities transactions. The banks cannot underwrite debentures. But in the past, the securities companies were regarded as too weak to underwrite securities; therefore, "commission banks" [Industrial Bank of Japan and others] were authorized to underwrite securities. At present, the Industrial Bank of Japan underwrites about 70 percent of the bond issues outstanding. These corporate bond issues are backed by mortgage collateral. The procedure requires the corporate issuer to give a list of collateral to the commission bank, and the latter decides whether the bond can be issued. Thus, the securities companies have been mere salesmen of the bonds. They had no underwriting obligation. The securities companies enjoyed this arrangement for the past 30 years or so.

The Bank of Tokyo acts as underwriter for Samurai bonds, which mostly are backed by no collateral.

Q: *Has liberalization resulted in any change in the balance of power between the Ministry of Finance and the Bank of Japan?*

A: In the future, there will be much less checking of foreign exchange matters by the Bank of Japan. Thus, the bank will have fewer personnel.

A: In former days, policy decisions were made in the Ministry of Finance; then the ministry asked the Bank of Japan to implement these decisions. Thus, there was a distinction in the type of control or authority exercised by each. However, there are examples of direct intervention by the Ministry of Finance in international affairs. For example, recently it whispered to the insurance companies, "Stop buying foreign bonds." Again, it whispered to the securities firms, "Stop the purchase of zero-coupon foreign bonds by Japanese residents."

The Ministry of Finance is in a state of confusion because it controls both the foreign exchange rate and the interest rate. In order to raise the value of the yen, it should raise the interest rate. But in order to stimulate business, it should keep the interest rate low. The low interest rate is also helpful to government deficit financing. Present emphasis is mainly on raising the value of the yen in order to reduce the trade surplus. However, because of the J-curve effect, there would be a lag [there are different opinions as to how long] before the adjustment of the trade account would occur. In any event, the income effect is stronger than the price effect, so I do not agree that the yen should be appreciated in order to adjust the trade balance.

A: This is not so easy. The Bank of Japan tries to get countervailing power through the use of its daily operating functions. It has the power to allocate yen funds to the various banks. This is especially effective when the banks experience an excess demand for funds. The Bank of Japan can cut you off if you displease it. Thus, its prerogatives lie primarily on the domestic side of the financial system.

Q: *Because of liberalization, to what extent do brokerage houses, trading firms, and other types of firms engage in foreign-exchange transactions that formerly were the exclusive monopoly of the foreign exchange banks?*

A: To a very limited extent. Despite liberalization, we still have the licensed foreign-exchange bank system. Only a small degree of liberalization was extended to the trading companies—the limit on permissible "marrying" of export proceeds and import expenses was extended somewhat. Otherwise, no foreign-exchange transactions can be performed outside the authorized bank system. However, there are many such authorized foreign-exchange banks, and their number is increasing. They include, for example, the Bank of Tokyo, all city banks, regional banks, trust banks, long-term credit banks, Sogo banks and Shinyo Kinko.

[Sogo banks are mutual loan and savings banks. They were established under the auspices of the Mutual Loans and Savings Bank Law of 1951. They conduct consumer-financing business as well as providing regular banking services for small business. The latter are defined as businesses with fewer than 300 employees or with capital less than ¥ 200 million. Besides ordinary commercial bank deposits, their clients may make regular monthly installment deposits, which after a time entitle them to take out loans.]

[Shinyo Kinko are credit associations, organized under the Credit Association Law of 1951. They are similar to credit unions in Western countries. They may receive deposits from either members or non-members, but as a rule, loans, discounts, and other credit services are provided only to members. They offer a slightly higher interest rate on deposits than those paid by Sogo banks or other banks. As in the case of Sogo banks, their loans are available only to small business.]

A Japanese resident can buy foreign securities through a securities company without restriction, but the securities company has to take the yen from the resident and buy dollars through an authorized foreign-exchange bank in order to pay for the foreign securities. In a similar situation, suppose the Mitsubishi Company wants to lend money to its subsidiary abroad. It can now do so merely by filing a small report. Formerly they had to get a Ministry of Finance license to do this. But in both cases, before and after liberalization, they have had to perform the foreign-exchange transaction through an authorized foreign-exchange bank. The "marrying" procedure does not apply to this transaction.

A: In the Tokyo foreign-exchange market, about 30 percent of trading is accounted for by actual business, that is, visible and invisible trade and capital transactions. The remaining 70 percent is done by banks to adjust their positions. Speculation is principally in the form of leads and lags by trading firms.

Q: *Because of liberalization, when there is a shift from the licensing procedure to the notification procedure, must the notification be "accepted" by the Ministry of Finance before the proposed action may proceed?*

A: There are two types of notification: first, prenotification of more than 21 days before the proposed action; second, prenotification immediately before the proposed action, as in case of the purchase of a foreign bond. The latter is just a "small" notification. The first type would apply in a case such as the proposal to issue your own bond in the Eurodollar market. In this case, the Ministry of Finance may not accept the notification, in which event the bond cannot be issued.

Q: *Since December 1980, what controls on international capital movements remain in effect?*

A: Many controls. Guidelines. These are not legal; they are by administrative guidance. If a bank wants to make a loan to a foreign country, it must present its proposed schedule at a "hearing" before the IFB of the Ministry of Finance. [The IFB doesn't like the word control.] The hearings may be quarterly or monthly. Where no foreign-exchange transaction is involved in a loan to abroad, in lending dollars or yen, the Short-Term Capital Department is in charge.

The Foreign Capital Department is in charge of bonds issued in foreign markets. The Securities Bureau is also involved in this. The approval for a given action is conveyed by a single department, but that department may consult with other departments or bureaus before giving its approval. Here again, although the Bank of Japan is operationally in charge, the policy is made in the IFB.

A: There are strong informal controls on capital outflow at present. There are few controls on inflow. But there are few capital inflows. Life insurance companies are making big investments in overseas dollar bonds.

Q: *What are the "voluntary," or self-regulatory, rules that the banking industry must observe with regard to international transactions?*

A: The Bankers' Association and the Securities Industry Association have a great deal of power. They decide the fees and the commission rates.

In a technical sense, the trade associations have a great deal of power. In accordance with the government's wishes, they impose ceilings and distribute quotas to each member of the association. They decide how many issues each securities house should handle. Similarly, the Bankers Association decides how much each bank should lend in yen to nonresidents.

Q: *Is it correct to say that capital movements are occurring at the present time primarily because of volatility in the foreign-exchange market rather than because of discrepancies between interest rates in Japan and those of other countries?*

A: Capital movements occur primarily because of huge differences in the long-term interest rate, which is the interest rate on bonds in the secondary trading market. The short-term interest rate affects market conditions through psychology or sentiment, but actual movements occur in response to the long-term interest rate differential.

A: In the short term, capital movements are primarily determined by foreign-exchange rate fluctuations. In the medium term, they are primarily determined by the interest rate. In the long term, they are primarily caused by a desire for asset diversification. From month to month, there are huge variations in both the short-term and long-term capital accounts. The long-term capital accounts are affected primarily by gensaki transactions.

Formerly, capital movements occurred in response to the funda-
mentals [the Consumer Price Index and the current account]. Now the
animating stimulus is primarily political.

Note that there is very little correlation between the overall balance of payments and changes in the foreign exchange reserves. Apparently the CD and foreign deposit data are not taken account of
statistically in the balance of payments.

A: Interest rate differentials have a stronger effect on capital
movements than do fluctuations in the foreign exchange rate.

A: For the short term, the interest rate is more important. For
the long term, the exchange rate is more important. The reason is that
in the short term, exchange rate fluctuations can be covered in the
forward market. For long-term transactions, exchange rate fluctuations
cannot be covered. Therefore, in the long term, the exchange rate
fluctuation is more important.

For long-term interest rates, you have to find the rates specified in
long-term contracts.

Q: *Will liberalization and internationalization increase the degree of potential instability in the Japanese economy?*

A: Again, you must take account of the "invisible handshakes"
in the Japanese economy. In the labor market, we have lifetime employment. In money markets, we have long-term controls. The maintenance of these long-term controls implies stability in interest rates
and in wages.

A: So far as monetary policy is concerned, liberalization and
internationalization imply some difficulty for interest rate policy.
However, while short-term money markets are free, long-term money
markets are regulated. The gensaki was defined as a long-term instrument prior to October 1981. Thereafter, it was redefined as a short-
term instrument. Now all gensaki are short term.

A: It depends on the degree of liberalization. If you totally liberalized capital outflows, everybody would be in here trying to borrow.
Interest rates would go up. Moreover, interest rates are bound to go up
when the bulk of the outstanding government debt begins to mature
in 1984. An enormous amount of bonds will mature.

Q: *When there is a question about the relative importance of
domestic versus international priorities, how does the IFB coordinate
with other bureaus of the Ministry of Finance concerning this question? What are the issues that divide the bureaus?*

A: A very interesting question. Establishment of the offshore international market would help mollify the Americans. The foreign banks in Japan have been complaining because their profits have been low. Also the United States has been badgering Japan to liberalize services imports. Establishment of an offshore dollar market would give foreign banks the upper hand and would give them more to do. Moreover, it would not hurt the Japanese banks. It would not take anything away from them.

A: This is becoming a very important question. Formerly, the domestic economy was more important than the international economy. Now, even the domestic bureau people understand that Japan is too big to be selfish.

Q: *What types of information necessary for forecasting Japanese interest rates and the exchange value of the yen are not publicly available?*

A: In Japan, various government bureaus keep statistical information that they collect and do not publish and that they may not even share with other government agencies. Thus, the necessary information for policymaking is often unavailable in various government agencies. It would be nice to know how much information of this kind is being withheld. The withholding, of course, is done for the purpose of inflating the importance of agencies that own the information.

Q: *How much control does the Ministry of Finance exercise over subsidiaries of Japanese banks and Japanese nonfinancial firms abroad?*

A: In the case of financial companies, the Ministry of Finance can "persuade" the parent firm. But it has less influence with nonfinancial companies concerning their subsidiaries abroad.

A: None.

A: A moderate amount of control. In their overseas operations, Japanese banks and securities companies are actively getting into each other's business. [They are crossing turf lines in Japan as well.] Eventually, Japanese banks will be "universal" banks.

A: Under the Foreign Exchange Law, the Ministry of Finance has no jurisdiction over the subsidiaries abroad of either banks or nonbanking firms. Foreign subsidiaries are under the control of the local law wherever they happen to be established. Nevertheless, by the ministry's control over the head office in Japan of the subsidiary abroad, the ministry may obtain information on a "nice to know" basis. In actuality, Ministry of Finance bank examinations do cover branch offices abroad of Japanese banks, but not bank subsidiaries incorporated abroad. The ministry sometimes asks for data on the "total exposure" of the bank, including its subsidiaries abroad. But we don't like this.

Concerning subsidiaries in Switzerland, Panama, and Luxembourg, we can do what we want in those subsidiaries because it is against the law for the business information of those countries to be communicated outside. Their laws forbid disclosure.

But of course, we understand the intentions of the Ministry of Finance and why they want what they want. And we cooperate. The ministry doesn't like uncontrolled transactions in yen outside Japan. So we don't do it. But the foreign banks do it.

We don't issue yen bonds by means of our subsidiaries outside Japan. And we don't make loans in yen by means of those subsidiaries.

Q: *In the event of the establishment of an International Banking Facility (IBF), who would be the winners and losers?*

A: Ah! Winners would be the foreign banks. Because the dollar is their home currency, the foreign banks can acquire dollar funds more cheaply than Japanese banks. In the United States, this is especially so because of Regulation Q.

Residents of Japan, however, will be able more readily than before to obtain information about international markets from the offshore dollar market. This may redound to the advantage of the Japanese banks with which they do business. Note, however, that the offshore market is an "out-out" market: It is not a market in which residents can operate, except indirectly by means of their subsidiaries abroad. Thus, Japanese banks will gain relatively less than foreign banks.

A: Winners: foreign banks in Japan and Japanese banks. Singapore will lose. Hong Kong will not suffer much. Some London business may be switched to the Far East. Largely, the losers will be institutions outside Japan. But even they will not lose much.

A: It depends on what kind of offshore market is established. It depends on whether or not the banks can engage in securities business. The securities industry needs long-term, face-to-face relations. If only banking is permitted, then the banks will gain. But if securities business is included in the offshore market, then there will be winners and losers.

A: Securities firms would become more active in the financing of Asian companies. Banks, too, would attract Asian clients for their banking activities. Asian companies would not have to go far away to Europe or the United States.

If a Tokyo offshore market comes to be like its New York counterpart (that is, only for short-term banking), the Banking Bureau would become busier. If the market became like its London counterpart [that is, long-term financing also allowed], the Securities Bureau would then also become busy.

A: Winners but no losers.

Q: *What effect would establishment of an International Banking Facility have on Japan's balance of payments?*

A: Again, it depends on what kinds of transactions occur in the IBF and what kinds of currencies are defined as eligible.

One effect would arise as a result of the instructions that would be given by head offices in Japan to their subsidiaries abroad with regard to the latter's transactions in the IBF. Electronic banking, which keeps head offices constantly in touch with their international cash position, would facilitate these instructions. Subsidiaries with extra cash would be told what to do in the IBF. By means of the electronic international cash-management system, there would not only be an effect on the balance of payments but there would also be some leakage from the IBF to the domestic monetary system.

Q: *Will internationalization of the money market undermine the government's control of domestic monetary policy?*

A: Yes. But keeping yen out of the offshore market will delay attenuation of the government's control over the domestic economy.

A: The demand function for money will change because of internationalization, but not as much as in West Germany. The reason is lifetime employment in major firms and the institutional practices associated with it. In the United States, for example, official A uses the services of bank Q. When official A retires or quits, official B comes in. B does not necessarily continue to patronize bank Q. In Japan, official C uses the services of bank X. When official C leaves, his successor continues to maintain the company's affiliation with bank X. Thus, in Japan there is an institutional memory: There is a permanent relationship between the company and its customers and suppliers. This stabilizes the demand function for money.

Q: *What are the considerations that are relevant to the decision as to whether or not Japanese firms should be allowed to issue commercial paper (CPs)?*

A: The Japan Bankers' Association strongly objects to the establishment of a CP market. They fear that it would mean a shifting of business from the lending market to the CP market. A CP market would create a more competitive environment for the banks. They would have to meet this competition, but the volume of their transactions would not change greatly.

The Ministry of Finance doesn't want rapid decontrol of the interest rate. Establishment of a CP market would decontrol interest rates too rapidly.

The Bank of Japan wants a treasury bill market, not a CP market. If a CP market were to gain rapidly, the effectiveness of monetary policy would decline.

A: The CP eliminates the bank as an intermediary; therefore, it is being fought by the banks. The CP is like a short-term bond. It enables the borrower to raise funds without going through a bank. You merely go to a brokerage house. It is like a debenture: there is no collateral. You have to have a good name to issue a CP. The broker finds a customer for your CP, and you raise money in that way. [On the other hand, a *tegata*, which is generally a claim on a deposit account, does go through a bank. The bank issues the tegata and charges a fee.] The CP, unlike a promissory note, is not associated with a specific trade transaction. A promissory note is trade credit: you buy something and promise to pay for it later.

A: A CP may be guaranteed by a bank, so the bank would get a small commission for performing this service. However, this fee is much less than the interest the bank would gain by extending a loan. Therefore, the banks do not like CPs and would rather extend loans. On the other hand, from the point of view of a firm, it would be cheaper to issue a CP than to borrow money from a bank.

The CP raises another issue as well. In Japan, there is no rating system for firms. For a bond issue, there are four categories: AA, A, BB, and B. They are based on the size of the firm's capital and the firm's financial results in the preceding four quarters. But these categories are not a real credit-rating system. We are not so concerned about ratings because most corporation bonds are collateralized [except Samurai bonds and bonds guaranteed by the Japanese government or foreign governments]. Thus, bonds in all four of the above categories may have the same price. Authorization of a CP market would require the establishment of a credit-rating system for firms.

The authorities have postponed liberalization not only with regard to establishment of a CP market but also of a bankers acceptance (BA) market. I am very concerned about developing a BA market in Japan. The interest rate in the United States is very high for refinance. We should shift part of the burden to a Japanese BA market. We should establish a proper market for the finance of international trade; foreign trade finance should not be mixed up with domestic finance; we need a BA market in yen. But the Bank of Japan is reluctant to allow this because they are worried about losing operational control. They say, why not include BAs in the bills discount market?

The absence of short-term financial instruments in the form of CPs and BAs, as well as the rudimentary nature of the treasury bill market, has given rise to the existence of the gensaki market.

Long-term credit banks and trust banks don't want the city banks or the foreign banks to issue long-term credit. For this reason, the permissible term of a CD is limited to six months.

Q: *Are exceptions permissible in the implementation of Bank of Japan controls?*

A: When "exceptions" occur, they are granted by the Ministry of Finance, not the Bank of Japan.

However, not all exceptions are authorized. Some occur by means of connivance between bankers and their customers. The bankers manipulate the balance sheets and make implicit loans that do not appear on the books.

Q: *Will the Postal Savings system be a loser in the liberalization process?*

A: They may perhaps be a loser. They are losing their market share. There is a shift in deposits between the Postal Savings system and the banks. However, the Ministry of Finance has no legal power to change Postal Savings interest rates.

Q: *What are the uses of dollar funds by the city banks?*
A: This information is not published.

Q: *What are the statistics concerning foreign exchange transactions by banks and by foreign exchange brokers as distinguished from other foreign exchange transactions?*
A: This information is not published.

Q: *What is the effect of liberalization on takeovers and joint ventures?*

A: Legally, takeovers are authorized. But if the Ministry of Finance feels that a proposed takeover is not in Japan's national interest, it will oppose it. For example, it will oppose if it seems that the takeover would result in confusion in the market, if it would create excessive competition, if it would give rise to "lack of cooperation" or "lack of friendliness" in the industry, or if it would precipitate complaints by competing firms about the threat to their market share. In such cases, the Ministry of Finance would object and would request MITI to object also.

Q: *What other changes do you see taking place in the banking industry and the securities industry?*

A: In the future, foreign banks will be winners if banks in Japan are allowed to engage in the securities business. American banks, which can engage in the securities business outside the United States, have a great deal of European experience that Japanese banks lack. American banks will put this to use in Japan. In another respect, however, foreign banks will continue to be disadvantaged. Japanese banks have close connections with large Japanese corporations; thus, they will have the inside track in handling the securities business of those corporations. On the other hand, foreign banks and Japanese banks can exchange favors: The former have the precious asset of experience in international markets; the latter have the precious asset of close connections with major Japanese business firms. An interesting legacy of the period when Japan was closed to foreign direct investment is the absence of foreign-dominated industrial groups in Japan. These would provide foreign banks with the access to securities-issuing corporations that they now lack.

A: The securities industry has more vitality than the banking industry. Nomura Securities is now bigger than the top Japanese bank; therefore, it has clout. At the moment, the banks have no political support, and they have a lot to lose. The securities industry does have political support, and they have nothing to lose. The Postal Savings system also has strong political support. These factors impel the Ministry of Finance to proceed gradually with regard to liberalization.

For example, whatever one may think of the merits of the bankers' case concerning CPs [as being damaging to their business], the results are very revealing as to the way in which policy changes actually occur in Japan, namely, step by step. The banks' fear of CPs is respected. There are no sudden great departures or dramatic changes in official policy. Instead, policy evolves in gradual stages from one point to the next. Moreover, this matter also illustrates the Japanese propensity for achieving a goal by indirection: First one step is taken in an indicated direction, followed by another step, possibly at a tangent rather than in a straight line.

A: The banking industry and the securities industry are invading each other's territory. This has repercussions on the Ministry of Finance. Where a securities matter concerns the banks, the Banking

Bureau has a voice in it. Where a banking matter concerns the securities industry, the Securities Bureau has a voice in it. This means that more issues will arise that concern both bureaus. Thus, there will probably be more conflicts between the two in the future than in the past.

Concerning changes that are taking place, the foreign banks lack the personnel and the contacts to call up the Banking Bureau or the Securities Bureau to find out what is going on. They lack the senior people who have known the ministry officials in the past and have ties to them. Therefore, they are left out of the pipeline of current information.

A: Japanese banks have been affected by change in several different ways. In the first instance, they were losers to the securities companies by virtue of a change in the environment rather than as a result of policy. As the assets of the private sector accumulated, firms moved away from bank financing in favor of self-financing. Later, liberalization made it possible for firms to have recourse to foreign financing and thus to further increase their independence of the domestic banks. Subsequently, there was a policy effort to redress the balance between the banks and the securities companies. For example, banks were granted the concession of being allowed to deal in gensaki transactions.

The securities companies are more difficult to control than the banks. The reason is that the banks can be controlled in terms of a few variables such as interest rates and access to funding, whereas the securities companies can invent new products or new means of utilizing old products. Moreover, the banks are used to being protected, whereas the securities companies are used to being independent and exposed. Securities companies, unlike the banks, are not at all protected from going bankrupt.

Q: *Among its other duties, the Banking Bureau of the Ministry of Finance administers the Insurance Law. To what extent does the insurance industry remain unliberalized?*

A: The law covers all insurance categories [casualty, fire, life, etc.]. Japanese insurance companies are not permitted to sell insurance outside of Japan. If this were permitted, it would not be profitable and thus probably would not be attempted. Nevertheless, it is prohibited.

Insurance companies are not allowed to determine their dividend policy without permission of the Insurance Division of the Banking Bureau. Premiums charged by the insurance companies are also determined by the Insurance Division. Purchase of real estate, either inside or outside Japan, of a value beyond some minor amount, requires permission of the Insurance Division. Participation of insurance companies in syndicated loans likewise requires permission of the Ministry of Finance.

In the life insurance industry, the ministry maintains that these controls are necessary in order to restrain excessive competition among Japanese firms and to enable the industry to withstand competition from foreign firms in Japan. Among the 21 life insurance companies in Japan, however, five majors *are* strong enough to withstand competition. The weak companies want the restrictions, while the strong companies want more freedom to compete.

Every three months, the major insurance firms are given a "hearing" by the Ministry of Finance regarding their lending quota. The Banking Bureau determines the quota, but it consults with the International Finance Bureau before doing so.

═ 4 ═

ADMINISTRATIVE REFORM

Administrative reform is more interesting for what it has proposed than for what it has accomplished. It is also interesting as an example of the contrast between appearance and reality in Japanese affairs. In its several aims, the proposed reform is a response to several conflicts: between government subsidies and fiscal balance, between government enterprise and business efficiency, between government intervention and the market system, and between Japan's domestic and international goals. By shrinking the size of government and the public deficit, as well as simplifying bureaucratic procedures, administrative reform proposes to reduce the burden of government on the private sector and to dissolve disincentives. Thus, although formally it has not been presented as such, administrative reform in effect could be an instrument of economic liberalization. As in the case of other such instruments, its task is both political and economic. The political motives of its sponsors, however, are not unambiguous. They concern matters of status, turf, and political power within the public and private sectors and prerogatives of government intervention in the private sector. In its desultory progress, administrative reform has clearly revealed disharmony—"Japan, Disincorporated"—as opposed to consensus in Japanese society.

Predicaments

In 1948, the Administrative Management Agency was established to keep the bureaucracy in check. The effort was not fruitful. In the next fifteen years, more than a dozen attempts were made to simplify the administrative structure, but they all ended in failure. In February

1962, a Provisional Administrative Study Council was established by Prime Minister Hayato Ikeda. In September 1964 (having expended ¥ 200 million), it rendered its report to Prime Minister Eisaku Sato, again with little impact. On the contrary, as the economic "miracle" blossomed, many new agencies were established, and many new burdens were assumed by the government in the expectation that the expanding GNP would pay for them. The government indulged in the creation of new public corporations, of new departments and bureaus within ministries, and in the expansion of employment throughout the public sector.

In March 1981, the second Provisional Commission for Administrative Reform—known as Rinchō (Rinji gyōsei chosakai)—was established by Prime Minister Zenko Suzuki and placed under the leadership of Toshiwo Doko, former president of Keidanren and one of Japan's most eminent and respected industrial statesmen.[1] Yasuhiro Nakasone, then director of the Administrative Management Agency, was the cabinet minister in charge of the program. When the Rinchō was inaugurated, Suzuki declared that he would stake his political life on the achievement of its objectives. In particular, he pledged that he would balance the budget by fiscal year 1984 without raising taxes.[2] In balancing the budget, he would terminate the issuance of "special" deficit-financing government bonds by that date.[3]

The Rinchō's first report, which called for an immediate reduction in public expenditure and curtailment of subsidies, was submitted in July 1981; it was largely ignored by the government. Its second report, submitted in February 1982, emphasized simplification of government procedures. Prime Minister Suzuki responded by repeating his pledge to balance the budget by fiscal year 1984. The third report, issued in July 1982, called for fundamental structural reforms, including dismemberment and privatization of three government enterprises. In September 1982, Suzuki announced that he would not stand for reelection as president of the Liberal Democratic Party and hence would resign as prime minister. Suzuki's departure absolved the LDP of its commitment to balance the budget by fiscal year 1984. The fourth report, issued in February 1983, called for the establishment of a new organization to promote and implement administrative reform programs. Upon being dissolved in March 1983, the Rinchō submitted its final report, mainly recapitulating its previous recommendations. The report was received by Yasuhiro Nakasone, who by then had succeeded Suzuki as prime minister.

The complexities of Japanese fiscal affairs include the distinction between the general and special accounts, regular versus supplementary budgets, central versus local expenditures, and activity in the Fiscal Investment and Loan program (FILP). Thus, comparison between Japanese and U.S. fiscal statistics presents some difficulties. At the national level, income taxes are the principal tax source. The prefectural level depends primarily on business taxes, and the local level (cities, towns, and villages) depends mainly on income and property taxes. Combined central and local government expenditures in Japan amount approximately to 35 percent of GNP. If military expenditures were excluded, the ratio would be approximately as high in Japan as in the United States.

Concerning Japan's phenomenal government deficits in recent years, there has been a clear propensity on the part of the authorities— as in 1981 and 1982—to overestimate prospective tax revenues. It has been questioned whether the EPA and the Ministry of Finance take their own forecasts seriously. Recent errors have been on the order of 10 percent.[4] In 1979, deficit financing provided 39.6 percent of the initial general account budget. (See Table 1.) Reliance on deficit financing declined to 33.5 percent in 1980 and to 26.2 percent in 1981.[5] In 1982, the deficit of ¥ 14.3 trillion was unprecedented in absolute terms. In that year, the budget deficit was 6 percent of GNP, compared with 3.5 percent in the United States. As amended, however, the 1982 budget showed a surplus of ¥ 190 billion. The total amount of the public debt outstanding rose from ¥ 4.0 trillion in 1971 to ¥ 100 trillion in June 1983.[6] At that time, it constituted almost 40 percent of the GNP, a higher ratio than in the United States or West Germany. If the average interest rate were 8 percent, payments on the public debt would amount to 3.2 percent of the GNP annually, or more than three times the amount of the defense budget.

In the Rinchō's various reports, it recommended ways of trimming waste from the bureaucratic structure and proposed rationalization of the system of licenses and permits. It also recommended termination of various activities, supported by government in the early postwar period, that had become obsolete.[7] In Japan, a public corporation (Tokushu Hōjin) is a corporation established by the national government for the conduct of business operations. There are nine specified types, whose Japanese names are only approximately translatable into English. The types are distinguished from one another by the source of their funds, scale of operations, nature of budgetary surveillance to which they are subject, nature of their management, and type of activity they perform. As of December 1981, Japan had 106 public corporations whose fields of operation ranged widely over social and economic policy areas, from public works to social welfare. A *public*

TABLE 1
JAPAN'S GENERAL ACCOUNT BUDGET, FISCAL YEARS 1946 TO 1984

FISCAL YEAR	REVENUE		EXPENDITURE		BUDGET SURPLUS OR DEFICIT (Billions of yen)
	(In billions of yen)	(Percentage change from previous year)	(In billions of yen)	(Percentage change from previous year)	
1946	74.4	413.1	115.2	435.8	−40.8
1950	716.8	−5.5	633.3	−9.5	83.5
1955	1,126.4	−5.0	1,018.2	−2.2	108.2
1960	1,961.0	22.8	1,743.1	16.6	217.9
1965	3,575.9	7.0	3,723.0	11.5	−147.1
1966	3,886.0	8.7	4,459.2	19.8	−573.2
1967	4,472.4	15.1	5,203.4	16.7	−731.0
1968	5,597.8	25.2	5,937.1	14.1	−339.3
1969	6,697.7	19.6	6,917.8	16.5	−220.1

Year					
1970	8,120.0	21.3	8,187.7	18.4	−67.7
1971	8,783.7	8.2	9,561.1	16.8	−777.4
1972	10,843.9	23.5	11,932.2	24.8	−1,088.3
1973	13,462.6	24.1	15,272.6	28.0	−1,810.0
1974	18,218.1	35.3	19,099.8	25.1	−881.7
1975*	16,192.9	−11.1	20,860.9	9.2	−4,668.0
1976	17,877.8	10.4	24,467.1	17.3	−6,589.3
1977	19,872.4	11.2	29,059.5	18.8	−9,187.1
1978	24,233.3	21.9	34,096.0	17.3	−9,862.7
1979	26,307.2	8.6	38,789.8	13.8	−12,482.6
1980	29,871.0	13.5	43,405.0	11.9	−13,534.0
1981	34,503.0	15.5	46,921.0	8.1	−12,418.0
1982	33,217.1	−3.7	47,562.1	1.4	−14,345.0
1983	37,034.6	11.5	50,379.6	5.9	−13,345.0
1984	37,947.2	2.5	50,627.2	0.5	−12,680.0

* In FY1965, business capital investment declined 14.4 percent from the previous year. Business inventory investment fell by a sharp 66.7 percent.

SOURCE: Ministry of Finance, Budget Bureau

corporation is an entity separate from the government and separate from the civil service. A *national enterprise* (such as the Postal Service, the Mint, or the Printing Office) is not a separate entity; it exists within the jurisdiction of a government ministry and in a broad sense is included within the civil service. In a narrow sense, the central government civil service excludes government enterprises as well as public corporations and the self-defense forces. In that sense, Japan's national civil service contains fewer personnel than the public corporations.

During each of the calendar years 1981, 1982, and 1983, Japanese government final consumption expenditures amounted to 10.2 percent of GNP. In addition, its capital formation expenditures (including inventories) amounted to 9.5 percent, 8.9 percent, and 8.4 percent of GNP during those years, respectively. In every year from fiscal year 1975 through fiscal year 1983, tax revenue constituted only about 60 percent of total government expenditures. The individuals and institutions that escape income taxation in Japan are numerous. Schools of flower arrangement, tea ceremony, and the like pay little or nothing in taxes. More important, a multitude of incorporated entities such as farm cooperatives, industry and trade associations, schools, and hospitals have accumulated substantial business assets and pay handsome salaries, but are exempt from taxes in whole or in part.

The fiscal year 1984 general account budget, however, was considered by Ministry of Finance officials "the most austere in nearly twenty years."[8] (See Table 3.) It called for a 7.9 percent increase in overseas economic aid and a 6.65 percent increase in defense expenditure, while social security expenditure increased by only 2.0 percent. Budgeted expenditures for agricultural price supports and public works were actually reduced. The budget as a whole amounted to ¥ 50.6 trillion, or approximately $225 billion at then prevailing exchange rates. The deficit amounted to ¥ 12.7 trillion, or approximately $56 billion. Table 2 shows the nature of the problem confronting the Rinchō in its effort to cut expenditures.

The budget politics of subsidies is of particular interest in the case of agriculture. One of the structural problems connected with the rice subsidy and the consequent excess of rice production arises from the fact that very few farm families depend exclusively on agriculture for their livelihood. Those who are also engaged in nonagricultural employment prefer to grow rice because rice is the easiest crop to raise on a part-time basis. Livestock, fruits, and vegetables require full-time attention. Thus, although most rural families depend substantially on nonagricultural sources of income, they do *not* take a nonagricultural point of view in their voting behavior. They retain a heavy stake in the rice subsidy.

The fiscal problem includes not only the maintenance of inappropriate subsidies but also their maladministration. As proposed by the *Rinchō*, many separately administered subsidies could be combined and simplified. This would be an important economy measure inasmuch as the process of applying for subsidies is usually complicated and time-consuming. In particular, subsidies to local governments need to be aggregated.[9] The many pilgrimages to Tokyo made by local officials applying for renewal of their subsidies is a further wasteful expenditure of time and money.[10] Moreover, if the central government were willing, it could remove itself from the procedure of deciding how subsidies are locally applied. Instead, it could simply hand over sums of money to the local authorities and let them decide the matter by themselves. Among the merits of doing so would be an improvement in the rationale of income redistribution in Japan. At present, in vying with each other for influence and political control, the education, labor, and agricultural ministries distribute subsidies to local areas. These are provided for specific purposes on a per capita basis without regard to existing variations in income levels. Thus, rich areas receive the same amount of subsidy as poor areas. For example, rich and poor areas may both receive a subsidy for the construction of swimming pools despite the fact that the rich area may already be well supplied with swimming pools. If local governments were in charge of allocating subsidies, they could presumably make better functional use of them. It could be further argued that rich local areas should receive no subsidies at all. Once a scheme of central government subsidies has been put in place, however, it survives by force of votes and becomes difficult to dislodge. Voting alliances make for strange bedfellows. Politicians, for example, have a positive interest in the continuance of subsidies, as does the Ministry of Education. Although educators and politicians are adversaries on many educational issues, they are allies when it comes to putting pressure on the government to maintain subsidies to education.

Aggregation, simplification, or reduction of subsidies, moreover, would not only threaten the prerogative of ministerial intervention but would shift the relative distribution of ministerial power. At present, many ministries have their fingers in the subsidy pie. Aggregation and simplification of the subsidy system require that the administration of subsidies be concentrated in fewer ministries. This would be negotiable only if *all* ministries—not only the culprits—were called upon to relinquish some of their prerogatives. If a particular ministry or only

TABLE 2

JAPAN'S GENERAL ACCOUNT EXPENDITURES, BY MAJOR CATEGORY, FISCAL YEARS 1950 TO 1984
(PERCENT OF BUDGET AND PERCENT OF GNP)

Fiscal year	Social security		Pensions		Debt service		Education and science		Local finance		Public works		Other	
1950	7.7	1.2	0.8	0.1	9.2	1.5	17.4	2.8	17.1	2.7	33.5	5.4	14.3	2.3
1955	13.8	1.7	8.7	1.1	4.3	0.5	12.3	1.5	15.7	1.9	19.6	2.4	25.6	3.2
1960	13.3	1.4	6.7	0.7	1.5	0.2	12.1	1.3	19.1	2.1	26.3	2.8	21.0	2.3
1965	14.6	1.6	4.6	0.5	0.3	0.0	13.2	1.5	19.1	0.9	19.8	2.2	28.4	4.4
1966	14.1	1.6	4.3	0.5	1.0	0.1	12.5	1.4	17.5	2.1	19.7	2.2	30.9	3.4
1967	14.2	1.6	4.2	0.5	2.0	0.2	12.4	1.4	18.7	2.1	19.6	2.2	28.9	3.2
1968	14.0	1.5	4.3	0.5	3.3	0.4	11.9	1.3	19.7	2.1	18.0	1.9	28.8	3.1
1969	14.1	1.5	3.8	0.4	4.0	0.4	11.8	1.3	20.7	2.2	17.4	1.9	28.2	3.0

1970	14.1	1.5	3.6	0.4	3.5	0.4	11.7	1.3	21.6	2.4	17.2	1.9	28.3	3.1
1971	14.1	1.6	3.5	0.4	3.3	0.4	11.7	1.4	20.0	2.4	19.5	2.3	27.9	3.2
1972	13.9	1.7	3.0	0.4	3.8	0.5	10.9	1.4	18.7	2.5	21.8	2.7	27.9	3.4
1973	14.5	1.9	3.1	0.4	4.5	0.6	10.6	1.4	21.0	2.8	18.7	2.4	27.6	3.6
1974	16.3	2.3	3.1	0.4	4.4	0.6	11.8	1.6	21.7	3.0	15.5	2.1	27.2	3.8
1975	19.4	2.7	3.6	0.5	5.3	0.7	12.7	1.7	15.9	2.2	15.9	2.2	27.2	3.8
1976	19.6	2.8	4.0	0.6	7.5	1.1	12.2	1.8	15.5	2.3	15.4	2.2	25.8	3.7
1977	19.5	3.0	4.0	0.6	7.9	1.2	11.7	1.8	15.4	2.6	17.0	2.6	24.5	3.7
1978	19.7	3.3	3.9	0.6	9.4	1.6	11.3	1.9	15.4	2.8	16.9	2.8	23.4	3.7
1979	19.3	3.4	3.8	0.7	11.0	2.0	10.9	1.9	14.9	3.0	16.8	3.0	23.3	3.8
1980	18.9	3.4	3.7	0.7	12.6	2.3	10.5	1.9	17.9	3.3	15.6	2.8	22.7	3.8
1981	18.8	3.5	3.8	0.7	14.1	2.6	10.2	1.9	18.5	3.4	14.9	2.8	20.0	3.7
1982	19.2	2.2	4.0	0.7	14.5	2.6	10.1	1.8	16.8	3.0	15.3	2.7	20.0	3.6
1983	18.1	3.3	3.7	0.7	16.1	3.0	9.5	1.8	15.1	2.8	14.2	2.4	23.8	4.4
1984	18.8	3.2	3.7	0.6	17.9	3.0	9.6	1.6	17.9	3.0	13.4	2.3	18.7	3.2
1985	18.5	3.1	3.5	0.6	19.1	3.2	9.2	1.5	18.2	3.0	13.0	2.2	18.5	3.1
1986*	18.7	3.0	3.4	0.6	19.8	3.2	9.1	1.5	18.1	2.9	12.9	2.1	18.0	2.9

* Estimated

SOURCE: Ministry of Finance, Budget Bureau

TABLE 3
JAPAN'S GENERAL ACCOUNT BUDGET, FISCAL YEAR 1984
(IN BILLIONS OF YEN)

	FY 1984	Percentage change from FY 1983
Revenue		
Tax Receipts	34,596	7.1
Nontax Receipts	3,351	−29.0
Proceeds From Bond Issues[a]	12,680	−5.0
Total	50,627	0.5
Expenditures		
Debt Service	9,155	11.7
Revenue Sharing	8,886	18.2
General Expenditures	32,586	−0.1
Social Security	9,321	2.0
National Defense	2,935	6.65
Overseas Economic Aid	544	7.9
Education and Science	4,867	1.0
Energy	603	0.9
Pensions	1,886	−0.2
Small Business	229	−5.5
Food Control Account	813	−11.0
Public Works	6,520	−2.0
Total	50,627	0.5

a. Includes 6,455 billion yen for purposes of deficit financing.
SOURCE: Ministry of Finance

a few ministries were singled out for reduction or removal of their controls over subsidies to local governments, they would strongly resist doing so. To achieve subsidy reform, it must be apparent that all ministries have agreed to make concessions. Further resistance to this proposal arises from fear on the part of the Construction Ministry, the Ministry of Health and Welfare, and others that the net result of simplification and aggregation of subsidies would redound to the advantage of the Ministry of Finance and the Home Ministry. These would be winners and the others would be losers. Many people, outside as well as inside government, believe that the Ministry of Finance is already too powerful in relation to the other ministries. Moreover, the ministries do not want reform, because if they had to cut back their spending, they would undermine the political support they receive from the subsidized sectors. As suggested above, the Japanese government works by collaboration between the ministries and the Diet. Even though the Ministry of Finance is a civil service organization, it depends for its clout on collaboration with Diet members. If government subsidies were curtailed, this collaboration would be undermined, and Diet members would not be able to assist their Ministry of Finance counterparts to the customary extent.

As previously mentioned, in recommending measures ostensibly designed to achieve reduction of the government deficit and simplification of government procedures, the *Rinchō* proposed various fundamental reforms. These proposals were described by terms such as *reform, reconstruction,* and *rationalization.* Operationally, however, the proposals implied adjustment of functions and redistribution of political and bureaucratic power. Before discussing the power struggle to which they gave rise, we should review the *Rinchō's* proposals.

Prescriptions

Even during his term of office, it was said that Prime Minister Suzuki did not really want administrative reform. Instead, many assumed he wanted the *appearance* of reform without much change in substance. If there were a significant change in substance, some people would be hurt and the support of the LDP would be impaired. Behind the scenes, the LDP itself was making recommendations different from those it made in public. In public, for example, it deplored the papering over of fiscal deficits by means of "construction bonds," but in a private document it recommended an increase in public works expenditure in lieu of deficit spending in the general account.[11] Among other interesting recommendations in the same document were the following:

The government should try to raise additional revenue by means of public monopolies and by selling national assets such as land and forests.

To avoid tax increases, there should be no inflation adjustment in government spending, no wage increases for government officials, cuts in traveling allowances and other office expenses, cuts in subsidies to special accounts and to private corporations, and expenditures should be shifted from the General Account to the FILP.

To raise government revenue, there should be less tax evasion, and excise taxes should be ad valorem rather than specific.

There should be no excess revenue estimate for 1983, as there had been for 1981 and 1982.

On the other hand, in its own reports, the *Rinchō's* recommendations included the following:

Attainment of modernization to the level of Western developed countries;

Construction of a vital welfare society;

Positive contribution to international society;

Fiscal rehabilitation without tax increase;

Growth in expenditure within the General Account to be kept below the growth rate of the national economy;

Ratio of government expenditure to GNP to be kept at a level considerably below that of European countries;

In agriculture: attainment of balanced supply and demand for rice and early reduction of dependence on subsidization;

In social security: reforming of the public pension scheme, including integration of various public pension systems and integration of pension administrative organization; medical costs to be financed by fees for service;

In education: review of the burden of the cost of higher education;

In land and housing: measures to promote the effective use of land and to supply better quality rental houses;

In science and technology: strengthening of cooperation among business, university, and government;

In diplomacy: integrated decisionmaking in formulation of external policies and in their dynamic and effective implementation;

In economic cooperation (economic aid): establishment of basic policies for economic cooperation and improvement of the administrative management of economic cooperation;

In defense: promotion of an efficient defense buildup, with emphasis on quality; vitalization of the National Defense Council;

In taxation: reduction of inequity in the tax burden by improvement of the system of self-assessment;

Administrative organization: establishment of a General Management Agency, integrating the duties and powers of the Personnel Bureau of the prime minister's office, the Administrative Management Agency, etc.;

Administrative organization regarding national land: unification of the National Land Agency, the Hokkaido Development Agency, and the Okinawa Development Agency;

Administrative system for implementing external policies: a system for dynamically dealing with important policy matters by a Ministerial Conference made up of a small number of ministers concerned and the active utilization of ministers without portfolio; strengthening of the planning function by reorganization and rationalization of the internal organs of the Ministry of Foreign Affairs;

Establishment of a Ministerial Conference for Economic Cooperation for discussion of fundamental policies for economic cooperation;

Public service personnel: salary and allowances paid to public service employees are to be based on the wage level for private sector employees;

The Personnel Bureau, prime minister's office: its coordinating function should be improved so as to break down excessive sectionalism;

Abolition of Japanese nationality requirement for teachers at national universities and for researchers of a similar status;

Measures for the division of functions between the central government and local governments: reform is to be carried out in terms of the principles of "regionality," "efficiency," and "integration"; integration and rationalization of services entrusted to local governments by the central government are to be achieved to the extent of at least 10 percent within two years;

Services other than standard services that may be desired by local inhabitants shall be financed by local taxation, according to the principle of "choice and burden";

Subsidies to local governments shall be integrated into the general revenue source system;

To achieve economies of scale, community services of cities, towns, and villages shall be integrated for joint operation;

Measures shall be taken for the reform and rationalization of local administrative work.

Policy measures for the reform of the three *kōshas*, which are the most public-service-oriented of the public corporations, as well as of the other public corporations:[12]

> (1) Japanese National Railways (JNR):
> (a) JNR should be divided into seven separate firms within five years; thereafter their shares should be sold to the public and their operations placed under private management.
>
> (2) Nippon Telegraph and Telephone Public Corporation (NTT):
> (a) NTT should be separated from its data-communication facilities and some other facilities;
> (b) NTT should be reorganized within five years into a central entity and various regional or local entities; the shares of both the central and regional entities should gradually be offered to the public and their operations placed under private management.
>
> (3) Japan Tobacco and Salt Public Corporation (JTSPC):
> (a) The structure of the JTSPC should be changed into a special business entity whose shares are offered for public subscription and whose operations are placed under private management;
> (b) The monopoly system for tobacco and for salt should be abolished, and tobacco imports should be handled by ordinary private companies.

Policy-reform measures for non-kōsha public corporations:

Criteria should be established for the integration, abolition, retrenchment, and transfer to private management of the business of the public corporations.

Issues for future consideration:

Rationalization of internal organs of ministries and agencies;

Review of the division of functions among ministries and agencies;

An overall approach to resolving problems of regional and local public administration;

Concerning public service personnel: examination of the scope and categories of employees, systems of recruitment, standards for promotion, and other matters requiring reform for the enhancement of efficiency;

Integration or abolition of public corporations;

Rationalization of public enterprises;

Rationalization of budgetary compilation and operations of the FILP;

Rationalization of the systems for granting permits or authorizations;

Rationalization of the subsidy system;

Elaboration of systems for dissemination of administrative information and procedures;

Establishment of an ombudsman facility;

Ensuring that military expenditure is exclusively for defensive purposes.

The Japanese government would be pleased to be able to claim credit for having accomplished even a small number of these proposals. Which, if any, it will actively pursue depends on the power struggle behind the scenes. The players represent miscellaneous branches of business, the bureaucracy, agriculture, and labor. Although their special interests may be inconsistent or antagonistic, each contrives to present his case in terms of the national interest. However, even the link to the national interest is not self-evident. At a particular moment, for example, it is arguable whether cyclical or structural matters should receive the highest national priority. In the power game, moreover, a typical tactic is for the parties to "agree in principle, but disagree in particulars" (sōron-sansei, kakuron-hantai).

In principle, for example, it is generally agreed that the government deficit is too high. Should the problem be solved by raising taxes or by reducing expenditure? The public is ambivalent about budget cuts. It does not want to pay more taxes, but it also wishes to retain its social security benefits. While beneficiaries of welfare fear the reduction of government expenditure, Keidanren advocates the "beneficiary-pay" principle. A large proportion of the Japanese public believes that the present level and incidence of taxation are unfair. Thus, it is opposed to raising taxes. Big business, which is seen as a beneficiary of the inequitable tax burden, is likewise opposed to raising taxes: It wants "small government" and less government intervention.[13] Perhaps the zaikai is more unhappy about taxes than about regulation. Regulations are in place; the firms have accommodated to them. But taxes eat up profits. Small- and medium-size business benefits from public works spending (as does big business) and would like the government to spend more; but it does not say this openly for fear of giving the government an excuse for raising taxes. Keynesians, on the other hand, argue that reduction of investment in public works may lessen effective demand through multiplier effects and that, moreover, exports would expand to restore the balance between supply and demand, thus provoking more trade friction. It is also argued that cutting expenditure does not by itself improve the equity of the tax burden.

There is much scope for improvement in efficiency as well as in equity. At present, for example, in civil service personnel matters, the National Personnel Authority handles salaries, the Ministry of Finance handles pensions, and the prime minister's office handles other retirement benefits. In military expenditure, which is steadily increasing, there are separate budgets for air, marine, and land forces. The Rinchō recommended that these be combined into a single budget, which would improve the efficiency of military spending. The Ministry of Finance is much tougher on other branches of the government than it is on the military with regard to spending of public funds.

Power Struggle

For the bureaucracy, the goals of reducing the government deficit and reducing the size of government have generated a power struggle. Within the bureaucracy there are strong conflicts concerning the revenue and spending aspects of administrative reform as well as the proposals for cutting red tape. Red tape is essential for maintaining the size of staff and programs. As an enemy of red tape, administrative reform is clearly linked to economic liberalization, to which the bureaucracy likewise is generally opposed. Within the Ministry of Finance, the Budget Bureau is especially resistant to the call for cutbacks in spending. The power of the Budget Bureau arises from its ability to grant budget increases to its clients. (In this, it resembles the politicians, who likewise gain strength from their ability to deliver benefits to their constituents.) As in the case of the subsidies mentioned above, it is essential not only that *all* agencies be cut but that they be cut *unequally*. In Japan, however, it is very difficult to discriminate among the various claimants for proportionate shares of the budget. Thus, the Budget Bureau resists this implication of administrative reform. Being pinched for revenue, the Budget Bureau already feels that it is losing its power. It also felt threatened by the proposal to privatize the tobacco and salt monopoly, which was a source of Ministry of Finance revenue.

If the budget is not cut sufficiently, the problem is shifted from the Budget Bureau to the Tax Bureau, which has to raise taxes to reduce the deficit. Meanwhile, the Budget Bureau says that the Tax Bureau should collect more taxes, while the latter says that it cannot increase the tax rate. On the other hand, a dilemma of the Budget Bureau is that, although in the event of a tax increase it would remain the most powerful bureau, the Tax Bureau would grow in power. On another front, the Financial Bureau, which floats the government debt, tells the Banking Bureau that it should not resist an increase in postal savings, which is another source of financing the deficit. A related problem is that although Japan's inflation was subdued from 1981 to 1983, the persistent massive issuance of national bonds and increase of the money supply during that period suggested the possibility that inflation would erupt again two or three years thereafter. In the event, the wholesale price index declined 10 percent from 1984 to 1986, while the consumer price index rose about 3.5 percent.

Three activities that should be largely, if not entirely, self-supporting contribute to the budget morass. These are sometimes characterized as the *san-K* or "three-K" problem: *kokutetsu, kome,* and *kempo* (railways, rice, and national health insurance). *Railways* here refers to the Japanese National Railways (JNR), a symbol of the 106 public corporations and the most notorious of them all. Reform of the JNR, which was the Rinchō's chief priority, constitutes perhaps the most difficult of all the problems of administrative reform.

Apart from its corrupt and inefficient practices, the JNR has suffered from three principal structural problems, namely, its pension obligations, the burden of its debt, and its unprofitable local lines. Its accumulated deficit since 1970 (when it was last in the black) amounted to ¥ 16.4 trillion (about $66 billion) at the end of March 1982, and in 1983 its annual losses were running at a rate of over ¥ 1.5 trillion (about $6 billion) a year. The deficit includes two components: a public-policy component (such as reduced fares for students) and a business component (rate structure, salary structure, inefficiency, corruption). The public-policy component of the JNR deficit has constituted about ¥ 700 billion annually; the remaining and principal component is largely attributable to the inefficiency of employees, incompetence of managers, and graft. Clearly there is a conflict of interest with regard to the use of its facilities. Which will assume the relatively heavier part of the burden of reducing its deficit? In absolute terms, obviously the business side will have to contribute the preponderant share. Inconveniently for those who regard Japan as a consensus society, however, the left-wing unionists who dominate the JNR, and who "make each workplace a Marxist battlefield," will bitterly resist this.[14]

Seeking a fundamental solution for the JNR difficulties, the Rinchō in July 1982 recommended that it be denationalized. As a transitional step, it should be dismembered into seven operating companies; thereafter, shares in each of the companies could be sold to the public. Although dismemberment is technically feasible, some of the successor companies would not be easily sold for this reason: because of political pressure, their lines were built in sparsely settled, unprofitable regions.[15] Presumably, however, private local management would be more innovative than the present national government and might be profitable by responding more effectively to local conditions. Be that as it may, no private interests would consider acquiring JNR properties unless its accumulated debts were assumed by the government.[16] Furthermore, no transfer of JNR to private ownership would be possible unless the domination of its left-wing unions were curbed. It is no secret that the dismemberment scenario contemplates smashing of the *Sōhyō* unions.[17]

A knowledgeable but ambivalent observer gave the following account of these matters.

You overemphasize the economic aspect. You neglect the political aspect.

The main incentive for big business in subscribing to administrative reform is *not* the matter of reducing taxes by reducing government spending. Big business can avoid or evade taxes to a substantial extent. Instead, the aim of big business is to break the unions.

This is the reason they want to break up JNR and NTT into smaller regional companies. To do so would have the effect of breaking up the JNR and NTT unions. These unions are the cutting edge of the labor movement throughout Japan. The private-company unions are their satellites. If the JNR and NTT unions are dismembered, then the private-company unions will likewise become more docile.

This strategy intersects the LDP's political strategy of gradually abandoning its rural constituency and cultivating the urban constituency. Notice, for example, that the Agriculture, Forestry, and Fisheries Ministry is *opposed* to raising the rice subsidy this year [1982]. In order to consolidate its power, the LDP is going to try to cultivate the urban workers. There are not many votes in the agricultural sector; moreover, the farmers are rich and have no alternative to voting for the LDP.

On the other hand, there is an inconsistency in the concurrent strategies of cultivating the urban workers and attacking the power of the labor unions. But by weakening the power of the labor unions, employers may be able to replace workers with machines and not worry about the struggle against robotics. The JNR and NTT unions are perfectly aware of this implication of splitting them up, and they strongly resist it.

Big business recently realized that the workers are not as strong as they may seem. This became evident when the spring labor struggles of the past several years were less successful than anticipated. Thus, the present seems a good time to attempt to break their power conclusively.

Breaking up the JNR and NTT unions has the further purpose of destroying strong bulwarks of the Japan Socialist Party, which is the chief adversary of the LDP. In any event, the LDP will remain in power for the indefinite future. This is regrettable because the Socialists, in being excluded from office, are by the same token deprived of the experience of assuming responsibility. Thus, the Socialists have remained doctrinaire and ideological, and this reinforces the impression gained from the economic failures of socialism all over the world, namely, that the Japan Socialist Party has nothing to offer.

Besides being ideological and lacking in responsible experience, the Japan Socialist Party has another handicap in lacking an effective or "charming" leader. Incidentally, it is not true that Japanese are allergic to charismatic leadership. They do not necessarily distrust the eloquent speaker. This legend has been propagated by American "experts" on Japan.

MacArthur's contribution was very great in giving Japan the democratic constitution: This is something that Japan could not have achieved for itself. His motives for doing this are another matter. The result, however, was to give Japan an escape valve for protest. You can protest against the system by voting for the Japan Socialist Party or the Japan Communist Party. But you cannot change the system by your votes. In fact, most of the people who vote for the left-wing parties do so not from ideological conviction but rather for the purpose of scaring the LDP. Inasmuch as protest is unavailing, by providing Japanese society with an escape valve, MacArthur helped to preserve a reactionary system.

Prewar Japan had its ideals. These were not ideals that I accepted. Nevertheless they served the purpose of building the nation. The war destroyed those ideals, and nothing has replaced them. Now there is alienation. Japan has become materialistic and disunited. There is a great generation gap and lack of communication, even within families. There is still respect for status—the status of government officials, for example—but less so. The chief object of respect these days is wealth.

In material things, we are flexible, energetic, adaptable. Underneath, however, we are chauvinistic, conformist, intolerant. The achievements of Japanese management are effective only in the sense that managers try to gain the highest efficiency in *method*. However, they suppress individualist thinking. Individualism has no place in Japan.

The main objective behind administrative reform, then, is simply to break the unions and to give the conservatives a stronger position than they already possess. The rest of the program is window dressing, designed to confuse the issue.

Apart from national politics, there is also a vein of bureaucratic politics in the JNR struggle. Vulnerable bureaucrats are keen on protecting the JNR because it is the first line of attack of the administrative reform program, whereas the bureaucracy is the second line. Thus, if JNR were to remain intact, the secondary line of attack would surely also be immune from reorganization.

Another controversial scenario of administrative reform in terms of "Japan, Disincorporated," is the following, which was offered by a sociologist.

There is a weak sense of grass-roots democracy in Japan. The ordinary person feels that he is powerless to affect the course of events. Control is exclusively in the hands of the powerful elite at the top. However, there are several elites, a premier and a secondary elite, or an insider and an outsider elite. The administrative reform movement is a reflection of competition and conflict between the inside and outside elites.

The Todai Law Faculty graduates are the premier elite. They run the government and they are the top business bureaucrats in key industries. A secondary elite is represented by Keio University. They are secondary in terms of their access to power and the instruments of control. One of the chairmen of the four subcommittees of the Rinchō is a professor from Keio University. Mr. Doko, chairman of the Rinchō, is not a graduate of an insider university. He graduated from the Tokyo University of Technology at a time when it was a school for middle-level technicians and engineers.

Keidanren itself is a curious mixture. On the one hand it is dominated by big business and the key industries within big business. Thus, it has ties with the government bureaucracy. However, it no longer feels itself to be in a tutelary relationship with the government. During the 1960s, it received government subsidies—the price of which was acceptance of government regulations and administrative guidance. Now it has its own capital reserves and does not need government subsidies. Therefore, it no longer acquiesces in regulations and guidance. Moreover, it resists government taxation. Thus, it argues for more efficiency in government. An important means of doing this is to cut off the quasi-governmental corporations that consume taxes and cause deficits in the government budget.

Keio graduates have dominated the business bureaucracy of the textile industry. But graduates of the Todai Law Faculty dominate the old-boy network within the key modern industries and the key ministries. Thus, Keio [graduates] attack the top Todai elite indirectly by means of administrative reform.

Symbolically, it is interesting to see where the various parties sit when they dine together. In former days, when businessmen ate with an official of the Ministry of Finance, the ministry official would always sit in front of the *tokonoma*. Recently, it has been known to happen that the businessman or banker would sit in front of the *tokonoma* even though he was younger than the ministry official.

The External Option

Some members of the Rinchō entertained a concept of its mandate that was different from that perceived by the public. Their concept referred to the twofold concerns of the Japanese government: (a) affairs of state, including foreign relations, military affairs, and police, and (b) regulation of industry, redistribution of income, and other economic functions. Hitherto, the government has concentrated on the second category, with chief emphasis on economic growth. In the view of those who advocate what this author has termed the *external option* (defined below), the first category has been neglected. In particular, Japan's external relations have been passive. The nation's international prerogatives were abdicated in the early postwar period, when Japan pursued an "after you" policy in relation to the United States. Beyond the "low posture" of "friendship with all" and pursuit of "mutual understanding," the Rinchō view affirms that Japan must play a positive role: In politics, in military defense, as well as in economic aid and international development, Japan must take sides.

The program of the external option takes "economic security" as its point of departure.[18] Its immediate operational objective is to steer Japan safely between two paradoxically conflicting trends in the world economy: increasing interdependence among nations, juxtaposed with increasing protectionism. The high level of actual and potential instability in world affairs compounds the difficulty of this task.[19] Pragmatically, and in a purely defensive manner, the Japanese government already had anticipated the rationale of the external option during the 1950s. For example, it sought to overcome excessive dependence on the United States by diversifying export markets and sources of import supply. There was also a systematic effort to reduce foreign trade dependence in general by transforming the structure of industry—traditional labor-intensive and light-industry products were phased out in favor of heavy-industry and chemical-industry products, followed by a shift to the high-technology field. At each stage, the degree of domestic value-added inputs was increased.[20]

In contrast with these inward-looking or defensive measures, the external option approach is probing and on the offensive. Moreover, it contemplates Japan's role in a multilateral rather than a bilateral context. The defensive strategy, for example, attempted to achieve external stability by means of long-term contracts between Japan and its individual trade partners. The new strategy attempts to create a world environment that indirectly as well as directly provides assurance for the future. Examples of the latter include the "national projects" (those too large for any single Japanese firm) and the Global Infrastructure Fund (GIF) proposal of Masaki Nakayama, former president of the Mitsubishi Research Institute.[21] Implementation of such proposals would augment world productive capacity as well as world specialization and complementarity, with accompanying benefit to Japan as manager and supplier.

The interests of Japanese business had become global before the government's abandonment of its defensive strategy in external affairs.[22] In its attempt to overcome "resources nationalism" and protectionism abroad, the private sector had launched a massive program of direct foreign investment. As the government's spokesman for industry, MITI in 1974 promulgated a "vision" of Japan as a headquarters country in charge of a network of basic materials, processing, and assembling industries abroad.[23] This touches the core of the external option strategy, namely, the re-allocation of resources from the domestic to the international sector of the Japanese economy. The concept of the headquarters country in charge of a global hinterland has now been sharpened by virtue of the growing sophistication of Japan's information and software technologies. Furthermore, whereas the government's foreign aid activities have been essentially limited to those that would be of direct benefit to Japanese construction firms and capital goods suppliers, the external option takes a wider view of Japan's self-interest in economic cooperation.[24] At the same time, beyond "dialogue," "economic diplomacy," "mutual understanding," and even "community involvement," the new era has been ushered in by outright lobbying on the part of Japan in foreign capitals.

Beyond "economic security," the external option contemplates "comprehensive national security." This scenario provides not only for a major expansion of Japan's international economic and political role but, more controversially, for an expansion of its military role as well. (The external option implies expansion of the military budget; however, this is not mentioned in the administrative reform proposals proper.) En route to administrative reform, growth in the military budget may be accelerated in an attempt to placate the Americans. As a parallel effort to co-opt American supporters—by giving them a stake in the welfare of the Japanese economy—the government should continue to liberalize capital inflow.

At the administrative level, pursuit of the external option requires augmentation of the resources of the Foreign Ministry. Its personnel and budget are conspicuously smaller than those of other major advanced nations.[25] In addition to increasing its budget and staff, and stationing more Foreign Ministry officials abroad, the Rinchō proposed adding to the cabinet a minister who would have direct access to the prime minister and who would relieve the present minister of foreign affairs of some of his burden. Simply to add another minister, however, would not have been in the spirit of administrative reform. Consequently, it was suggested that the Economic Planning Agency, the Hokkaido and Okinawa development agencies, and the National Land Agency be consolidated. This would have removed one minister from the cabinet and made it possible to include the new minister for foreign affairs with no net addition to the size of the cabinet. The EPA, however, strongly objected to the proposed merger, and the proposal was dropped.[26] An even greater obstacle to the external option, however, is the fact that the re-allocation of resources from Japan's domestic sector to the international sector would not be acceptable to the Socialist members of the Diet. Japan is not like the United States, where the party in office can proceed to implement its program without regard to the wishes of those in opposition. In Japan, it is necessary for the party in office to achieve some degree of consensus with the opposition on matters of fundamental importance.

In any event, within its own establishment, the LDP has taken a strong stand on the transfer of resources from the domestic to the external sector. Under the chairmanship of former Foreign Minister Toshio Kimura, the Committee to Strengthen Japan's Diplomatic Capabilities of the LDP Foreign Affairs Research Council prepared a document (dated 17 June 1982) expressing this position. The author's translation of the document can be found in Appendix A.

Winners and Losers

> We must reform now, because this is an exceptional situation. In the past, Japan received help from abroad. But if the present situation is not remedied, we will be alone and can expect no help from outside. We must anticipate the crisis that will occur if we do not reform now. [Remarks by Toshiwo Doko, chairman of the Provisional Council for the Promotion of Administrative Reform.]

Administrative reform is perhaps innocuously named. Its proposals are by no means mere formalities of administration; they call for political and economic reforms as well.[27] In August 1983, the Economic Council of the Economic Planning Agency submitted an "Outlook and Guidelines for the Economic Society of the 1980s" to Prime Minister Nakasone. The document was endorsed by the cabinet on 12 August 1983. It stated that administrative and fiscal reforms are Japan's "most important tasks" and should receive top priority. How will administrative reform interact with economic liberalization at large in producing winners and losers in Japan's present transition? So far, its chief accomplishments have been moves in the direction of privatizing the three kōshas—the Nippon Telegraph and Telephone Public Corporation (NTT), the Japanese National Railways (JNR), and the Japan Tobacco and Salt Public Corporation.[28] Its "priority" proposals, therefore, are interesting for the difficulties they reveal in Japanese society and the conflicts that emerge in attempts to resolve those difficulties.

There are supporters and opponents of administrative reform among the ministries, in the political parties, and within the private sector. Among the ministries, the chief proponents are the Foreign Ministry and MITI. As noted above with regard to the "external option," in some respects administrative reform is expansionary rather than contractional. The Foreign Ministry would gain from the proposed reinforcement of its diplomatic service and the transfer of resources from the domestic to the external sector. The Foreign Ministry, however, has no domestic support for this shift; its constituency is external, primarily the United States. Because of its concern with private sector international activities, MITI has been a rival of the Foreign Ministry and might share the benefits of a transfer of official resources from the domestic to the external sector. MITI would also gain from the contractional effects of administrative reform because of their relatively sharper incidence on the Ministry of Finance than on itself. Fiscal reconstruction would probably deprive MITI of some of its budget for subsidies.[29] The primary source of MITI's power, however, lies not in its subsidies but rather in its *gyōsei shidō* activities. Despite the termination of its price control, foreign exchange control, and rationing authority since the occupation, MITI continues to play a key role in industrial policy, foreign economic policy, and economic development. These functions give MITI a place in coordinating the struggle among major private corporations, which has taken new forms since the end of the economic miracle.

MITI's rivalry with the Foreign Ministry arises in terms of the overlap between its assigned mission in international trade policy and the economic affairs jurisdiction of the Foreign Ministry.[30] MITI participates (with the Foreign Ministry, the Ministry of Finance, and the Economic Planning Agency) in the committee that determines the allocation of Japan's foreign aid. It also collaborates with private enterprise in identifying foreign projects that are worthy of Japanese government participation. It has been accused of being reluctant to share its foreign-trade information with the Foreign Ministry. In making its choices among projects and countries, MITI has in effect been making foreign economic policy for Japan, often to a degree greater than that of the Foreign Ministry itself. Part of the incentive for the Foreign Ministry to support administrative reform is its rivalry with MITI and its desire to overwhelm MITI's role in the foreign policy field.

A decade ago, it was said that MITI's power would decline because of liberalization and the contraction of its regulatory authority. As direct controls were abolished, however, MITI sought new ways in which to apply guidance and new areas in which to become influential. Evolving from an inquisitor of business, MITI became an ally of business. On the international plane, for example, MITI has extended its assistance to firms in their development of foreign markets. It opposes the Ministry of Agriculture, Forestry, and Fisheries concerning the restriction of agricultural imports (foreign retaliation being directed chiefly against MITI's industrial clients). In a controversy with the Ministry of Posts and Telecommunications, MITI argues that data processing and other functions of NTT should be liberalized. (In this case, liberalization is in MITI's interest because such functions would then fall within the orbit of its own industrial "protection.") Likewise, MITI adopts a partisan attitude toward industries in distress and poses as a protector of small- and medium-size firms. In the 1970s, MITI won friends and influenced people by its prominent role in the antipollution movement. Recently, MITI has adopted an important new approach that may be described as a strategy of "pooling brains." Acting as a "brain secretariat," MITI has organized working groups of academic and industrial experts who collaborate in high technology and other projects. MITI's Industrial Structure Council has numerous subcommittees (to which neutral persons are assigned as chairmen) that investigate promising new topics from MITI's point of view. MITI's energy and initiative in the policy field should stand it in good stead in the era of liberalization.

Being more international minded and more probusiness than other ministries, MITI sees as another favorable interaction effect of liberalization the opportunities for placing its retiring bureaucrats (amakudari) in desirable positions in the private sector. Major corporations seeking pipelines into the bureaucracy welcome amakudari with experience and contacts in MITI. These placements benefit MITI itself as well as the private sector. They are of special benefit in relation to MITI's rivalry with the Ministry of Finance. The constituents of the Ministry of Finance are largely banks, securities companies, and insurance companies. The ministry's amakudari are primarily found among these institutions or in politics, rather than in the industrial sector. The Ministry of Finance alumni in the Diet are financed primarily by MITI's industrial corporate clients.

The Ministry of Finance, however, remains pre-eminent. Before World War II, the two principal ministries were the Ministry of Finance and the Home Ministry (Naimushō). During the occupation, the Home Ministry was abolished, and all other ministries except the Ministry of Finance were "reformed." Thus, the dominance of the Ministry of Finance was enhanced. Many observers, outside as well as inside the Japanese government, believe that the power of the Ministry of Finance is excessive. The most powerful bureau within the ministry is the Budget Bureau. As mentioned above, it is reluctant about administrative reform. Elsewhere in the government, with few exceptions, administrative reform meets further resistance.[31] Among its supporters are some younger members of the bureaucracy, whose confidence in the efficacy of regulation is less fervent than that of their seniors.[32] The younger staff of the Rinchō itself were enthusiastic supporters, as well as the Administrative Management Agency, under whose auspices the Rinchō operated.

Outside the government, administrative reform is widely approved by the general public. It is also supported by younger intellectuals who maintain that firms should be relieved from excessive regulation and that the private sector would gain vitality from fiscal reform. In the aftermath of the economic miracle, the strategy of business enterprise shifted from quantitative goals (expansion of market share) to qualitative goals (improvement of productivity and increase of profits). Business support, especially by Keidanren, for "government reform without tax increases" is in accord with this shift. The growing importance of international profits in the business performance of major firms also conforms with the rationale of the "external option."

Among the political parties, the Democratic Socialist Party is the most supportive of administrative reform. Komeito, the New Liberal Club, and the United Social Democratic Party are also supportive. Within the Liberal Democratic Party, some members support, others oppose, depending on the issue.[33] Only the Japan Socialist Party and the Japan Communist Party openly oppose administrative reform.

Does administrative reform, as well as economic liberalization in general, imply a gain for politicians at the expense of the bureaucracy? Some bureaucrats, especially those of the Foreign Ministry, tend to think so. However, in various respects, their answer to this question is not clear—or if clear, the answer may vary depending on where the observer sits in Kasumigaseki. At the top of the political pyramid, and apart from matters of personality, the Japanese prime minister often appears to be relatively weak and passive as compared with his counterparts elsewhere. His personal office is thinly staffed, including only about 80 members; its lacks the competence to coordinate policy. The LDP, on the other hand, has ample staff. It has been in power since 1955. It knows all that is to be known about the bureaucracy; many of its senior members are former bureaucrats. These factors, together with the help of its Diet members, enable the LDP to take the initiative and play an increasingly larger role. Since the early 1970s, moreover, the clashes of various parties affected by liberalization and internationalization have created a power vacuum into which the politicians have been able to enter. They are able to play upon rivalries and preside over negotiations to accommodate differences among the parties. In providing coordination and reconciliation services, the politicians have increased their ability to determine the outcome of struggles for status and turf.

In the particular matter of solving Japan's present fiscal crisis, however, which is at the core of administrative reform's concerns, the LDP has been accused of failing to provide leadership. Indeed, the actual seat of LDP leadership is itself often in doubt. Partly, perhaps, this may be accounted for by the dissonance between senior LDP politicians, who may take a more national point of view, and junior LDP politicians, who take a more particularistic, local point of view. Partly it may be accounted for by the fact that local interests are rising in importance in relation to interests of the center. Partly it may be accounted for by the fact that characteristically the LDP and its Diet members do not intervene in such prominent aspects of Japan's economic transition as industrial policy or international finance. The lack of LDP leadership on the fiscal issue, however, is egregious in view of the kind of previous experience and practical preparation that Diet members bring to their task. As already observed, the most important retiring members of the Ministry of Finance come 'from its most important bureaus—namely, Budget, Financial, Tax, or Banking—and many of these choose politics or banking as a second career. Because of their Ministry of Finance background, key members of the LDP and of the Diet would appear to be ideally equipped to cope with problems of taxation and budget, the two components of the fiscal crisis. The failure of the Diet to assume leadership in an area in which it possesses enormous expertise may help account for the perception on the part of some that the balance of power between politicians and bureaucrats has not shifted.[34]

In the words of an Expert Member of the Rinchō, the "unholy alliance" against administrative reform includes the principal potential losers: government bureaucrats (in 1981, the Rinchō announced the goal of reducing the number of government employees by five percent during the following five-year period); the trade unions of the public sector (affiliated with Sōhyō)[35]; so-called progressive intellectuals who support Sōhyō and who favor big government (despite, paradoxically, their simultaneous contempt for the government); and the Socialists and the Communists. Apart from the above, in the short run, the general public would be a loser because of the reduction in government services (or introduction of the "beneficiary-pay" principle); in the long run, it would gain. Politicians would lose as a result of the curtailment of public-works expenditure: They receive political contributions from construction companies that are awarded contracts. The income of physicians would be reduced in accordance with plans to reform the medical insurance system. Many small- and medium-size businesses—and the Japan Chamber of Commerce and Industry, which represents them—oppose administrative reform because they favor government spending, which they believe to be in their interest. Education, social security, and agriculture would likewise be losers, as well as the ministries by which they are represented. Among this group, the principal losers would be the Ministry of Transportation; the Ministry of Health and Welfare; the Ministry of Education; the Ministry of Agriculture, Forestry, and Fisheries; the Ministry of Posts and Telecommunications; the Ministry of Construction; and the Ministry of Labor.

The Ministry of Transportation is listed as the chief potential loser from administrative reform because of the plan to privatize the JNR. The proposed curtailment of public corporations in general, however, bodes ill for other ministries as well. Among the chief losers would be the amakudari. Unlike those described above, who as star performers go on after retirement to illustrious second careers in business or politics, the bureaucratic deadwood floats into the public corporations. Some of the key jobs in these corporations are highly desirable.[36] MITI controls 23 public corporations; the Ministry of Finance controls 16. (In some cases, control is exclusive; in others it is shared.) The Administrative Management Agency and the Ministry of Justice are the only major Japanese government agencies that control no public corporations. Of course, if retirement were postponed to age 60, the problem of finding places for the amakudari would be reduced, and the issue concerning public corporations would shrink.[37]

The squeeze on the amakudari reflects the problem of aging in Japan, which in turn is an aspect of the liquidation of the monolithic structure of interests in Japanese society. As shown above, the attack on monolithic interests has been accelerated by the process of economic liberalization. Floating exchange rates (inaugurated in 1973) have divided the interests of protection-minded domestic industries from those of the export industries; the former favor an overvalued yen, while the latter favor the opposite. Small regional banks have a vested interest in the status quo with regard to interest rate controls, while major banks favor liberalization of interest rates and internationalization of the yen. Deregulation has put the securities industry and the banking industry at loggerheads. Agriculture and industry have opposing interests with regard to import liberalization. Labor and management are at odds concerning the concept of Japan as a "headquarters country" and the liberalization of direct investment abroad. The interests of small- and medium-size business are different from those of big business in the fiscal context of administrative reform. The interests of Keidanren are increasingly different from those of the government. The problem of governability increases.

The Japanese economy emerged from its economic miracle into a world of economic and political instability. Externally, exchange rates, interest rates, and debt structures were in volatile disequilibrium. Domestically, the fiscal system was in disarray, the demographic transition was destabilizing, the rate of saving was declining, and the rate of increase in productivity was faltering. These were only a few of the most obvious difficulties. In the midst of adverse indicators, and largely against its inclinations, the government pursued economic liberalization. The present study has been an attempt to describe the policymaking process and the extent of institutional change associated with liberalization. As a nation, Japan has displayed remarkable powers of accomplishing institutional change in response to its historical predicaments. In the 1980s, Japan's predicament concerned the threat of external protectionism to its basic national interest in achieving comprehensive security. In this context, Japanese economic liberalization was a non sequitur. As discussed in the introduction and the final chapter of this study, Japan's institutional response can be logically anticipated.

═ 5 ═

RETROSPECT AND PROSPECT

In attempting to cope with its external dependence, Japan since the reign of Meiji (1867–1912) has gone from one extreme to another. Invariably, however, its strategies have aimed at internationalization, seeking by various means to firmly secure foreign markets and sources of supply. Following the period of *sakoku* (national isolation) in the Tokugawa era (1603–1867), internationalization took the form of territorial conquest. During Showa, the imperialist approach culminated in the Tokyo-Rome-Berlin Axis and the disaster of World War II. To overcome the isolation that followed the war, Japan attempted to internationalize by means of membership in organizations such as the International Monetary Fund, the General Agreement on Tariffs and Trade, and the Organization for Economic Cooperation and Development. But the Japanese government was reluctant to pay the price of such memberships—namely, external economic liberalization, which by linkage implied a threat to the maintenance of domestic controls as well. Hence, Japan entered the club of the "advanced," liberalized nations through the back door, and with reservations. The government's misgivings were magnified when, in the miraculous 1960s, big business became less needy of government favors and more resistant to government controls. Recently, under the pressure of the protectionist tide that is seeping through Europe and America, Japan's task of managing its dependence on the world economy has raised new anxieties.

Reflections on the Study

As shown in this study, the policy of liberalization has been a divisive force in Japan for various reasons. It creates dissonance between cultural norms and institutional arrangements. The entry of foreigners and foreign investment into Japan induces a form of dualism in a traditionally xenophobic society. Liberalization threatens the traditional role of the bureaucracy as leader and planner, a role that was established at the outset of the Meiji Restoration (1868). Liberalization threatens the traditional principle of an assumed identity between national interests and the interests of the firm, or between macro and micro interests. It brings the conflict between Japan's domestic and international policies, as well as between economic and political goals, into the open. It brings inter- and intra-ministerial conflict into the open. It creates conflict between the financial and nonfinancial sectors of the economy. Hence the disruption of consensus and the advent of "Japan, Disincorporated."

There are two schools of thought about how Japan achieved its postwar success. One emphasizes the social and cultural characteristics of the Japanese people; the other emphasizes the institutional arrangements by which Japan allocates and organizes its resources. Of course, both are relevant. Both, moreover, are germane to an explanation of the process of liberalization and the "deliberate speed" with which it has been implemented. Behind both of these explanations, however, lie Japan's basic national interests—survival, independence, continuity, stability, and security—which are unambiguous and which when seen from a Japanese point of view can clarify much that often baffles Western observers. With regard to liberalization, for example, continuity implies incrementalism, the "step-by-step" approach. Stability has both domestic and external objectives, which may or may not be compatible. Security has economic, political, social, and military dimensions that likewise may or may not be compatible. In given circumstances, Japan's actual policy will be determined by a weighting of these various factors.

Japan's national interest in stability has had a dominant effect in shaping its economic institutions. Historically, its confined space and scanty resource endowment gave rise to institutions that were conditioned by poverty. In the interest of achieving social stability, the Japanese economy was managed by a system of "fair shares" within segmented market positions. These positions were established by means of customary relationships and "channels" that all parties observed. In broadly social and cultural terms, the system was dedicated to the proposition of "sharing the poverty" rather than "sharing the wealth." Traditional virtues included the constraint of consumption. The system was characterized by the gemeinschaft nature of group organization and the avoidance of "excessive competition." In the present approach toward liberalization of the banking system, the traditional principle can be seen in the "convoy" policy publicly espoused by the government, which restricts the pace to that of the slowest member. It can be seen in the system of indirect finance and "socialization of risk" that characterized the reconstruction of Japanese industry following World War II. In providing stability of shares, if not of absolute income, the system was also compatible with the maintenance of control by the authorities. The liberalization policy implies destruction of established channels and customary relationships, thus disrupting Japan's "communitarian" economy.[1]

These considerations have provided the context of the present study. It has interpreted the liberalization process in terms of Japan's national interests, in terms of the interaction between cultural and institutional factors in the public and private sectors, and in terms of bureaucratic politics. Despite Japan's genius for institutional innovation, the process of achieving it is not necessarily immune to conflict among vested interests and to disruption of consensus. This study has been especially concerned with the inter- and intra-institutional relationships of the Ministry of Finance and the Bank of Japan, key players in the financial stage of the liberalization process. In the external sector, the liberalization of commodity flows has in general been well advanced. International capital flows and flows of services are the last to be liberalized. Because of financial linkages between the external and domestic sectors, however, the former cannot be liberalized without liberalizing domestic money and capital markets as well. Altogether, therefore, financial liberalization threatens to invade the ultimate stronghold of authority of the Ministry of Finance.[2] One of the arguments raised by the Ministry of Finance concerning liberalization of external capital flows is that liberalization should occur in domestic markets first. This is another way of saying that the entire process should be deferred. From the institutional point of view, moreover, the ministry is averse to losing power in relation to MITI, whose important prerogatives in the field of industrial policy would be unimpaired by financial liberalization.

While the Ministry of Finance always justifies its decisions in terms of the national interest, the form and timing of those decisions are determined largely by its own interests. The more directly an essential national interest is affected by a policy decision, the more justification the ministry can muster for deliberate and prolonged incremental change. As a complex policy matter, the objective merits of economic liberalization can be seen from various points of view. It is interesting that in the frank and confidential interviews that provided much of the basic material of this book, a respondent would typically evaluate the objective merits of any question in ways compatible with the interests of the section of which he was a member. One result of the study is the demonstration that with regard to liberalization, there are as many points of view in Japan as can be found among interested observers anywhere. Differences refer even to the policy interpretation of narrow technical matters. This illustrates the observation that whatever may be said about Japan, the opposite may also be true.

Instability: The Central Predicament

Beyond cultural and institutional reasons for the laggard pace of liberalization, the Japanese case for delay also rests upon other difficulties both at home and abroad. Overshadowing all, perhaps, is the paradox of a world in which nationalism and protectionism are growing side by side with the deepening of interdependence among nations. While Japan has embarked upon liberalization, its major trade partners have been restricting its access to their markets. It is evidently true that despite the rise of protectionism, Japan has some "catching up" to do before it reaches the level of liberalization that still prevails elsewhere. Nevertheless, the inconsistent trends at home and abroad are ominous. From a Japanese point of view, instability arises chiefly from foreign rather than from domestic sources, and the government maintains that its need to resist the external threat to Japan's national interests requires discretion in the abandonment of controls.

In the first half of the 1980s, external sources of instability were numerous. Most nations were in monetary and fiscal disarray. Their budgets were in deficit and their price structures were inflated. The debt crisis of the developing nations was acute. Both interest rates and foreign-exchange rates were misaligned and their fluctuations were erratic. World commodity and energy prices were unstable. A high degree of uncertainty and risk prevailed in international markets as well as trade-policy friction between Japan and most other governments. Japan's international economic relations, moreover, were highly politicized, which made it increasingly difficult to appraise the purely economic component of its external difficulties. As Japan's international role increased, external economic-political-military interactions became potentially more disruptive.

In both domestic and foreign markets, the increasing competition of newly industrializing countries was a destabilizing factor. Japan's dependence on a relatively narrow range of key export products, in which exports were a high proportion of output, was also potentially destabilizing. The shift in the structure of trade from consumer goods to producer goods, moreover, increased the income elasticity of demand for Japan's exports, which increased its variability over the business cycle.

The services sector of Japan's balance of payments has been markedly unstable and in deficit. In the capital account, the potentially destabilizing effect of Euroyen transactions is of great concern. In recent years, sharp fluctuations have occurred in the trade account and in the current account. For example, the current-account surplus of $16.5 billion in fiscal year 1978 was followed by a current-account deficit of $8.8 billion in fiscal year 1979 and a deficit of $10.7 billion the following year. In the overall balance of payments, the deficit of $5.0 billion in 1982 was followed by a surplus of $5.2 billion in 1983.

In the early 1980s, there were indigenous sources of instability as well. An important structural problem was the aging of the population, which implied an impending burden of fiscal adjustment and institutional change. Social security expenditures were already contributing to inordinate budgetary deficits, which in turn reduced the flexibility of the government's macroeconomic instruments. The decline in the growth rate after the 1960s has made economic adjustments of all kinds more difficult to accomplish. The savings ratio, while still high, has been declining. The increasing complexity of economic adjustment lengthens the amount of lead time required in the decisionmaking process; accordingly, it increases the amount of uncertainty and risk in decisionmaking as well. The preposterous price of land—a legacy of the inflation of the 1970s—contributes to economic imbalance. A deterioration has occurred in the capital structure of small- and medium-size firms that have attempted to survive by modernizing their equipment. Fluctuations in inventory cycles are accelerated because, apart from opportunity cost considerations, there is a greater reluctance to hold inventory by means of borrowed funds than with self-supplied capital.

Underlying these directly economic problems were social and cultural developments such as the decline of the extended family, the rise in crime and delinquency, protest movements, and the like, which in various ways reflected conflict and the shrinkage of consensus. These destabilizing trends compound the problem of "governability" in Japan. Combined with external sources of instability, they constitute a national predicament to which foreigners are largely oblivious.

Liberalization and Deliberalization: The Unfinished Agenda

Given the circumstances mentioned above, it is timely to review the annual changes in Japan's capital markets in recent years and to identify the residual controls still maintained by the Ministry of Finance. In what sequence have controls been lifted, and to what extent? In which matters is the ministry most reluctant to yield? A chronology of liberalization and deliberalization compiled by the author and by the Japan Economic Institute is to be found in Appendix B.[3]

Classified by type, the measures listed in the chronology fall into three categories. One type refers to widening the limits of permissible financial action to Japanese residents. A second type refers to authorization of new financial markets and financial instruments. A third type refers to providing foreigners with greater access to Japanese financial markets. United States pressure on Japan has been exerted largely in behalf of market innovation rather than access, the former being calculated to yield quicker liberalization benefits from an American point of view. Some other steps in the liberalization process, moreover, are hardly voluntary. For example, deregulation of interest rates is essential in order to refund the enormous volume of national bonds maturing in 1985 and thereafter. (In March 1984, the outstanding total of long-term national government bonds amounted to the equivalent of approximately $500 billion, about one-half the GNP.) Interest rate deregulation, in turn, implies deregulation and integration of financial markets as well. Before Japanese fiscal year 1984 (beginning April 1984), the most important liberalizing measures included the removal in 1979 of restrictions on bank participation in the gensaki market, the establishment of a market for bank CDs in 1979, and the lifting of controls from 1978 to 1981 on the operation of the interbank money markets.

The strength of vested interests in the old order, however, is reflected in the restrictions still maintained at the outset of Japanese fiscal year 1984. The following six categories of restrictions were compiled by the Japan Economic Institute:[4]

1. The "real demand" rule prohibited forward exchange market hedging that was not related to a merchandise or service-trade transaction. [This was dropped during 1984.]

2. Payment of interest on nonresident accounts could be restricted if necessary to prevent drastic fluctuations in the exchange rate (a provision that as yet had not been used).

3. MITI approval was required on contracts calling for import prepayments more than one year before customs clearance, or exports to be paid for more than one year after shipment.

4. For purposes of monitoring and controlling capital transactions, the Ministry of Finance (or the Bank of Japan as its agent) required prior notification followed by specified waiting periods concerning the following, to provide time for studying the proposed action and time to forbid it:

   a. Acquisition of shares of unlisted companies.

   b. Acquisition of 10 percent or more of the shares of a listed company by a single foreign investor.

   c. Acquisition of loans with a maturity of more than one year or securities privately placed in Japan.

   d. Changes in the business objectives of a company with more than one-third foreign ownership.

   e. Acquisition of securities other than through designated securities companies.

   f. Issues of securities overseas by Japanese enterprises.

   g. Acquisition of real estate in Japan by nonresidents.

   h. Foreign investment by residents in the form of loans; usance exceeding one year; issuance of yen-dominated bonds by nonresidents in Japan; direct investment abroad.

5. In addition to notification requirements, the following transactions required actual government approval in advance:

   a. Foreign-currency deposits overseas by residents; borrowing and lending in foreign currency between residents.

   b. Issuance of Euroyen bonds by nonresidents.

6. Controls were in effect concerning the following types of actions:

   a. The overall net position of foreign-exchange banks in foreign currencies (with reference to their oversold or overbought position).

   b. Establishment of new branches by Japanese banks abroad.

   c. Eligibility of foreign issuers of yen-dominated bonds in Japan.

   d. Investment by foreigners in ten specified companies (total foreign ownership limits being restricted to a maximum of between 25 and 50 percent).

The restrictions are evidence that as of April 1984, privileges accorded to Japanese financial and nonfinancial firms in the United

States were not reciprocated to U.S. companies in Japan. An American company could not raise money in Japan for use outside of Japan either by borrowing from banks or by issuing bonds. The banking authorities enforced a large number of minor regulations that prevented American banks in Japan from utilizing their full competitive capacities. Moreover, there were many unpublished guidelines to which all banks were expected to conform. Establishment of an international banking facility, or offshore banking market, had no imminent prospect of being authorized. A market for yen-denominated bankers acceptances had not been authorized. Permission for American banks to join with Japanese securities companies in the trust banking business had not been granted.[5]

Before fiscal year 1984, all banks in Japan were subject to swap quotas on the amount of foreign currency they could convert into yen. These quotas were an inconvenience chiefly to latecomer foreign banks in Japan; long-established foreign banks had largely managed to overcome the problem. The "swap" limits were to have been removed in fiscal year 1984. Another restriction concerned the 190 foreign-exchange banks in Japan. Although licensed to deal in foreign exchange with the public, they could not engage in direct foreign-exchange transactions with one another. All such transactions had to be performed through one of Japan's ten licensed foreign-exchange brokers as an intermediary. In the securities field, as in banking, theory and practice frequently diverged. For example, although the Tokyo Stock Exchange revised its articles in April 1982 to permit membership by non-Japanese securities companies, in practice no such membership had occurred or was in prospect due to the limit on membership to 83 companies and to the unlikelihood that a vacancy would occur. Any attempt by a foreign firm to obtain membership by taking over a Japanese firm had been strenuously opposed by the Japanese securities industry. Foreign investment banks and securities houses faced a further difficulty in attempting to obtain permission to upgrade their representative offices in Japan to the status of full securities branches.[6] Among other restrictions in the services sector, narrow limits were placed on foreign lawyers who wished to practice in Japan. There were similar limits on foreign activities in the fields of marketing, information, and communications.

As of April 1984, although secondary-market transactions in treasury bills were becoming active, there still existed no new issues market for TBs. The minimum denomination permitted for negotiable yen CDs was ¥ 300 million ($1.34 million). The minimum authorized size of an overseas CD transaction was likewise ¥ 300 million. Dollar CDs were about to be authorized. Trading in foreign commercial paper was restricted to transactions of at least ¥ 200 million ($890,000) in size. As of October 1984, three foreign banks were permitted to begin dealing in Japanese government bonds over the counter and to bid on new issues of medium-term government bonds. It was presumed that those banks would subsequently be allowed to buy or sell previously issued government bonds. The minimum size regulations with regard to "liberalized" transactions served several purposes. First, it was in accord with the "step-by-step" regimen that enabled the authorities to feel their way in making an innovation. Second, it reduced the immediate impact of liberalization on vested interests that faced an impending loss of exclusive privileges. Third, and perhaps most important, it was conducive to economic concentration by implicitly restricting the number of firms that could participate in the liberalized activity. The initially eligible firms were always the largest and already the most favored of all firms in their respective fields. (A rationale for the government's deliberate encouragement of economic concentration is suggested below.)

A typical example of favoritism to large companies occurred in the course of liberalizing the issuance of Euroyen bonds. These are unsecured yen-denominated bonds issued by Japanese firms to tap the pool of yen funds abroad. The yen proceeds of such bonds are held largely by Japanese banks abroad, thus being indirectly subject to Ministry of Finance control.[7] Euroyen bond issuance, inaugurated on 1 April 1984, was subject to highly restrictive guidelines that permitted only 30 Japanese companies to issue straight Euroyen bonds and about 100 others to issue convertible Euroyen bonds.[8]

Because of administrative guidance, which by definition lacks "transparency," many of the restrictions imposed upon Japan's financial industry are not public information. Some come to the surface in the course of U.S.-Japan controversies about financial liberalization. Administrative guidance has wide scope and is often inherently ambiguous. Sometimes it is given explicitly in the form of a bulletin or notice to banks; sometimes it is given verbally or merely implicitly. In substance, it may cover such matters as deposits, lending, funding, or accounting methods. For example, banks have been "guided" to suppress loans for the purpose of financing acquisition of land; to suppress loans to *sarakin* ("salary-loan") companies; to observe guidelines with regard to compensating balances (compulsory deposits maintained by borrowing clients); and to observe guidelines with regard to minimum spreads on long-term impact loans. An ambiguous situation exists concerning requirements of the Temporary Interest Rate Adjustment

Law, in accordance with which interest rate ceilings are imposed on both Japanese banks and foreign banks for all loans and deposits in yen. There is no legal interest rate ceiling on foreign currency loans or on yen loans with a maturity of more than one year. In fact, however, if either Japanese banks or foreign banks charge undue or "out-of-market" interest rates, they are very likely to receive strong guidance or a reprimand from the monetary authorities. Administrative guidance to Japanese banks is more direct and comprehensive than that to foreign banks because of the wider scope and greater volume of their transactions. Foreign banks receive guidance when they visit the Ministry of Finance or the Bank of Japan for consultation about specific transactions, as well as on other occasions.

In presenting its case for liberalization of Japanese financial markets and internationalization of the yen, the United States argues in terms of increasing the relative attractiveness of yen-denominated assets. If such assets were more attractive, of course, the yen would rise in value, and the competitive position of U.S. exports would improve. Liberalization of Japan's domestic financial markets is the key to making yen assets more attractive. It is also the means by which U.S. financial institutions could find new competitive opportunities in Japan. Even in the absence of direct financial controls, however, foreign outsiders would remain at a disadvantage in relation to Japanese insiders because of the latter's access to information concerning administrative decisions that influence interest rates and exchange rates.

At any event, in 1984, U.S. banks were using their scarce political capital in Japan to urge the adoption of various measures to enhance the role of market forces in Japan's domestic financial system, especially with regard to short-term financial instruments. It is interesting to note the rank order of their priorities as specified in a memorandum prepared following discussions of five major U.S. banks and transmitted in February 1984 to Beryl W. Sprinkel, under secretary for monetary affairs, U.S. Department of the Treasury, for his use in negotiating with his Japanese counterpart. As a first priority, it was the consensus of the banks that a treasury bill market should be established in Japan, with participation not limited to resident financial institutions and prices freely determined by market forces. The banks stated their belief that a relatively "deep and free" market in treasury bills would accelerate financial market liberalization more effectively than establishment of a yen-denominated bankers acceptance market, although the latter would be desirable as well. Second, it was urged that the primary issue of government securities should be by auction rather than by allocation, and that foreign banks should be allowed to underwrite such issues. Third, it was argued that "window guidance" imposed upon the allegedly free call-money market should be eliminated. Such guidance was transmitted by means of the brokers (tanshi) who performed transactions ordered by the banks. In the procedure of generating funds in the interbank market, abolition was also urged of the current practice of requiring promissory notes to be backed by collateral. Fourth, it was urged that controls over the minimum size, maturity, and total volume of various financial instruments be substantially liberalized. It was argued that the steps already taken to reduce the minimum size and maximum issue of bank CDs were not particularly meaningful. Fifth, it was argued that banks should be allowed to price loans on bases other than the formulas for Japanese short-term or long-term prime. Sixth, it was proposed that a financial futures and options market be developed in Japan for national bonds, local money-market instruments, and foreign exchange instruments. Seventh—a proposal that would incur relatively severe political opposition in Japan—the U.S. banks urged that all banks and securities companies be allowed to perform trust activities. Finally, it was advocated that regulations concerning purchase of membership in the Tokyo Stock Exchange be relaxed. It was also observed that the price of membership, approximately $5 million, was designed to exclude new entrants even if an opening should occur.

The memorandum further remarked that rules and regulations prevailing at the outset of 1984 unfairly discriminated against foreign banks in Japan. In this context, it was argued that foreign banks should be allowed to borrow from the Bank of Japan at the official discount rate, using government securities as collateral. Second, it was argued that foreign banks should pay the same bond-transfer tax as Japanese syndicate members. Third, it was maintained that foreign banks should be allowed to become members of the Tokyo yen-clearing house.

Apart from actions to enhance the role of market forces, a second main category of issues concerned actions to encourage international capital mobility. Of particular importance was the prospective elimination of the "real demand" rule governing forward foreign-exchange transactions. When implemented, this would allow cross-currency hedging and currency and interest swaps. The easing of guidelines on the issuance of Euroyen bonds by Japanese residents had already had the effect of allowing swaps of yen-denominated bonds issued by residents for foreign-currency denominated bonds issued by nonresidents. The priority list with regard to eliminating remaining barriers to international capital mobility was headed by the demand for establishment of an offshore banking facility in Tokyo. Second, limitations on yen-dollar swaps by banks should be eliminated. Third, it was urged that Japanese residents should be allowed to participate in financial futures markets outside Japan. Fourth, nonresident investors should be allowed to purchase all yen-denominated financial instruments without limitations. Fifth, the rules limiting nonresident purchases of the equity of Japanese companies to a maximum of 25 percent (in "unrestricted" industries) should be relaxed to permit majority ownership. Sixth, the remaining limitations on resident purchases of foreign financial instruments should be eliminated.

These measures advocated by the five major U.S. banks would be insufficient to resolve the yen-dollar problem in the absence of harmonization of U.S. and Japanese monetary policies. Such harmonization, moreover, could be achieved only if monetary and fiscal policies in the United States itself were harmonized beforehand. The prevailing conflict between monetary and nonmonetary forces in the U.S. economy makes the early achievement of such harmony extremely unlikely.

A Scenario

As shown above, Japan's liberalization progress is very uneven in various commodity and services categories and in the domestic and external economic sectors. The government is obviously ambivalent in responding to foreign demands that its policies conform to Western textbook principles of a market system. Is the government's spotty performance consistent with its primary mission of internationalizing the Japanese economy?

Although Japan responds to the circumstances of its environment, as does any other nation or individual, this is not to say that it is merely "reactive" in a passive sense. On the contrary, Japan's previous and prospective response to prevailing world trends may be interpreted as showing enormous initiative and innovative capacity. The present scenario begins with the stagflation among the advanced industrial nations in the first half of the 1980s. In 1983, the foreign trade of the industrial countries declined for the third consecutive year.[9] In the future, Japan will no longer be able to overcome its domestic recessions by means of supply-oriented exports.[10]

As described in a previous chapter, more and more industries in Japan are being forced to accept "voluntary" export restraints. The restrictions cover a wide array of products, including automobiles, motorcyles, machine tools, quartz watches, forklifts, television sets, stereo equipment, and video tape recorders.[11] The export quotas distributed by MITI to producers of these products constitute a set of implicit cartel assignments. MITI has also been a party to the cartelization of the world steel industry. In October 1983, the U.S. Trade Representative's Office announced that it had secured arrangements with seven specialty steel-exporting companies, including Japan, that entitled them to assigned shares of total U.S. imports of alloy tool steel and stainless rods and bars. Japan received specific tonnage quotas on a quarterly basis through July 1987.

Neo-cartelism may be defined as cartelism in which governments play an operational role and in which private oligopolies implicitly approximate cartel behavior. It reinforces "new protectionism" and "organized free trade." The scope of neo-cartelist activities may be surmised from an estimate that as of February 1983, at least 30 percent of world trade was "managed."[12] In October 1980, for example, the European Economic Community (EEC) adopted the Davignon Plan for cartelization of steel producers within the EEC. In January 1984, the life of the cartel was extended until the end of 1985. The plan imposed compulsory production quotas, mandatory minimum prices (since January 1984), and import quotas. In October 1982, the EEC adopted quotas on exports of steel to the United States, to be effective until December 1985.

Such cartels are altogether familiar in Japan and are consistent with its cartel tradition. They are also consistent with the interests of the major groups in the business community because they reinforce and perpetuate the dominant positions of the leading firms. They are congenial likewise to the government authorities, especially MITI, whose role is enhanced by the augmentation of its guidance prerogatives and by its participation with foreign governments in establishing and allocating quotas and prices for production and exports. Thus, MITI, which prospered by presiding over Japan's export-promotion drives in the 1960s, is now a beneficiary of the restrictionist policies imposed upon Japan by the new protectionism abroad. MITI's principal prospective role, accordingly, will be to formulate and implement Japan's industrial policy not only at home but also on the international plane. In seizing its new role, MITI will aspire to gain stature in relation to, and possibly at the expense of, the Ministry of Finance.

A well-known Japanese economist told the author, "I am more or less informed about the real liberalization story, but I am not free to talk about it." It may be speculated that MITI's contemplated role is foreshadowed in the vague phrases—such as "international industrial adjustment" and "comprehensive economic security"—recently coined and publicized in terms of its "visions" of the future.[13] Clearly, these phrases must be defined in the context of international realities. These include the oil crisis, rising competition from newly industrializing countries, and the revolution in information technology and other high-technology sectors. The new industries foster infant industry protectionism, which complements the protection of declining industries, such as the manufacturers of automobiles, ships, and steel, in the advanced nations. Protectionism promotes defensive foreign investment, designed to circumvent external trade barriers. It promotes international tie-ups, mergers, and globalization of enterprise. It promotes economic concentration and market sharing. Economic concentration, furthermore, is implicit in the nature of high technology, such as sophisticated electronic telecommunications systems, which incur enormous development costs. In Japan, where "scale optimism" has always been an article of faith, this comes as no surprise. In practice, moreover, according to studies of the Fair Trade Commission, it has been shown that due to mergers and bankruptcies in declining industries, economic concentration in Japan increases during periods of slackened growth. The same phenomenon has been observed in other industrial countries.

In support of the economic-concentration movement, Keidanren has strongly urged the government to relax the Anti-Monopoly Law.[14] (A parallel movement in favor of relaxation of the antitrust laws in the United States received considerable attention during the early 1980s.) In April 1983, the Temporary Measures Law for Structural Adjustment of Specific Industries ("Industrial Structure Law") was enacted by the Japanese Diet, becoming effective in May 1984. The law revised, extended, and strengthened the Law on Extraordinary Measures for Specific Depressed Industries ("Specific Depressed Industries Law"), which expired in June 1983. With regard to specific depressed industries (electric furnace steel making, aluminum smelting, chemical fiber, chemical fertilizer, ferro-alloys, paper and paperboard, petrochemicals, and other industries to be designated by government ordinance), the Industrial Structure Law provided for the following steps, which fall into two categories: (1) disposal of excess capacity; prohibiting or restricting the construction or remodeling of facilities; (2) arrangement for business tie-ups (by means of joint production, sales, purchasing, etc.); arrangements for restriction of production of special items; grouping of businesses, including mergers and transfers of business. Measures in the first category, subject to agreement by the Fair Trade Commission, were authorized as exceptions to the provisions of the Anti-Monopoly Law. Measures in the second category, while not authorized as exempt from the Anti-Monopoly Law, were permissible with the concurrence of the FTC. Thus, in effect, if not in name, the Industrial Structure Law maintains the tradition of the "anti-depression" cartel in postwar Japan.

Apart from MITI's administrative guidance concerning production quotas, pricing policies, and the establishment of sales "channels," concerted business behavior has recently escalated to a new level through collaboration among the chief industrial groups in the Japanese economy. Six major groups dominate the economy, including three zaibatsu successors (Mitsubishi, Mitsui, and Sumitomo) and three bank-oriented groups that emerged after World War II (Fuyō, Dai-Ichi Kangyo, and Sanwa). Because of the need to pool technological and financial resources in the development of frontier industries, there has been a breakdown of the boundaries among these major groups. Numerous important examples of collaborative projects that cross group lines have recently been reported.[15] Intergroup collaboration has profound implications for the future of economic concentration and neo-cartelism in Japan. The latter, as defined above, is implicit rather than explicit cartelism, and it is characterized by international as well as national economic concentration in which oligopolies, usually with government collaboration, perform effectively as cartels.

Ideologically, MITI's readiness to play a role in neo-cartelist "voluntary" export restrictions has been long in the making. In an ironic sense that is not apparent to Japan's trade partners, these arrangements are indeed voluntary. Since the 1960s, the concept of "agreed specialization" has been publicly advocated by various authorities in Japan. The purpose of agreed specialization is to contract the vertical structure of world trade, especially between Japan and developing countries, in which the latter have been confined largely to a primary product role while Japan has attempted to sustain a complete set of "self-contained" modern industries.[16] Its further purpose is to achieve an agreed international dispersal of productive activities within the manufacturing sector in such a way as to create a network under Japanese management. The author's earliest acquaintance with this concept came in an interview on 3 August 1964 with Hiroshi Hiyama, former president of the Marubeni Company, in which he said, "Ultimately, there will be an arranged division of labor among the advanced countries in terms of categories of products." On the academic level, Professor Kiyoshi Kojima wrote an essay entitled "An Approach to Integration: The Gains from Agreed Specialization."[17] When Yoshizo Ikeda became president of Mitsui & Co. in the spring of 1973, he was described as "an enthusiastic proponent of 'international division of labor by mutual agreement.'"[18] Operationally, Japan is already deeply committed to this way of thinking because of the high ratio of exports to output in many of its key export products.

It is noteworthy, however, that the international joint ventures, shared production and marketing enterprises, pooling of research and development ideas, and other forms of business association into which Japan has entered in recent years refer primarily to what may be described as the declining industries of Japan's heavy-industry and chemical-industry sector. The 1984 Toyota–General Motors joint venture to launch a small-car production operation in California is a typical example. In the high-technology and services sectors, there has been no agreed division of labor or assignment of specialties between Japan and its trade partners. On the contrary, Japan's high-technology protectionism (as in the case of Nippon Telegraph and Telephone) has been one of the most prominent sources of friction between Japan and the United States. The liberalization process has been highly selective. Japan's aspirations in the information and communications field, and in financial, insurance, and other services, have not been curtailed for the sake of international division of labor.[19]

An explanation of this discrepancy may lie in a three-phase scenario described in the Introduction, of which liberalization constitutes phase two. Clearly, as Japanese authorities are fully aware, Japan's liberalization program is inconsistent with major prevailing trends in the world economy. But they are not pursuing liberalization out of philanthropic motives concerning world welfare. Indeed, the liberalization upon which Japan is embarked is not of the textbook type that envisages a universe of atomistic firms, practicing free competition in markets where entry is open. Instead, liberalization will be contrived to generate a high degree of economic concentration. By means of selective liberalization, Japan's domestic secondary industries will be exposed to foreign competition, ostensibly in support of a multilateral, nondiscriminatory, free-trade system in the world economy. In the sectors where it is allowed, however, liberalization will be the means by which minor firms will be merged or bankrupted. Minor banks will be exposed selectively to domestic rather than foreign competition, and they too will be either merged or extinguished. (This scenario for domestic liberalization, followed by domestic economic concentration, helps to explain the argument of the Ministry of Finance that financial liberalization must occur at home before being allowed in the external sector: Small- and medium-size banks must be assimilated by major domestic banks before they become prey to foreign banks.) As the financial partner of big business, Japanese banking in the future will be dominated by a handful of institutions that will be able to offer a complete range of services worldwide. The rationale for huge size includes not only economies of scale (where obtainable) but also the benefits of raw business power in the international arena. By presenting liberalization as something that has been forced on Japan by outside pressure, Japanese authorities can escape censure for permitting the extinction of small- and medium-size enterprises, which is essential for the fulfillment of their own objectives.

Thus, the transition to phase three includes both economic concentration at home and direct investment abroad. Cheered on by the new protectionism of the United States and Western Europe, and solemnly carrying the banner of "economic cooperation" with developing countries, the neo-cartelists will transfer much of Japan's smokestack industry elsewhere. Their announced purpose will be to advance "horizontal division of labor" in the world economy. Horizontal division of labor, however, will be an intermediate step toward creation of a new vertical relationship between headquarters and plant in which those foreign investments will be coordinated and integrated as parts of a world network controlled by Japan. Formation of this network will be facilitated by the desire of many middle advanced countries, as in Latin America, to diversify their international relations away from overdependence on the United States.

The debt crisis of the developing countries provides another motive for their collaboration in the Japanese scenario. It will be noticed, incidentally, that in the art of combining export credits and grants with export sales to developing countries, and using technological transfers as bait for the tender of joint-venture investment opportunities in those countries, Japan has few if any peers. It will be noticed further, however, that in preparation for things to come, Japan has been chary—to the expressed displeasure of countries such as India and South Korea—of transferring technology or know-how of a sophisticated kind to newly industrializing countries. In general, advanced Japanese technical information is proprietary and thus not in the public domain. (This may partly explain how Japan acquired its undeserved reputation for lacking creative talent in science.)

Operationally, then, liberalization promotes economic concentration, which promotes cartelization (explicit or implicit), giving rise in turn to an international network. In this scenario, the logics of the technological imperative (economies of scale), of industrial evolution (toward tertiary-sector development), and of the bureaucratic propensity (toward engrossment of controls), combine to generate the concept of Japan as a headquarters country. The headquarters manipulates a world network of primary and secondary activities by means of information, finance, and other high-technology services. In the culminating stage, MITI becomes a coordinator of Japan's international cartel arrangements. It serves as a partner with Japanese business and banking in negotiations with foreign governments. "Japan, Incorporated"—or rather, "Japan, Reincorporated"—emerges. And again the term is validly descriptive in the sequel to the "disincorporation" of the liberalization phase. The domestic administrative reorganization implied in the course of Japan's progress toward becoming a headquarters country suggests promising possibilities for administrative reform. It is easier to achieve reform by reallocating resources during growth than by making cutbacks in a steady state.

The scenario suggested here is consistent with the traditional oligopolistic propensity of Japanese society. Traditionally, the convenience of the ministerial oligopolies has been well served by collaboration with private oligopolies, such as the zaibatsu, through which orders could be efficiently conveyed and imposed upon the private sector as a whole. Administrative guidance is most effective in an economy of the few. In the culminating stage of the scenario, controls would be primarily administrative rather than legal, thus sidestepping the legal formalities of liberalization, and providing another typical example of the separation between appearance and reality in Japan. The scenario would be fulfilled when liberalization in Japan has achieved its own demise. At that point, Japan would be in a position to internationalize by other means.

In the meantime, Japan is in turmoil. It is engaged in a race against time to put the foundations of its strategy in place before rising external opposition smothers its emergence as a headquarters country.

APPENDIX A

Committee to Strengthen Japan's
Diplomatic Capabilities
LDP Foreign Affairs Research Council
17 June 1982

A DECLARATION RELATING TO
STRENGTHENING OUR DIPLOMATIC SYSTEM

Part 1. Our Basic Posture

Our country, which has reached an economic scale which places it number two in the free world, must fulfill an international role suitable to that position.

We anticipate that all the countries of the world will also make contributions according to their powers [in accordance with their abilities] through economic, cultural, scientific technological, etc., cooperation and other kinds of cooperation with Japan, and that as a result monetary responsibilities and contributions towards international agencies, etc., and sharing of responsibilities in the international community will increase. The political role that Japan should play in the complicated and multivaried international society is rapidly enlarging in scope. Nevertheless, Japan's diplomatic system has not gone outside the framework that was established during the occupation. In a comparison with the levels of 1931, even though every other ministry has increased its number of personnel four to five times, the Ministry of Foreign Affairs has not increased any more than a mere 400 employees, going from 2,300 people to 3,632 [at the present time]. Of course it is necessary to continue our efforts in the administrative reform program to make an effective small government in order to put our money into financial recovery. The problem is in the contents of the administrative reform. We won't be able to meet the demands of the times with the kind of indiscriminate reduction of public officials seen in the past. This time we have got to put our efforts into placing our personnel into the proper positions and creating a functional government through a bold process of scrap and build. Article 73 of the Japanese Constitution set up a new item called "Handling of Diplomatic Relations" with respect to duties and jurisdiction of the cabinet, and by doing so distinguished it from other administrative departments. This is proof that the constitution places importance on diplomacy in particular within the duties and jurisdictions of the cabinet. This must be kept in mind as one of our principles today, when our country, as "Japan in the World," holds a position of importance in international society.

When we take a direct look at the reality from a concerned point of view, the public's eye is in agreement with the fact that Japan's present diplomacy is by no means strong [or outgoing] [healthy or robust], and it is necessary to put together a strong, robust diplomatic system as quickly as possible. This committee will investigate from all angles what it should do in order to strengthen the diplomatic system and herein puts forth this [our] declaration.

Part 2. Establishing a Comprehensive Diplomatic Function (Centralization of Diplomacy)

(1) We are at the present time at the threshold of the age of international politics, and are now in the age of summit diplomacy. While we keep a sharp eye on domestic developments, it is therefore extremely necessary to thoroughly analyze and evaluate the world situation and possess the strategic type of coping ability. In order to do this it is necessary to establish a strong comprehensive diplomatic function to cope with this [the world situation]. The Ministry of Foreign Affairs should indeed be the strongest and most comprehensive government office in handling this. We have got to have the backbone [self-respect, spirit] that will completely transform [change over to] an ability, a function, and a structure for this purpose in order to be prepared for the demands of the age. Again, in order to do this, we should assign someone to the minister of foreign affairs who has the rank or the qualifications of vice prime minister. As someone who has been assigned the responsibility of long-term diplomacy, this person would instigate the holding of meetings of the cabinet ministers related to diplomacy. These meetings would include only a small number of ministers, including the minister of foreign affairs himself, and would be held under the leadership of the prime minister, and with agility would cope with external problems based on high-level decisions. Additionally we will establish [set up] a *minister* in charge of external matters or a government *representative* in charge of foreign economic matters [emphasis added]. And together with striving for their positive [active, affirmative] application, it is necessary to increase by one the number of employees in the General Affairs Division of the Ministry of Foreign Affairs Secretariat, and station him permanently in the prime minister's official residence and assign him to liaison between the prime minister and the minister of foreign affairs.

(2) The present age is one in which diplomatic problems are always intimately linked to economic problems. Therefore, there has to be stronger teamwork between the Ministry of Foreign Affairs and the other ministries. In order to do this, we think that we should set up a [provisionally named] Department for General Government Affairs within the Ministry of Foreign Affairs, and make adjustments among the various ministries and agencies. In other words, we should establish ahead of time a system of adjustments among the ministries and agencies.

Part 3. Strengthening the Implementive Function of Diplomacy

(1) Organizational Reform

(i) One of the big criticisms with respect to the Ministry of Foreign Affairs is that there is a very obvious sectionalism in both the geographical departments and the functional departments. This has become at the same time a deficiency in the ability to investigate diplomatic problems from the medium- to long-term point of view and horizontally among the departments because each of the departments is swamped with its daily work. In order to resolve the related problems, we will set up the provisionally named Department for General Government Affairs within the Ministry of Foreign Affairs, to be in charge of overall planning and adjustments.

(ii) In order for Japan, which does not have military powers, to survive strongly in international society, great expansive leaps in economic cooperation are indispensable, and are, moreover, an international responsibility that has come to us by virtue of our being a great economic nation. In order to meet this demand [of the times] we should upgrade the present Economic Cooperation Bureau to being the International Cooperation Bureau and strive to unify both economic and cultural aspects by putting under that umbrella [of the bureau] both an Economic Cooperation Department and a Cultural Cooperation Department.

(2) Reform of Personnel and Appointment Systems

Not only organizational reforms but raising the quality of diplomatic services [the diplomatic corps] is an important point in smoothing out the handling of diplomatic problems and in assuring foreign trust. The actual proposal is as follows:

(i) To drastically re-evaluate the diplomatic corps examination system and to take in personnel who are equipped with the qualifications and discernment to be professional diplomats.

(ii) To assign personnel to the diplomatic corps from the private sector who have acquired a high level of expert knowledge and linguistic ability.

(iii) To assign [promote] superior individuals from the private sector as ambassadors and ministers. To open the way for promotion of younger members of the diplomatic corps to be ambassadors in malarial regions.

(iv) It is difficult to establish trust with the country of assignment if the representative is replaced after two years, which is the standard principle for overseas assignments. Assignment periods must be lengthened.

(v) To set up regional specialists and to educate the diplomatic corps with a high level of expert knowledge related to that region.

(vi) In order to acquaint a diplomatic serviceman with the domestic situation of a country, he should undertake a re-studying [of the foreign country] during an appropriate period of time.

(vii) As is seen with present-day attachés, we should change the transfer style of personnel–foreign exchange to a mutual type of foreign exchange.

(3) Increasing permanent employees and the budget

The number one condition for strengthening the implementive function of diplomacy is to secure basic personnel. If we remember that the number of people in the Ministry of Foreign Affairs before the war was 2,300, the present 3,632 is far too small. We must take advantage of this administrative reform and carry out a bold "scrap and build" operation in the entire government and work to secure a major increase in the number of personnel in the Ministry of Foreign Affairs and the budget for it.

(4) Promotion of Foreign Public Relations and Cultural Diplomacy:

Japan has been told that we are incompetent at foreign public relations. That insufficiency of public relations has brought on a large disadvantage concerning problems of the security treaty and trade friction. For example, compared with the advertising expenditures of ¥ 18.2 billion of one of the large domestic automobile manufacturers, the Ministry of Foreign Affairs foreign public relations expenditure was only ¥ 2 billion. And cultural diplomacy expenditures were ¥ 5 billion. It is an urgent duty to add a major increase to that amount. The government should also strive for a positive use of international broadcasts and mass communications media of every country and seek on this point in particular the cooperation of the private sector.

Part 4. Strengthening the Information-Gathering Functions

(1) Information is the life of diplomacy. Diplomacy would be completely incapacitated without information. Compared with our country before the war or compared with any of many foreign countries, the budget that is provided for information gathering is surprisingly small. It would shock you. We cannot allow this situation to continue. We should correctly acknowledge the things that cost money in terms of information gathering and greatly increase that budget. With striving for the enlargement of the Ministry of Foreign Affairs as a given in terms of the budget and personnel, we should set up inside the ministry an information and investigative bureau and conduct information gathering and analyses along with becoming more scientific in informational analysis.

(2) At the present time, when diplomacy problems and domestic prob-

lems are intimately linked, the Ministry of Foreign Affairs should provide every ministry and agency with the information related to it that has been received from diplomatic establishments abroad, and other sources of information, and should establish a system wherein things related to diplomatic problems amongst the information obtained by all the other ministries can flow swiftly to the Ministry of Foreign Affairs.

(3) It is necessary to establish a system that absorbs [obtains] private sector information thought to be important in terms of diplomacy, in the present day in which the amount of foreign information obtained by the private sector has increased dramatically, accompanying our country's economic development. We must substantially increase the mechanism and function of the Japanese International Problem Research Institute, which is an auxiliary organization to the Ministry of Foreign Affairs, in the fields of long-term positive technical approaches related to information surveys. We also think that it is necessary to legislate it into a special *hojin* [corporation].

Part 5. The Positive Application of Dietmen's Diplomacy and Private Individual's Diplomacy

Looking at the process that brought us to the present position in the international community, one realizes the large role played by private individuals in creating international inroads [in making us a part of the international community]. In other words, since diplomacy is the entirety of association between two countries, it is an urgent duty not only to assign capable private individuals with expert knowledge to the diplomatic corps, but also to promote private diplomacy and strive for its positive application. The role of Dietmen in diplomacy is also extremely large. The establishment of tight linkages between the activities of Dietmen and the diplomatic activities of the government will undoubtedly have a large effect on the promotion of positive diplomacy. In particular, we should take advantage of the power of Dietmen's diplomacy in approaching the parliaments of the various countries.

APPENDIX B

A CHRONOLOGY OF
LIBERALIZATION AND DELIBERALIZATION

1949

Foreign Exchange and Foreign Trade Control Law was enacted.

1950

Foreign Investment Law was enacted.

1952

Foreign Investment Law was amended to permit remittance abroad of foreigners' proceeds from sales of stock investments. Initial remittance was permitted only from sale of securities that had been held for a period of two years, and only by five-year installments thereafter.

In "nonrestricted" industries, foreigners were permitted to hold a maximum of 8 percent of the outstanding shares of any individual company. In "restricted" industries, they were permitted to hold 5 percent of outstanding shares.

1960

In "nonrestricted" industries, foreigners were permitted to hold a maximum of 15 percent of the outstanding shares of any individual company. In "restricted" industries, they were permitted to hold 10 percent of outstanding shares.

1963

Restrictions on foreign investors' remittances were abolished.

1967

In "nonrestricted" industries, foreigners were permitted to hold a maximum of 20 percent of the outstanding shares of any individual company. In "restricted" industries, they were permitted to hold 15 percent of outstanding shares. Restricted industries included banking, electric power, gas, waterworks, railroads, tramways, marine transportation, road transportation, air transportation, forwarding, fisheries, mining, and broadcasting. Unrestricted industries included printing ink, household appliances, phonograph records, soups, radio receivers, beer, and ice.

1970

Japanese investment trusts and insurance companies were permitted to hold foreign stocks.

In "nonrestricted" industries, foreigners were permitted to hold a maximum of 25 percent of the outstanding shares of any individual company.

Lending by foreign branches of Japanese banks (Genchi-Kashitsuke), mainly to Japanese nonfinancial corporations, and standby credits of foreign branches of Japanese banks were somewhat liberalized.

1971

Japanese individuals were permitted to hold foreign securities listed on foreign securities exchanges.

The Ministry of Finance prohibited purchase of Japanese treasury bills by nonresidents.

Restrictions on Genchi-Kashitsuke were reinforced.

Restrictions on conversion of foreign currency into yen (Yen-Tenkan) by Japanese banks and branches of foreign banks were strengthened.

The Bank of Japan freed the yen from its parity of ¥ 360 = $1.

As per the Smithsonian Agreement, the yen was revalued at ¥ 308 = $1.

1972

The Yen-Tenkan foreign-exchange controls were mitigated and then again reinforced.

A license for establishment of a Tokyo branch was granted to Merrill Lynch.

Restrictions on purchase of foreign securities by Japanese residents were relaxed. Purchase of unlisted foreign securities in secondary markets became permissible.

Foreigners were required to convert the yen proceeds of sales of Japanese securities within one month of sale.

Net increases of foreigners' investments in Japanese bonds were prohibited.

1973

The yen float was inaugurated.

Issuance of yen-denominated foreign bonds was prohibited.

Purchase of U.S. Treasury securities by Japanese securities companies was restricted.

Japanese nonfinancial corporations were permitted, with restrictions, to issue bonds in foreign markets.

1974

Yen-conversion ceilings on impact loans (foreign currency loans from foreign banks to Japanese nonbank institutions) were raised.

Japanese residents allowed to purchase foreign short-term securities (one year or less), subject to case-by-case screening and official discouragement of such transactions.

Foreign-currency lending by government financial institutions and Japanese foreign-exchange banks for foreign direct investment and import prepayment were restricted.

Ceiling for convertibility to yen of foreign-currency prepayments to Japanese exporters was raised twice (to $500,000).

Rules requiring the conversion of the proceeds of securities sales by nonresidents to foreign currencies within one month were revoked.

A ceiling was imposed on resident foreign-currency deposits at banks, while a similar restriction was placed on foreign-currency holdings of corporations (requiring them to convert or reinvest abroad within seven days).

Conversion into yen of proceeds of advance payment for exports in excess of the established ceiling ($100,000) subject to automatic approval by the Bank of Japan if received less than six months before export shipment.

Requirements for listing foreign stocks on the Tokyo Stock Exchange were relaxed.

Purchases of foreign currency for travel became subject to validation or approval (including approval from the Bank of Japan for amounts in excess of $1,500).

Maximum amount of yen allowed to be taken out of the country by resident and nonresident travelers was lowered (to ¥ 30,000).

Ceiling on "small-lot" remittances to abroad was lowered to $200.

Bond issues abroad were facilitated by removal of withholding tax on interest payments.

Export-Import Bank was instructed to operate its lending for investment abroad in a restrictive fashion.

Yen-conversion quotas for foreign banks in Japan were increased twice.

Restrictions on portfolio investments in Japan by nonresidents were relaxed, including automatic licenses for purchase of short-term government securities, automatic approval of unlisted bonds and debentures redeemable within a year (all previously prohibited), plus other changes.

The 10 percent reserve ratio on free yen deposits held by nonresidents was eliminated.

Controls on interest payable on resident and nonresident foreign-currency deposits at Japanese banks were withdrawn.

Conversion into yen of proceeds of bond issues made abroad now allowed on a case-by-case basis.

Restrictions were reinforced on Eurodollar market borrowing by Japanese banks.

Japanese banks were prohibited from medium- and long-term lending in foreign currencies.

The prohibition against purchase by foreigners of Japanese treasury bills was rescinded.

1975

Inward investment in real estate, retail trade, and twelve other "restricted" industries was fully liberalized (allowing 100 percent foreign ownership).

Request to securities dealers and foreign-exchange banks not to encourage public purchases of foreign securities was revoked.

Foreign-exchange banks were allowed to issue certificates of deposit in Singapore and the United States.

First life insurance company with partial foreign ownership was allowed; first fully foreign-owned, non-life-insurance firm was licensed.

Temporary prohibition (dating from 1973) on issuance of bonds by foreigners was lifted.

Approval policies for certain invisible transactions were eased.

Ceiling was eased on total amount of foreign currency that foreign banks could convert into yen.

Restrictions were intensified on the issuance of impact loans.

Restrictions were intensified on the issuance of bonds in foreign markets by Japanese nonfinancial corporations.

Restrictions were eased on the purchase by Japanese residents of U.S. Treasury securities.

1976

Foreign banks in Japan were permitted to increase the outstanding total of their conversions of foreign currency into yen.

Inward direct investment in the computer industry (including software) was fully liberalized.

Japanese banks were subjected to administrative guidance on foreign investments, including a requirement to file regular reports with the Ministry of Finance on the financial standing of their overseas subsidiaries.

The Bank of Japan introduced a new system for accepting accommodation drafts for yen-denominated, export-usance bills designed to encourage yen-denominated exports.

The basic exchange allocation for travel abroad was raised from $1,500 to $3,000 per person per trip; the amount of yen allocated to resident and nonresident travelers was increased from ¥ 30,000 to ¥ 100,000.

Permissible level for residents' foreign-currency bank deposits in banks in Japan was raised from $10,000 to $20,000.

Limit on remittances abroad by residents was raised from $200 to $1,000 per remittance.

Japan informed the OECD of removal of its reservations to the Code of Liberalization of Capital Movements on both inward and outward portfolio investment and on short- and medium-term export- and import-usance credits.

The Ministry of Finance revoked its instruction to commercial banks to refrain from financing "non-urgent" investment projects abroad.

Several measures were introduced to promote yen financing of imports, including the Bank of Japan's acceptance of accommodation drafts for yen-denominated import-usance bills and flexible consideration of window-guidance limits for banks shifting import financing from foreign currencies to yen.

Limits on issuance of yen bonds in Japan by foreign borrowers were eased.

Restrictions imposed in 1974 on medium- and long-term lending in foreign currencies by Japanese banks to overseas customers were eased, but that lending remained subject to government approval.

The Bank of Japan was authorized to impose reserve requirements on commercial banks' foreign-currency liabilities (except foreign-currency guarantees) if warranted by market conditions.

Restrictions on issuance of bonds in foreign markets by Japanese nonfinancial corporations were eased.

1977

The ceiling on bonds issued abroad by government-owned enterprises was eased for fiscal 1977 (allowing a total of ¥ 190 billion).

Guidelines were placed on bonds issued in the Euroyen market, restricting issues to international organizations that had previously issued yen bonds in the Tokyo market, with a further requirement that Japanese financial institutions be the head managers and that nonresidents not issue such bonds without approval of the Ministry of Finance.

Interest income on yen-denominated bonds issued in Japan by government-guaranteed foreign borrowers and international organizations were exempted from income tax (joining the previously exempted foreign central and local governments).

The ceiling on free transactions related to invisibles was raised from $1,000 to $3,000.

The ceiling on remittances to relatives abroad was eliminated.

Japanese nationals traveling abroad were allowed to take out $3,000—with larger amounts subject only to verification by foreign-exchange banks (eliminating Bank of Japan approval).

The amount of foreign currency nonresidents were allowed to purchase upon exit from Japan without approval from foreign-exchange banks was raised from $1,000 to $3,000.

The requirement of validation by the Bank of Japan for payments on overseas contracts was eliminated.

A 0.25 percent reserve requirement was placed on foreign-exchange banks' liabilities in foreign currencies, on free-yen liabilities, and on residents' external foreign-currency deposits with foreign-exchange banks. Control over conversions by banks of foreign currencies into yen was replaced by control of spot foreign-exchange positions (with oversold spot positions not allowed for Japanese banks).

Japanese foreign-exchange banks were allowed greater freedom in extending medium- and long-term loans in foreign currencies.

Control over short-term loans to nonresidents by Japanese foreign-exchange banks was abolished.

Partially convertible deposit accounts of nonresidents were abolished, with the proceeds from the principal sources of these accounts (sale of debentures and beneficiary certificates within six months from date of purchase) allowed to be deposited in fully convertible free-yen accounts.

The restriction was eased on purchase by Japanese residents of foreign securities with maturities of one year or less.

The ceiling of $20,000 on foreign-currency deposits held by residents was abolished.

Restrictions on the maturity or amount of foreign-currency deposits held abroad by Japanese security, insurance, and transportation companies were abolished.

Restriction on the acquisition of real estate abroad by Japanese residents not being put to direct use was abolished.

Ministry of Finance approval for any purchase of foreign stock under stock-sharing plans for Japanese employees of foreign-affiliated companies was abolished.

Two temporary controls were placed on inflow of short-term capital: (1) public sales of short-term treasury bills were stopped after November 21; and (2) a reserve requirement of 50 percent was placed on increases in free-yen deposits from the average level held in October.

The reserve ratio on nonresidents' free-yen deposits was raised.

1978

A reserve requirement of 100 percent was placed on increases of free-yen deposits over average holdings of February.

Nonresidents were precluded from purchasing Japanese bonds with a remaining time to maturity of less than five years and one month.

A package of measures intended to reduce Japan's trade and current-account surpluses was announced and implemented, including measures to expand credit available for import financing; relaxation of the standard settlement system; an increase in the ceilings for remittances; liberalization of regulations on foreign-currency deposits of residents; relaxation of restrictions on forward foreign-exchange transactions. Intention to create a new foreign-exchange control law was announced.

Expanded swap quotas for foreign banks operating in Japan were announced.

Ministry of Finance granted blanket approval to Japanese foreign-exchange banks to lend abroad.

1979

Japanese banks were required to match 60 percent of their outstanding medium- and long-term loans denominated in foreign currency with foreign-currency financing of maturities greater than one year.

Reserve requirement on increases in nonresidents' free-yen deposits was reduced from 100 percent to 50 percent, and later eliminated (leaving the basic 0.25 percent reserve requirement on total deposits).

Ban on nonresident purchase of bonds with a remaining maturity of five years and one month was lifted, first allowing nonresidents to purchase bonds with remaining maturities of greater than one year and one month (January) and then allowing purchases of any maturity (February).

Permissible period for conversion to foreign currency of proceeds of foreigners' yen-denominated bond issuance in Japan was increased to 30 days.

The ceiling on oversold spot positions (swap quotas) for foreign banks was raised twice. Japanese banks were allowed to be in oversold spot positions under ceilings set for individual banks.

Maximum import-usance period was extended from 140 days to 180 days.

Requirement of government approval for export prepayments exceeding $500,000 was lifted.

Restriction on the maximum conversion period for proceeds of foreigners' yen-bond issues or syndicated loans was lifted.

Curbs on the use of impact loans with a repayment period exceeding one year were eased.

Ban on short-term impact loans (of less than one year) by foreign or Japanese banks was lifted.

The 25 percent limit on the share of nonresidents in subscriptions to foreigners' yen-bond issues was lifted.

Nonresidents were given permission to participate in the gensaki market.

Japanese and foreign banks were allowed to issue yen-denominated negotiable certificates of deposit with minimum denominations of ¥ 500 million and limits on total issues by each bank (25 percent of shareholder equity or net assets, and for branches of foreign banks 10 percent of outstanding yen-denominated loans and security holdings).

Foreign-exchange banks, trading companies, and securities companies were required to report on certain foreign-exchange dealings for purposes of monitoring capital flows.

Administrative guidance was applied to the interest rates on Japanese banks' overseas foreign-currency lending, effectively bringing a temporary halt to such loans.

The new Foreign Exchange Control Law was passed by the Diet, with implementation set for December 1980.

Syndicated yen loans to nonresidents were prohibited.

Medium- and long-term loans by Japanese banks to nonresidents, denominated either in yen or in foreign currencies, were prohibited.

1980

Window guidance was applied to medium- and long-term overseas foreign-currency loans by Japanese banks (in February) and later eased somewhat (October) as the temporary halt in lending imposed in October 1979 ends. Yen-denominated loans were also resumed.

Ceilings on issuance of negotiable certificates of deposit were raised (to 50 percent of shareholders' equity or net worth and to 20 percent of yen assets for foreign banks).

Overseas lending by Japanese banks was subjected to guidance on total lending by country (to reduce the proportion of loans to potentially risky developing countries).

New Foreign Exchange Control Law goes into effect. The guiding principle is that all transactions are unregulated unless excepted. Government reserves the right to impose controls under certain emergency situations, but in general the law removes many previous restrictions and requirements.

1981

Temporary suspension of private placement of bonds in Japan by nonresidents was lifted (imposed in 1979). Monthly limit on the number and size of monthly public offerings of bonds by nonresidents was eased.

Japanese banks were allowed to guarantee their overseas subsidiaries' bond issues in foreign capital markets.

Reserve requirement ratios for foreign-currency deposits held by Japanese residents were raised (to 0.5 percent on time deposits and to 1.25 percent on other deposits) in February and then reduced again in April (to 0.375 percent on time deposits and to 0.5 percent on other deposits). Deposits held by nonresidents were unaffected.

New banking law goes into effect, allowing credit associations to handle foreign-exchange operations and, in principle, allowing banks and securities firms to buy and sell in the domestic market commercial paper and certificates of deposit issued abroad.

Foreign branches of Japanese banks were allowed to freely make to nonresidents Euroyen loans with maturities of one year or less for financing international trade.

Administrative guidance was applied to Japanese corporate bonds issued abroad, limiting both the number and value of monthly offerings.

1982

Ministry of Finance lends from its foreign-exchange special fund account for emergency imports.

Permission for sale of foreign issues of zero-coupon bonds to Japanese residents was suspended.

Maturities for yen-denominated loans to nonresidents were reduced from fifteen years to twelve years for borrowing by international agencies.

Yen–dollar swap limits for foreign banks operating in Japan were increased.

Priority categories on overseas yen lending were removed, permitting Japanese banks to lend yen on a long-term basis to borrowers of their choice.

Japanese banks were permitted to open two additional overseas branch offices in fiscal years 1982 and 1983. Establishment of representative offices was unrestricted.

Window guidance on overseas lending by Japanese banks was tightened to slow capital outflow.

Limits on issuance of yen-denominated foreign bonds in Japan were tightened to slow capital outflow.

Administrative guidance was applied to reduce overseas securities purchases by Japanese insurance companies.

Limits on Japanese bank lending by country (established in 1979) were expanded to include short-term lending as well as the previously restricted medium- and long-term lending.

The annual queueing system for issuance of yen-denominated bonds in Japan by nonresidents was eliminated, substituting a quarterly issuance program decided by the main Japanese securities firms.

NOTES

INTRODUCTION

1. For further details, see Leon Hollerman, "International Economic Controls in Occupied Japan," *The Journal of Asian Studies*, August 1979.

2. For details, see Chalmers Johnson, *MITI and the Japanese Miracle* (Stanford: Stanford University Press, 1982).

3. See article by Peter F. Drucker, *Wall Street Journal*, 6 January 1987.

4. The rationale of U.S. demands for Japanese economic liberalization, however, has been subject to change. In the 1960s, it chiefly reflected the desire of U.S. firms for privileges of direct investment in Japan. Later, it was based on U.S. official displeasure with the state of the bilateral trade balance and complaints by U.S. firms about their difficulties in penetrating the Japanese distribution system.

5. Symbolically, perhaps, the breakdown of bureaucratic boundaries may be suggested by the striking change in appearance of the large office compounds of the Ministry of Finance. In the 1960s, bookcases and mountainous piles of documents were used to partition desk space, suggesting the establishment of personal empires. Nowadays, the barriers have been leveled, and there is more or less a clear view from one end of an office to the other.

6. With regard to the politicization of Japan's economic issues, see Leon Hollerman, "The Politics of Economic Relations Between the United States and Japan," in Leon Hollerman, ed., *Japan and the United States: Economic and Political Adversaries* (Boulder, Colo.: Westview Press, 1980).

7. Remarks by Glen S. Fukushima, director of Japanese affairs in the Office of the U.S. Trade Representative, in an address to the Japan Society, New York, 10 February 1987, reported in *The Journal of Commerce*, 17 February 1987.

CHAPTER 1

1. See Leon Hollerman, *Japan's Dependence on the World Economy: The Approach to Economic Liberalization* (Princeton, N.J.: Princeton University Press, 1967).

2. The "locomotive" thesis was propounded by the secretariat of the Organization for Economic Cooperation and Development (OECD) in the summer of 1976. It argued that the United States, West Germany, and Japan should adopt expansionary monetary and fiscal policies to stimulate their own economies and thus to act as locomotives in hauling other countries out of the world recession of 1974–1975. It was argued further that such policies would not be inflationary because of the existence of unutilized productive capacity in the leading countries. The United States adopted the locomotive policy and urged Germany and Japan to do likewise. After initial resistance, both Germany and Japan went along with the proposal. According to the Industrial Bank of Japan, "At that time, our financial position was sound because of little fiscal dependence on national bonds. So in line with President Carter's locomotive theory, fiscal policy was used to stimulate domestic demand, while overseas, America's expansionary economic policy encouraged the recycling of oil money into developing countries to create a development investment boom, which in turn helped to increase exports of Japanese industrial goods. Thus the Japanese economy was helped tremendously by Carter's 'locomotive theory' and by the development investment boom in the developing countries." (*IBJ Monthly Report*, January 1983).

3. In the economic summit meeting at Versailles in June 1982, then Prime Minister Suzuki expected to personally receive pressure for liberalization from others at the meeting. To the openly expressed relief of the Japanese government, he was saved by the problems of East-West relations and high U.S. interest rates, which distracted the attention of the delegates. On the other hand, in accordance with his commitment to administrative reform and pursuit of what is called here Japan's "external option," Prime Minister Nakasone took a positive attitude toward the liberalization process at the Williamsburg summit in May 1983.

4. C. Fred Bergsten, "What to Do About the U.S.–Japan Economic Conflict," *Foreign Affairs* (Summer 1982).

5. In June 1982, the MITI minister, Shintaro Abe, strongly recommended that defense of the yen should be enforced by means of foreign-exchange controls. In West Germany, in a parallel case, it was decided to raise the interest rate to defend the mark.

6. In the Ministry of Finance, the length of time that top career officials spend in each job has diminished. There is also more reshuffling in the ranks below the administrative vice minister than formerly; it produces a cascade of replacements below. At present, the administrative vice minister holds his office for one or two years (two years is the maximum in the Ministry of Finance; in the EPA it is two and a half years.) A month or so after the

administrative vice minister is replaced, his subordinate is replaced. In the month thereafter, the latter's subordinate will be replaced. Through the accelerated turnover of its officials, the personnel policy of the Ministry of Finance has become more fluid.

7. The "balanced budget principle" is emphasized as one of the main criteria of the Budget Bureau in John C. Campbell, *Contemporary Japanese Budget Politics* (Berkeley: University of California Press, 1977).

8. At the Versailles summit conference of June 1982, MITI promoted the concept of U.S.–Japan collaboration in science and technology as a means of distracting attention from the chronic controversy about Japan's imports of beef and citrus fruit. A MITI representative was present at the conference for the purpose of proposing this concept. (Normally, Japanese representatives at the summit include only the prime minister and members of the Ministry of Finance and the Foreign Ministry.) It may be argued, on the other hand, that while Japan was anxious to deflate controversy at the summit, it keeps the issue of citrus fruit and beef alive for the express purpose of masking its planned assault on the high-technology sector in world markets.

9. Before the oil shock in 1973, the Bank of Japan excessively bought dollars to prevent revaluation of the yen. This caused an unwarranted expansion of the money supply and consequent inflation, from which the Bank of Japan learned a lesson.

10. From the nuance of conversations at the Bank of Tokyo, this author inferred that there is not much love lost between that institution and the Ministry of Finance as well. The same impression is conveyed by a speech of Yusuke Kashiwagi, President of the Bank of Tokyo, at a meeting of Asian-Pacific bankers in Hong Kong on 26 April 1982, reprinted in Bank of Tokyo, *Tokyo Financial Review* (June 1982).

11. However, in a FTC survey of 612 companies in 16 industries, plus 162 others with which they have dealings, it was found that only 7.7 percent of the respondents favored a "substantial reduction" of government regulations. According to the survey, most firms believed they were benefiting from existing regulations and administrative guidance. The survey was performed in December 1981.

12. It would be an interesting exercise to investigate whether imports of manufactured goods by Japanese head offices from their subsidiaries abroad encounter the same sort of nontariff barriers that U.S. exporters of manufactures profess to encounter in their attempts to export to Japan.

13. The "paper-stone-scissors" analogy for the relations among bureaucrats, politicians, and businessmen is too simple. According to the analogy, politicians control bureaucrats, bureaucrats control businessmen, and businessmen control politicians.

14. According to some observers, the Japan Tobacco and Salt Public Corporation is highly inefficient. Dean Kenzo Hemmi of Tokyo University disagrees with this assessment.

15. *Keidanren* (abbreviation of *Keizai Dantai Rengōkai*) is the Federation of Economic Organizations. It was founded in August 1946 by uniting major pre-existing economic organizations. It represents big business rather than small or medium-size enterprises. Its membership is of two types. First, it includes over 100 organizations representing major industries (manufacturing; banking, insurance, and securities; other services; mining, forestry, and fisheries) and regional interests. Second, its membership includes approximately 800 of the major individual corporations of Japan. It performs research on domestic and international issues, the results of which form the basis for recommendations presented to various government agencies. Keidanren often takes initiatives and adopts positions in foreign as well as domestic affairs that eventually determine the shape of formal government policies. Keidanren also acts as a mediator in disputes among major interest groups. It has a close relationship with the Liberal Democratic Party (LDP), which depends heavily on it for financial contributions. Within the Japanese government, Keidanren collaborates most closely with MITI. Its junior rival is the Japan Committee for Economic Development *(Keizai Dōyukai)*, the membership of which is comprised of individuals rather than of organizations or firms.

CHAPTER 2

1. For example, in its brochure on the new Foreign Exchange Law, the Bank of Japan states that international transactions "may be carried out freely in principle except in cases of emergency." *Outline of Foreign Exchange Control in Japan* (Foreign Department, the Bank of Japan, March 1981): 2.

2. *Foreign Exchange and Foreign Trade Control Law*, as amended by Law no. 65, dated December 18, 1979 (Legal Division, International Finance Bureau, Ministry of Finance, March 1980).

3. As noted above, in its brochure on the new Foreign Exchange Law, the Bank of Japan states that "these transactions may be carried out freely in principle except in cases of emergency." Thus, with regard to both elements of the description, "freely in principle" and "cases of emergency," the brochure differs from the law. *Outline of Foreign Exchange Control in Japan* (Foreign Department, the Bank of Japan, March 1981): 2.

4. It is rumored, however, that if the foreign-exchange reserves fall below $20 billion, the Ministry of Finance will treat this as an emergency. Another rumored criterion concerns the ceiling that is still imposed on new overseas syndicated lending by Japanese banks. Since Japan accounts for approximately 10 percent of world GNP, the Ministry of Finance is alleged to limit banks to a 10 percent share of the world syndicated loan market. Officially, the Bank of Japan maintains that syndicated lending in yen or dollars and issuance of Samurai bonds are restricted by administrative guidance purely for purposes of "traffic control."

5. The charge was ¥ 3 for each $1.00 of foreign currency deposited. A fee of ¥ 3 was likewise charged for each $1.00 of foreign currency withdrawn. For small deposits or withdrawals (less than $100 or the equivalent in other foreign currencies), an additional fee of ¥ 100 was charged.

6. As of October 1981, banks were obliged to receive clearance from the Ministry of Finance for any loan of more than $15 million.

7. No bank could extend loans to a single country in excess of 20 percent of that bank's own capital.

8. In the case of another minsitry, it may be noted that MITI's "superior information" as a basis for advising the Mitsui Company to go ahead with its Bandhar Khomeini petrochemical project left something to be desired.

9. Because of the low GNP growth rate, domestic demand for the funds of the insurance companies had been weak. Therefore, financial institutions, including insurance companies, had been eager investors in dollar bonds. These investments were also based on the assumption that the dollar would remain strong.

10. "If it is a routine matter, or a small amount, the Bank of Japan takes care of it. If it is a large amount, or something unusual, the Bank of Japan refers the matter to the Ministry of Finance," said a high official of the International Finance Bureau of the Ministry of Finance.

11. The interest rate on dollar funds was substantially higher than the interest rate on yen during this period. However, since the forward dollar rate was lower than the spot rate of exchange, the forward discount margin on dollars was often larger than the differential between the yen and the dollar interest rates. Therefore, if the impact loan was a covered transaction (the borrower simultaneously converting dollars into yen and purchasing forward dollars for repayment of the yen loan), it was often cheaper to borrow dollars than to borrow yen.

12. *Balance of Payments Monthly* (The Bank of Japan, April 1982).

13. See the article by Tsuneo Fujita in the *Nihon Keizai Shumbun* (25 May 1982).

14. These data were supplied by the Ministry of Finance, the Bank of Japan, the IMF, the Bank of England, and the Bank for International Settlements.

15. The fact that traders do not invariably cover is seen in the fact that the forward market is much smaller than the spot market.

16. An IFB official asked some petroleum people why they exposed themselves to the risk of unhedged commitments to purchase petroleum in dollars. They replied that it was a bureaucratic rather than an economic matter. The petroleum refiners are large companies. The officers of such companies are judged on the results of their actions. If a petroleum bureaucrat decides to purchase petroleum with forward cover, and if the value of the yen should rise by the time of payment, his action would be seen retrospectively as an error, for which he would be given a demerit. On the other hand, if he takes no action—that is, does not cover—and if in that event the yen should decline in

value, this would be considered a *natural hazard* for which he could not be blamed. In the bureaucracy, if you take no action, you can incur no blame. Covering a foreign-exchange transaction is an *action*. Consequently, the petroleum bureaucrats avoid it. According to the Bank of Japan, in the summer of 1982 the petroleum bureaucrats were beginning to avoid it less. Approximately 30 percent of their foreign-currency transactions were hedged at that time.

17. In September 1982, the Dai-Ichi Kangyo, Japan's largest commercial bank, announced that it had lost ¥ 9.7 billion (approximately $37 million) due to "unauthorized" foreign-exchange speculation in its Singapore branch. Earlier in the year, the Nissho Iwai trading company, the sixth largest in Japan, reported that it had lost ¥ 16 billion (approximately $61 million) because of "unauthorized" speculation in its Hong Kong branch.

18. On their own account, commercial banks in Japan are subject to a limit on uncovered foreign-exchange positions "at the end of a day." Thus, their speculative losses are limited during the hours in which they are not open for business. However, there is no limit on the amount they may lose through uncovered positions in the course of the day.

19. If a nonresident wants to invest in gensaki or Japanese treasury bills (the latter are not liberalized and do not carry a market-determined interest rate), he converts dollar or other foreign currency into yen and then performs the transaction.

20. The Tokyo offshore market (IBF) was launched on 1 December 1986. The restrictions imposed upon it, however, limited the benefits it provided to its participants. Removal of restrictions was constrained by the pace of liberalization in Japan's domestic financial market.

21. At present, there is a 20 percent withholding tax on interest income in Japan.

22. It was anticipated that establishment of an IBF would enhance the use of reserve requirements as a policy tool of the Bank of Japan in the domestic banking system.

23. According to the Bank of Japan, the amount of yen outside Japan in 1982 exceeded the equivalent of $30 billion. "The Euroyen market is like an 'unauthorized child': we cannot destroy it, but we are not so happy about it," said an assistant to the Governor of the Bank of Japan.

24. The IBF in New York excludes securities companies.

25. Establishment of an Ombudsman Office was one concession to the foreigners. However, according to a Japanese official who should know, "The Ombudsman Office is largely window dressing. It doesn't accomplish much."

26. For purposes of import usance, the present source of most dollar financing of Japanese banks was the London Eurodollar market or the New York IBF rather than foreign banks in Japan. Incidentally, the disadvantage of using Western bankers' acceptance refinancing was augmented by the anomaly known as the "Japanese premium," which was charged in those markets for

paper accepted by a Japanese lending bank. For the Bank of Tokyo, the premium was 0.5 percent; for other Japanese banks it was 1 percent.

27. Statement of Yusuke Kashiwagi, president of the Bank of Tokyo, as cited in Eric W. Hayden, "Internationalizing Japan's Financial System" (Occasional paper of the Northeast Asia–United States Forum on International Policy, Stanford University, December 1980), p. 18.

28. The figure was quoted by then Ambassador Mike Mansfield in response to a question following his speech at the Foreign Correspondents Club in Tokyo, 6 January 1982. Cited by Kazuo Nukazawa, "Japan-Asian Trade Relations" (unpublished paper, May 1982): 32.

29. Apart from residual import restrictions as such, their restrictive impact is increased because agricultural import quotas are disproportionately distributed in accordance with political influence to a tightly limited group of agents. Sometimes foreigners do exceptionally well under these circumstances. California and Florida, for example, as rivals for the orange-import market of Japan, also have rival congressional supporters. Japanese orange importers likewise form two groups, each with its rival supporters in the Diet. (Separation of the rival parties on this issue in the Diet, incidentally, has no functional basis; members of the respective groups cross factional lines.) Sunkist of California was allied with importers who had strong contacts in the Diet and large quotas. Florida producers did not. Thus, Sunkist dominated the market; despite aggregate import quota limitations, it was not anxious to have the quota increased. Opposition of Japanese farmers to increased quotas could be bought off by the allocation of increased quota allocations to farmers themselves. As an alternative scenario, perhaps the Japanese wish to keep attention focused on beef and citrus while matters of much greater importance are brewing, as in the high-technology field.

30. At its board of directors meeting on 27 April 1982, Keidanren adopted a "View Concerning the Improvement of External Economic Friction," which called for complete liberalization of agricultural and non-agricultural residual restrictions.

31. Recently, the Socialist and Communist parties have been embarrassed by disclosures of corruption in the JNR unions, a principal source of their support. With regard to military defense, however, the apparent confusion in U.S. military policy has given them a chance to attempt to distract the public's attention from the matter.

32. Another example of mixed attitudes is the sympathy on the part of right-wing Diet politicians toward Cuba—which they see as the "underdog" in relations with its big neighbor to the north—while simultaneously they favor U.S. proposals for large military expenditures. However, in a statement in Tokyo on 3 March 1982, Deputy United States Trade Representative David Macdonald asserted that "the U.S. government has no intention whatsoever of linking together the defense problem and the trade problem."

33. The major trading companies, however, still handle over 90 percent of Japan's total food imports.

34. From the fixity of its national interests and the stable nature of its institutions and cultural characteristics, the course of Japanese economic strategy ought to be fairly obvious. While this strategy is being formulated, however, U.S. officials continue to fret about relatively minor matters such as Japanese import quotas for oranges and beef. The tactical benefit to Japan of this distraction may be one of the chief reasons such quotas have not yet been removed.

35. Increasingly, in domestic transactions, the financial intermediation of the trading companies in behalf of their small- and medium-size clients is being superseded. The sluggish state of domestic growth has induced the city banks to solicit new customers among minor firms.

36. However, the process is burdensome because of the eligibility requirements for such marrying.

CHAPTER 3

1. The Bank of Japan Law of 1942 remains in effect today. It is a nationalistic law, having been patterned after its counterpart in Nazi Germany. Article II emphasizes that the Bank of Japan "should be operated with the chief mission of achieving national objectives." Accordingly, it was placed under the supervision of the Ministry of Finance, which controls its policies as determined by the government in power at the time. The Bank of Japan Law of 1942 pays no attention to the concept of central bank independence, which had been advocated in Japan in the 1920s. (But it must be acknowledged that a case can be made for subordination of central bank policies to the policies of a democratically elected government.)

2. In terms of relations with government, the securities industry is influential with more Diet members than is the banking industry. The bankers are supposed to have more clout with the bureaucrats. Yet it was the Ministry of Finance that forced the banks to accept the unfavorable formulation of the new Bank Law with regard to their freedom to engage in securities transactions.

3. The Bank of Japan claims to have no specific target for the money supply. Instead, it says it is primarily interested in the Wholesale Price Index (WPI); it is less interested in the Consumer Price Index (CPI).

4. Banks are differentiated and restricted in the functions they can perform. Through this segmentation, the bureaucracy applies the strategy of "divide and conquer." It takes various forms. For example, the city banks historically have financed large-scale business and foreign trade; regional banks have financed local business and small- and medium-size enterprises. Mutual banks and credit depositaries also take care of small business. The government is

particularly concerned to maintain separation between the short-term and long-term banking business. Long-term credit banks (the Industrial Bank of Japan, the Bank of Tokyo, the Long-Term Credit Bank, Norin Chukin, and Shoko Chukin) are permitted to issue debentures for funding purposes; other banks may not do so. Some long-term financing is also done by trust banks. Only trading companies and the top sixteen securities companies are permitted to "marry" export proceeds and import obligations in foreign currency to reduce the amount of their foreign-exchange transactions with the banks. Article 65 of the Securities Trading Law has been applied to bar banks from engaging in the securities trade. The Banking Law, the Securities Trading Law, and the Commercial Code are used to legally exclude nonfinancial companies from performing transactions reserved for the financial community. The financial activity of nonfinancial firms, such as it is, is supervised by MITI.

5. Actually, by receiving subequilibrium rates of return on their savings, it is the banks' depositors rather than the banks that subsidize the government.

6. It was unlikely, however, that the government would be able to roll over the huge amount of national bonds approaching maturity in fiscal year 1985 if it insisted on the old rates. To this extent, liberalization would be involuntary. In the event that the issuing rate rose to the secondary-market rate of interest on national bonds, the winners would be primary purchasers of these bonds (city banks and institutional investors). Regional banks, which were not required to underwrite government bonds, would make no advance and thus would relatively lose. Besides the government, debenture-issuing banks and corporations, whose cost of funding will rise, would also lose.

7. For nonbanks abroad, the government exercises direct control only over securities companies. However, when nonfinancial Japanese firms abroad do business with branches or subsidiaries of Japanese banks abroad, they indirectly come under the control of the Ministry of Finance.

8. A director at the Bank of Japan was asked where he drew the line between intervention in a free economy and controls in an administered economy. He replied, "We are not academics. We are not attempting to draw the line. *Internationalization* and *liberalization* are not sacred words."

9. One reason for this is that Japan lacks a satisfactory rating system for the creditworthiness of corporations. Collateral obviates the need for credit ratings.

10. In March 1982, their share of assets reached the record level of 5 percent due primarily to their deposits in Japanese banks, deposits designed to promote reciprocal business.

11. In Japan, the transfer of funds from foreign banks to domestic banks is accomplished largely by the latter overdrawing their accounts. In the accounting statement, this is classified as "due from" or "due to." This procedure, however, is not popular with the lender, because overdrafts cannot be funded. (A bill, on the other hand, can be discounted in the bill discount market.)

12. Before the establishment of a bankers' acceptance market (inaugurated

1 June 1985), U.S. banks acted as intermediaries in putting Japanese commercial paper into the New York money market.

13. According to the senior vice president of a leading U.S. bank in Japan, foreign banks in Japan in 1981 earned 80 to 100 basis points before taxes and 40 to 50 basis points after taxes. In the United States, banks earned 60 basis points. Japanese banks earned 22 basis points after taxes in 1981.

14. In competition with U.S. banks, Japanese banks may offer lower interest rates on loans, but they plan to make it up through the collateral deals that will arise from cementing a relationship with the client. From the client's point of view, however, the lower interest rates that may beguile it into doing business with Japanese rather than foreign banks may be spurious. Once heavily involved with a Japanese bank, the client may be required to borrow money it does not need to help window-dress the bank's books at quarterly accounting time, when the amount of its loans outstanding determines the bank's rank in terms of market share. On bank anniversaries and the like, pressure may likewise be applied to the client to take out additional loans. U.S. banks are not involved in this market share competition and in any event have no such power over their clients.

15. On occasion, the authorities are not above manipulating that environment for their own purposes.

16. In June 1981, there were thirteen major domestic banks ("city banks") operating 2,780 nationwide branch facilities. The 64 foreign banks in Japan on that date operated a total of only 85 branches.

17. Investment restrictions on acquisition by foreigners of controlling interests in major Japanese industrial firms have hitherto prevented the formation of foreign-controlled groups. Close ties with such groups would provide foreign banks with loan and deposit business corresponding to that enjoyed by Japanese city banks with *keiretsu* groups.

18. The swap limit for Japanese banks is based on a percentage of their capital. Foreign banks, however, are only branches or representative offices because hitherto the Ministry of Finance has not allowed them to become domestic corporations; thus, they have no capital. (Theoretically, a foreign bank may now acquire a Japanese bank by purchase or merger.) Accordingly, the swap limit for foreign banks is based on some other criterion, undisclosed by the ministry. The government asserts that foreign banks have an advantage over Japanese banks in the calculation of the swap quotas. Except during periods of tight money, however, Japanese banks are already well supplied with yen as compared with foreign banks. Swap funding, moreover, is expensive because it requires forward cover. Before liberalization, when yen and nonyen currencies were segregated, swap funds were the only source of yen available to foreign banks. At that time, the swap operation was very profitable because the cost of swap-yen was 1 percent less than the cost of domestically acquired yen. At present, the bill discount market is the principal yen source for foreign banks, but it is an expensive source and highly subject to Bank of Japan manipulation.

19. City banks, on the other hand, acquire about 40 percent of their yen funds from their branches.

20. In 1980, there were three cases of cofinancing by foreign banks and the Export-Import Bank of Japan. In 1981, there were six cases.

21. In the United States, Japanese banks have equal access with American banks to funding from standard sources such as CDs or Fed funds. They also are permitted to establish interstate branches, as domestic U.S. banks are not.

22. Masumi Esaki, "Treatment of Foreign Banks and Foreign Insurance Companies in Japan" (A briefing paper prepared for the Esaki Mission to the United States and European Economic Community during February and March 1982). Esaki, a prominent Diet member, was formerly minister of International Trade and Industry and formerly director general of the Defense Agency.

23. Likewise, foreign banks were formerly told that they could not advertise. Now they have permission to advertise but refrain from doing so. In the words of one eminent American banker, "It would be like pissing out of the window."

24. "Even before the liberalization, there was no *written* prohibition against our opening new branches. But we could not even get the application to open a new branch accepted. Recently it was whispered to us that such an application might be accepted," said the senior vice president of an American bank in Tokyo.

25. The IFB is in charge of the matter of country risk and the exposure or overexposure of Japanese banks in their foreign lending. In this case, the Bank of Japan is responsible only for reporting the statistics.

26. A private U.S. corporation, other than a bank, is legally entitled to issue debentures in Japan, provided the issuance criteria are satisfied. In practice, however, only firms such as Sears, Dow Chemical, NCR, and Procter and Gamble have been able to do so. Effective 1 December 1984, the Ministry of Finance authorized the issuance by nonresidents of unsecured Euroyen bonds.

27. Emissaries of the American banks to the government include Japanese who prefer to work for foreigners because they have in some way rejected the Japanese system. These mavericks may rub traditional-minded Ministry of Finance officials the wrong way.

28. Established procedures are followed in the issuance of impact loans, syndicated loans, and straight commercial loans. Guidance falls heavily on foreign banks when they attempt to create new bond-issuance techniques, as in zero-coupon bonds, yen bonds, or hedged bonds.

29. Expansion of the impact-loan business during this period partly reflected attempts of borrowers to maintain their profit level by foreign-exchange speculation in the recession and exchange-market turbulence that followed the oil crisis. Impact loans would be converted to yen and left uncovered in anticipation of a rise in the value of the yen.

30. According to an estimate by the Bank of Tokyo, about 70 to 80 percent of these loans were covered in the forward market.

31. In factoring, American banks discount the foreign receivables of Japanese firms. In leasing, they relieve Japanese firms of the problem of purchasing equipment abroad for use abroad, removing the risk to such firms of receiving damaged or otherwise unsatisfactory equipment.

32. *Tatemae* refers to the official or public reason, as opposed to *honne*, which refers to the real reason for such an action.

33. Deposit interest rates are controlled. Lending rates are subject to an upper limit, but actual market lending rates are nowhere near the upper limit; therefore, the lending limit is of no practical effect.

34. The gensaki market was originally managed only by securities companies. Recently, banks have begun gensaki transactions directly with their customers. Banks can operate on either side of the gensaki market. The market is restricted to transactions in Japanese bonds only.

35. Through the Reserve Deposits Law, for example, the Ministry of Finance was able to impose reserve requirements of up to 100 percent on convertible yen deposits, which would make the banks reluctant to accept such deposits. (At present, all yen are convertible.)

36. Government bonds are issued to fill the gap between revenue and expenditure over a period of several years. Thus, the issuance of such bonds requires the approval of the Diet as part of the budgetary process. Treasury bills, however, are a 60-day instrument issued to fill the gap between seasonal revenue and expenditure within the boundaries of a single fiscal year; they do not require Diet approval. In the money markets, TBs contribute to the promotion of arbitrage. In practice, almost all TBs are sold initially to the tanshi companies; thereafter, they are usually bought by the Bank of Japan.

37. Major foreign banks disagree on this point.

38. Gensaki funds are expensive. Thus, only marginal amounts would be borrowed by high-rated borrowers. Gensaki funds may be more heavily borrowed by low-rated borrowers who cannot find accommodation elsewhere.

39. The real interest rate to individual customers, however, may vary because of differences in compensating balances, amount of collateral required, and the like.

40. Trade bills (on accounts receivable) or general promissory notes of major corporations are the instruments mainly transacted. The call and bills markets use similar collateral.

41. July 1982.

CHAPTER 4

1. The Rinchō was commissioned for a two-year period. It was dissolved on 15 March 1983. Thereafter, an Extraordinary Administrative Reform Promotion Council was inaugurated for the implementation of the Rinchō's recommendations.

2. In 1980, according to the OECD, the burden of taxes and social security contributions in Japan was 30.1 percent of national income, as compared with 34.8 percent in the United States. Fear of emulating the United States in this respect arises from a conviction in Japan that excessive taxation has impaired the vitality of the American private sector.

3. There was some sleight of hand here. Of the ¥ 10.4 trillion deficit in fiscal year 1982, ¥ 6.5 trillion was for public works; this was covered by the issuance of "construction bonds" and thus technically was not part of the deficit. The remaining ¥ 3.9 trillion constituted the deficit proper and was covered by "deficit-financing bonds." It was the latter that Suzuki committed himself to reduce to zero by fiscal year 1984.

4. Another interpretation is that the government's target for a GNP growth rate of 5.2 percent for 1982 (of which domestic demand was to account for 4.1 percent and external demand for 1.1 percent) deserved praise because it represented an effort to break free of excessive dependence on exports.

5. *Administrative Reform in Japan* (Administrative Management Agency, Prime Minister's Office, Government of Japan, March 1982).

6. *Monthly Finance Review* (Research and Planning Division, Minister's Secretariat, Ministry of Finance, June 1983).

7. For example, although Japan has not exported silk since 1974, the government continued at least until 1980 to support 533 public servants whose duties were to enforce quality standards in the export of silk. Nikkeiren, *Report of the Committee for the Study of Labor Questions* (March 1982).

8. On 20 December 1986, the Japanese cabinet adopted for fiscal year 1987 the most austere budget in 32 years, providing for an increase in government expenditure of only 0.02 percent.

9. According to a survey performed throughout Japan in 1980 by Professor Tokio Sakata of Tōyō University, more than half of the work done by village, town, and city governments is performed in behalf of the central or prefectural governments, and 37 percent of their total duties is concerned with the administration of subsidies. Sōichirō Tahara, "An Administrative System that Breeds Waste," *Japan Echo*, Vol. 8, No. 3 (1981): 26.

10. For making these pilgrimages, many local officials receive travel and per diem allowances both from the central and the local governments. This helps finance the customary presentation of gifts and entertainment by local officials to central officials in the course of negotiations.

11. Private memorandum of the Liberal Democratic Party Public Finance Reconstruction Committee, 24 June 1982.

12. A kōsha's capital is fully financed by the national government, its budget is subject to approval by the Diet, and its labor-management relations are governed by the Public Corporation and National Enterprise Labor Relations Law, under which the right to strike is not granted. The term *kōsha* applies only to the three public corporations listed here.

13. This is a complete reversal of the attitude of big business since the first

oil crisis. In the ensuing recession, Keidanren was the chief proponent of government deficit financing. The price of government support, however, is government intervention and administrative guidance, from which business wishes to be emancipated.

14. The quote comes from a member of the Rinchō commission. The unionists include the members of *Kokurō* (National Railway Workers' Union) and *Dōrō* (National Railway Locomotive Engineers' Union), the two largest JNR unions, affiliated with *Sōhyō* (General Council of Trade Unions of Japan). Although the Communist and Socialist parties are losing public sympathy, their core support in the JNR and postal workers' unions remains steadfast. It is not lost on the voters that as opposition parties advocating large-scale nationalization, the Communists and Socialists are supported chiefly by the most corrupt and inefficient unions in the nationalized sector.

15. Part of the rationale for denationalizing the JNR is to relieve the government of such pressure in the future. However, an opposite argument has been advanced with regard to the proposal for privatizing the Nippon Telegraph and Telephone Public Corporation (NTT). If it were private, and if it were not dismembered, NTT would be the largest private monopoly in Japan. As a public corporation, NTT could make contributions to politicians. As a private corporation, it could do so, with consequent political effects. Press and television pressure groups, accordingly, would become relatively weaker, and thus they opposed NTT privatization. Further considerations include the fact that proceeds of the sale of NTT stock would provide welcome revenue to the Ministry of Finance, which is attempting to rehabilitate the national finances. Another point concerns NTT rate schedules, which have been subject to scrutiny in public meetings. As a private corporation, role of its public meetings might be abridged.

16. Among its other financial problems, the JNR pension fund was on the point of collapse in 1983.

17. *Tetsurō* (Japan Railway Workers' Union) affiliated with *Dōmei* (Japanese Confederation of Labor), is exceptional in its positive attitude towards JNR labor-management relations. With only 50,000 members out of JNR's 400,000 employees, however, it is the smallest of JNR's five unions. On Japanese public corporations and their labor relations, see Chalmers Johnson, *Japan's Public Policy Companies* (Washington, D.C.: American Enterprise Institute and Hoover Institution, 1978).

18. During Prime Minister Suzuki's term of office, a special subcommittee of MITI's Industrial Structure Council was appointed to devote itself exclusively to economic security.

19. In 1982, MITI bureaucrats devised a timely tactic. With much publicity, they promoted the slogan of "international cooperation in science and technology" to distract attention from trade friction between Japan and Western nations.

20. Products of the new high-technology industries are described as *keiha kutansho* (light, thin, short, and small).

21. National projects are arranged on a government-to-government basis. The Nakayama GIF proposal was conceived in 1978. It includes a plan for a second Panama Canal, construction of a canal in the Isthmus of Kra in the Strait of Malacca, and a Himalayan hydropower-generation project.

22. As we have seen, both in liberalization and internationalization, the private sector led and the government followed.

23. The basic-materials industries transform raw materials into intermediate products, such as vinyl resins, ethylene, ferroalloys, or aluminum.

24. Linkage of another sort lies in the fact that, in bestowing its scholarships on foreign students, the Ministry of Education favors those from countries to which Japan extends economic cooperation.

25. In terms of personnel, in 1982 the United States had 13,601 diplomatic staff; England, 10,037; France, 6,801; West Germany, 6,118; Italy, 5,156. Japan had 3,580. Nobutoshi Nagano, "Geography of Personnel Veins in the Bureaucratic World—Central Government Agencies: The Foreign Ministry," *Kankai* (April 1983).

26. It was contemplated that the proposed foreign affairs cabinet member would have not only economic duties, as were assigned to Saburo Okita when he occupied a similar post, but political duties as well. According to an informed source, however, the EPA's rejection was primarily a bargaining tactic, based on the principle "never accept the first offer."

27. Analogously, Japan's principles concerning military defense (Japan will attack no enemy but will only maintain a defensive posture; Japan will defend only its homeland and adjoining islands; Japan will not send troops abroad) are political, not strategic principles.

28. Symbolically, some recent measures are noteworthy. On 1 September 1982, there came into effect a new law of the National Diet entitled "Law Concerning the Special Measure for the Appointment of Foreign Nationals as Faculty Members at National and Public Universities." Thus, for the first time, Japanese citizenship was no longer a prerequisite for such appointments. As another step toward internationalization, in July 1983 the Justice Ministry decided that naturalized citizens (most of whom are Korean) would no longer be required to adopt Japanese names.

29. Thus, its department in charge of the coal-mining subsidy, for example, might object. Anticipating a cut in the size of its subsidy budget, MITI in 1982 inaugurated two new councils that would effectively offset the reductions and leave its total budget intact. The first of these was the *Kokusai Keizai Kōryu Zaidan* (Japan Economic Foundation); the second was *Bōeki Sangyō Kyōryoku Zaidan* (Japan Trade and Industry Cooperation Foundation).

30. MITI has an International Trade Policy Bureau and an International

Trade Administration Bureau. The Foreign Ministry has an Economic Affairs Bureau and an Economic Cooperation Bureau.

31. According to an Expert Member of the Rinchō, for example, the Defense Agency has not been cooperative with the administrative reform program. However, the Defense Agency is pleased at the prospect of an increase in military spending. According to the same authority, although the Rinchō's program called for relinquishing some central government functions to local government, the former, including Prime Minister Suzuki himself, was opposed to such transfers. (It might even be inferred that Rinchō proposals for "removal of overlapping local jurisdictions," "combination of local offices," and the like were actually proposals for centralization in disguise.)

32. The younger bureaucrats, who are favorably disposed to the U.S. version of the free market, are often also more nationalistic and more hostile to the United States than are their elders.

33. Concerning reform of the JNR, about 80 percent of the LDP have been in favor.

34. Both the Ministry of Finance and the LDP have advisory councils bearing the same name, *Zeisei Chosa-kai* (Taxation Council).

35. Dōmei (Japanese Confederation of Labor), the second leading association of trade unions, with about half as many members as Sōhyō, is mainly in the private sector and is a proponent of administrative reform.

36. In 1982, the president and the executive director of the Japan Tobacco and Salt Public Corporation (usually referred to as the Tobacco and Salt monopoly) were retired officials of the Ministry of Finance. This public corporation (*Kōsha*) is exclusively under the control of the Ministry of Finance. JETRO (Japan External Trade Organization), a corporation exclusively under the control of MITI, was an optional landing place for MITI amakudari. Despite the tight budget policy of the government, JETRO's budget was increased in 1982 due to the intervention of a former MITI minister, Masumi Esaki.

37. Takeshi Watanabe once remarked that his two most important duties as personnel director at the Ministry of Finance were finding jobs for retiring officials and finding mates for young single members of the ministry. It is alleged that the Ministry of Finance gives special protection to major banks that provide post-retirement positions for its senior officials.

CHAPTER 5

1. Eisuke Sakakibara contrasts the "communitarian" system of financing in Japan with the "capitalist" system of financing in the West.

2. Segmentation of the banking system, for example, enables the Ministry of Finance and the Bank of Japan to channel and regulate the flow of funds to targeted sectors. The system includes four principal categories: city banks,

regional banks, long-term credit banks, and trust banks. The banks have their own vested interest in segmentation because it establishes barriers to competition (as, for example, in the separation of long-term from short-term financing) and because maintenance of the controlled interest rate structure provides them with a guaranteed margin of profit.

3. See Japan Economic Institute Report 10A, March 9, 1984.

4. Ibid.

5. Trust banks, which together with life insurance companies enjoyed a monopoly as managers of tax-exempt pension funds in Japan, resented the tactics of securities companies, which enlisted foreign pressure in favor of entry of American banks into the $50 billion pension fund business. In response, the trust banks threatened to enlist foreign pressure in favor of deregulating securities company commission fees, an eventuality much dreaded by the securities industry.

6. As of April 1984, there were 103 representative offices of foreign securities firms in Japan, but only nine full securities branches. Full-branch status entitled a securities firm to receive a commission of 73 percent on Japanese stock transactions, compared with only 20 percent for a representative office. The commission is paid by the Japanese securities company that is a member of the Tokyo Stock Exchange and that executes the trade.

7. When overseas branches of Japanese authorized foreign-exchange banks extend loans in foreign currency to nonresidents, no administrative procedure is required. However, if the loan is denominated in yen, the Bank of Japan requires prior notification, except for short-term, trade-related loans.

8. Issuers of convertible bonds were required to have either a net worth of more than ¥ 150 billion ($667 million) or a combination of more than ¥ 55 billion ($244 million) net worth and a stockholders equity ratio greater than 50 percent. The attractiveness of the bonds to nonresidents was greatly reduced by the refusal of the Japanese tax authorities to exempt interest payments on Euroyen bonds from the 20 percent withholding tax. Moreover, a 180-day waiting period was imposed on the entry into Japan of capital raised by means of Euroyen bond issues.

9. *International Financial Statistics*, (International Monetary Fund, March 1984).

10. In April 1984, for example, there was strong protest from the European Economic Community against the export drive of Japanese producers of hydraulic excavators, who had sustained declining domestic sales for three consecutive years (from fiscal year 1980 to fiscal year 1982). MITI invoked the Export and Import Transaction Law to impose a floor price on exports of this equipment. Producers were also "guided" by MITI to "voluntarily" raise their export prices.

11. In its February 1983 agreement with the EEC, MITI agreed to restrict exports of video tape recorders from Japan to the EEC as a whole for a period of three years.

12. *The Economist* (February 19, 1983): 48.

13. These phrases are quoted, but not defined, in Miyohei Shinohara, *Industrial Growth, Trade, and Dynamic Patterns in the Japanese Economy* (Tokyo: University of Tokyo Press, 1982). Shinohara is chairman of the Institute of Developing Economies, a MITI thinktank. See also, the Ministry of International Trade and Industry, *The Vision of MITI Policies in the 1980s* (March 1980).

14. Keidanren has urged the following: (1) elimination of the requirement for reporting concurrent price increases; (2) abolition of penalties for illegal cartels; (3) elimination of controls on stockholding of giant corporations and elimination or relaxation of controls on stockholding of monetary institutions; (4) extension of the authorized existence of antidepression and rationalization cartels from three months to six months; and (5) relaxation of the conditions under which cartel formation may be authorized. Proposal submitted to the Anti-Monopoly Law Special Study Committee of the Liberal Democratic Party, July 1983.

15. See Dodwell Marketing Consultants, *Industrial Groupings in Japan*, Revised edition, 1982–1983 (Tokyo, 1982).

16. See Miyohei Shinohara, *Industrial Growth, Trade, and Dynamic Patterns in the Japanese Economy* (Tokyo: University of Tokyo Press, 1982): 16, 33.

17. The essay appeared in W.A. Eltis, M.F.G. Scott, and J.N. Wolfe, eds., *Essays in Honor of Roy Harrod* (Oxford: Clarendon Press, 1970).

18. *Mitsui Trade News Supplement* (December 1975).

19. High technology and services are combined in the financial field, where advanced communications provide substantial economies of scale.

GLOSSARY OF JAPANESE WORDS
AND PHRASES

Amakudari

"Descend from heaven." The government career civil service is alluded to as heaven, from which high officials retire at about age 55 to take senior positions in private business.

Bōeki masatsu

Trade friction. Refers to adversarial relations between Japan and its trade partners arising from their offensive or defensive strategies respectively.

Bōeki Sangyō
Kyōryoku Zaidan

Japan Trade and Industry Cooperation Foundation. A MITI consultative council.

Dōmei

Japanese Confederation of Labor. Established in 1964, it backs the Democratic Socialist Party, representing right-wing socialists. Most of its membership is in the private sector, predominantly in blue-collar occupations. As of March 1985, it had a membership of 2.2 million.

Dōrō

National Railway Locomotive Engineers Union. Affiliated with Sōhyō.

Denka no hōtō

A samurai family's heirloom sword. Its function is to symbolize status rather than to serve as a weapon.

Genchi-kashitsuke

A lending commitment by the foreign branch of a Japanese bank.

Gensaki	Known in the United States as a "repo," it refers to the sale of a long-term bond subject to a repurchase agreement. Thus, it serves to transform a long-term bond into a short-term instrument.
Gyōsei shidō	Administrative guidance. This is a nonstatutory regulatory technique used by administrators to secure "voluntary" compliance with their wishes.
Hiragana	Japanese cursive characters.
Hōjin	A juridical person (corporation).
Jiyūka	Economic liberalization. Remission of economic controls.
Kanji	Chinese ideograph.
Kasumigaseki	A central district of Tokyo where the principal government ministries are located.
Katakana	The Japanese syllabary written in square form.
Keihakutansho	Refers to the physical characteristics of the products of Japan's new high technology industries: light, thin, short, and small.
Keiretsu	Oligopolistic financial-industrial conglomerate "groups"; successors to the prewar zaibatsu. The technical distinction between the two lies in the means by which they were respectively coordinated. The zaibatsu combine was coordinated by its top holding company. The postwar keiretsu "group" was (initially) coordinated by its common bank.
Kinyū-kikan Shikin Shingikai	A "deliberation council" of the Ministry of Finance concerned with the lending policies of financial institutions. Deliberation councils are composed of civilian experts appointed by a minister to investigate assigned topics and to provide the ministry with policy advice.

Kisai kai	Council on bond issues. An advisory council to the Ministry of Finance composed of representatives of leading financial institutions.
Kōgō keisan kanjō	A provision of the foreign exchange control system of the early 1980s that allowed eligible trading companies to offset their export proceeds in foreign currency against their foreign currency obligations, thus reducing the volume and cost of their foreign exchange market transactions.
Kokurō	National Railway Workers Union. Affiliated with Sōhyō.
Kokusai Keizai Koryū Zaidan	Japan Trade and Industry Cooperation Foundation. A MITI consultative council.
Kokusaika	Internationalization of the Japanese economy. For example, it contemplates widening use of the yen as an international currency.
Konnyaku	Devil's tongue, from which a traditional Japanese edible paste is made.
Kōsha	A public corporation that is oriented to public service. Its capital is fully financed by the national government. Prior to their (partial) privatization, the Japanese National Railways, the Japan Tobacco and Salt Public Corporation, and the Nippon Telegraph and Telephone Public Corporation were designated by this term.
Kyokuchō	Director general of a bureau of a Japanese government ministry.
Madoguchi shidō	"Window guidance." Administrative guidance as applied by the Bank of Japan. During times of monetary restraint, for example, credit rationing is effectively imposed by the allotment of quarterly lending quotas to individual banks.
Naimushō	Prewar Japanese name for the Ministry of Home Affairs. Following World War II, its Japanese name became Jichishō, although in En-

glish it continued to be known as the Ministry of Home Affairs (sometimes also referred to as the Ministry of Local Autonomy).

Nemawashi

"To dig around the root of a tree to prepare it for transplanting." By analogy, the term refers to groundwork to enlist the support or informal consent of those concerned with a pending matter before asking for a formal decision. In the *nemawashi* process, a proposal is revised until it assumes acceptable form.

Rinchō

Abbreviation of *Rinji Gyōsei Chosakai*, the Provisional Commission for Administrative Reform. It was established by Prime Minister Zenko Suzuki in March 1981.

Sakoku

National isolation and exclusion of foreigners during Japan's feudal period.

Sangyō Gōrika Shingikai
Sangyō Shikin Bukai

Subcommittee on Industrial Finance of the Council on Industrial Rationalization, Ministry of International Trade and Industry (MITI).

"San-k" problem

The "three-k" problem of administrative reform. It concerns the fiscal burden of *kokutetsu* (railways), *kome* (rice subsidy), and *kempo* (national health insurance).

Sarakin

Abbreviation of *sarariman kinyu*, "salaried man's finance company." These companies make unsecured consumer loans for unspecified purposes, often at usurious rates of interest. Many are notorious for their collection methods.

Shingikai

A government advisory council established under Article 8 of the National Administration Organization Law, which specifies that it is to be composed of "persons of learning and experience." (See Chalmers Johnson, *Japan's Public Policy Companies*, AEI-Hoover Policy Studies, 1978.)

Shinyū kumiai

Association of small local banks.

Sōgō shosha

General trading company. Its traditional functions have been transaction intermediation, financial intermediation, and information gathering. Recently, general trading companies have undertaken additional activities, including manufacturing, technical assistance projects, organization and coordination of development projects, construction of infrastructure, and managerial and consulting services.

Sōhyō

General Council of Trade Unions of Japan. Established in 1950, it backs the Socialist Party, representing left-wing socialists. As of March 1985, it had a membership of 4.4. million, more than half of which was in the public sector, including many white-collar workers.

Sōron-sansei, kakuron-hantai

A bargaining tactic: to agree in principle, but disagree in particulars.

Tamamushi iro no kaiketsu

An ambiguous or "iridescent" solution, in which each party to an agreement can find what he is looking for.

Tanshi

A money market house, of which there are six. (In Japanese, nouns are identical in the singular and plural.) They act mostly as brokers (intermediaries) but also as dealers. They perform a vital role in the institutional arrangements by which the Ministry of Finance and the Bank of Japan implement their policies. They operate in all money markets as well as the foreign exchange market, and may purchase and sell securities. They have borrowing privileges at the Bank of Japan. They receive meticulous daily instructions from the Bank of Japan on how to perform their duties of coordinating government policies in the various money markets. The tanshi take positions in the money markets in which the Bank of Japan intervenes most—namely, the call market, the bill discount market, and the certificate of deposit market—thus enhancing their role as servants of government policy. The Bank of Japan frequently carries out its open market operations through the tanshi. The largest of the tanshi is Tokyo Tanshi, followed by Ueda Tanshi, Nippon Discount, Yamane Tanshi, Yagi Tanshi, and Nagoya Tanshi.

Tegata

Draft or promissory note.

Tetsurō

Japan Railway Workers Union. Affiliated with Dōmei.

Todai

Abbreviation of *Tokyo Daigaku*: Tokyo University.

Tokonoma

An ornamental alcove in which family treasures are displayed.

Yen tenkan

Conversion of foreign currency into yen.

Zaibatsu

Financial clique. The term refers to large industrial and financial combines formed during the Meiji era, controlled by top holding companies. During the occupation, holding companies were abolished, thus formally dispersing the combines.

Zaikai

Financial world (circles). The term refers to elite business leaders who exercise special influence in politics and the government bureaucracy.

Zaisei-saiken

Reconstruction of public finance. This objective of the administrative reform program implies balancing the national budget by reduction of spending and severance of personnel.

Zeisei Chosakai

Taxation Council. An advisory council to the Ministry of Finance.

Zōshi tō Chōsei Kondankai

Council for Coordination of Stock Issues. Composed of representatives of leading financial institutions that advised on the allocation of capital funds during the early 1960s.

INDEX

Administrative guidance (gyōsei shidō): and information, 32; self-restraint as, 33; and trading companies, 48–49; and banking, 50–59 *passim*, 67–68, 79, 131–32; and foreign banks, 67–68, 132; and oligopolies, 140. *See also* Controls

Administrative Management Agency, 118, 121

Administrative reform: attempts, 93–94; and Rinchō, 94, 95, 99, 104–20 *passim*; and budget deficits, 94–95, 98; and subsidies, 98–99, 102–3; and ministerial prerogatives, 99, 102–3; LDP recommendations for, 103–4; and power struggle, 107, 108–13; and JNR, 109–12; and external option, 113–15; winners and losers from 116–22

Advisory councils, 9–10

Agreed specialization, 137–38

Agricultural imports, 44, 45, 117

Anti-Monopoly Law, 136, 137

Antitrust Law, 19

Asian Development Bank (ADB), 5

Balance of payments: volatility in, 17, 127; and Foreign Exchange Law, 25, 26; U.S., 44; and IBF, 87; and foreign exchange, 81, 84

Bank Law, 2, 50–52, 54, 77–79

Bank of Japan: and Ministry of Finance, 16–17, 52–53, 56–57, 60–61, 72–73,

80–81; institutional memory of, 23; opposition to IBF, 42; and BA market, 43; window guidance, 52–53, 58–59, 61, 69, 71; interview with, official, 56–61; discounting facilities of, 64; and money markets, 71–76 *passim*; and Foreign Exchange Law, 79; intervention, 79

Bank of Japan Law, 164n.1

Bankers' acceptance (BA) market, 43, 88–89

Banking Bureau, 20, 22, 40, 90–91, 91–92, 109. *See also* Ministry of Finance

Banks: and liberalization, 14–15, 30, 50, 61, 77–79; and Foreign Exchange Law, 15, 77–79; conflict with Ministry of Finance, 20, 21; and securities, 21, 27–28, 51, 78, 90–91, 164n.4, 173n.5; and Postal Savings system, 22–23, 89; and foreign lending, 29, 30–31, 58–59, 60; and bond issues, 30–31, 80; and Bank Law, 50–52, 77–79; and administrative guidance, 50–59 *passim*, 67–68, 79, 131–32; foreign, 61–71, 77, 85, 90, 91, 132–34; and subsidiaries abroad, 84–85; and CP, 87–89; restriction of, 164n.4; segmentation of, 172n.2

Bergsten, C. F., 2

Bond repurchase agreement, *see* Gensaki

Bonds: Samurai, 5, 27–33 *passim*, 58, 80; zero-coupon, 5, 27, 33–34; na-